7 Keys to Hearing God's Voice

Craig von Buseck

7 Keys to Hearing God's Voice

Craig von Buseck

HENSLEY
PUBLISHING

Tulsa, Oklahoma

Unless otherwise noted, Scripture quotations are taken from the *New King James Version* of the Bible © 1979, 1980, 1982 by Thomas Nelson, Inc.

Scripture quotations marked NIV are taken from *The Holy Bible, New International Version* ® NIV ®, copyright © 1973, 1978, 1984 by the International Bible Society.

Scripture quotations marked NASB are taken from the *New American Standard Bible* copyright © 1960, 1962, 1963, 1968, 1971, 1972, 1973, 1975, 1977, 1995 by the Lockman Foundation.

Scripture quotations marked AMP are taken from *The Amplified Bible, Old Testament* copyright © 1965, 1987 by the Zondervan Corporation. *The Amplified Bible, New Testament* copyright © 1958, 1987 by The Lockman Foundation.

Scripture quotations marked NLT are taken from the *Holy Bible, New Living Translation,* copyright © 1996 by Tyndale House Publishers.

Scripture quotations marked KJV are taken from the *King James Version* of the Bible.

Scripture quotations marked Weymouth are taken from *Weymouth's New Testament in Modern Speech.* Copyright by Harper and Row Publishers and James Clark and Company.

Scripture quotations marked NRSV are taken from The New Revised Standard Version, © 1989 by the Division of Christian Education of the Normal Council of the Churches of Christ in the USA.

HENSLEY
PUBLISHING

ISBN 1-56322-087-3

7 Keys to Hearing God's Voice

About Photocopying

First Timothy 5:17-18 instructs us to give the laborer his wages, specifically those who labor in the Word and doctrine. Hensley Publishing has a moral, as well as legal, responsibility to see that our authors receive fair compensation for their efforts. Many of them depend upon the income from the sale of their books as their sole livelihood. So, for that matter, do the artists, printers, and numerous other people who work to make these books available to you. Please help us by discouraging those who would copy this material in lieu of purchase.

Contents

Introduction

It was a peaceful Virginia morning. I awoke with a sense of anticipation — that feeling of serenity that you have as you prepare to take a long-anticipated journey. My boss, Tim, and I would be flying to Chicago that morning to be part of an Internet evangelism consultation. As the programming director for CBN.com I had been eagerly awaiting the arrival of September 11, 2001.

The night before I had plugged in my cell phone to recharge it for the trip. I placed it on the window ledge in the living room so that I would remember to pick it up on the way out the door the next morning. The stars still filled the blackened sky when Tim arrived. The Virginia air was already warming — it would be a beautiful day.

Still rubbing sleep from my eyes, I boarded the plane at Williamsburg Airport and settled into my seat. It was just after 6 A.M. The first sliver of turquoise-colored sky began to inch upward from above the tree line at the edge of the runway. I picked up the in-flight magazine and thumbed through it for a moment. I looked up to see the other passengers brushing past me in the aisle. Suddenly my eyes caught the gaze of a young man who seemed to be of Middle-Eastern descent. He wore a long robe and a turban on his head. Part of my job includes staying up-to-date on current events in the news. For my entire adult life I had followed the turbulent events in the Middle East. And since 1983, when a friend of mine was killed by terrorists in the Beirut Marine Corps barracks bombing, I had become very aware of the threat of terrorism. When this man walked down the aisle of that aircraft my first thought was, *Could this person be a terrorist?* Later my boss told me that he had had the very same thought.

Despite my concern, the flight to Atlanta was without incident, and we arrived just after 7 A.M. with a layover before our flight to Chicago. Tim and I grabbed a light breakfast and discussed the upcoming meeting before we boarded the second plane and settled in for the flight. A passenger had left a copy of that morning's *New York Times* on my seat, so I decided to thumb through it. One of the headlines was of the assassination of Afghan opposition leader Ahmed Shah Massoud, a veteran commander in the 1979-1989 war against Soviet occupation. In the months leading up to September 11, 2001, a confrontation had been growing between the Taliban leadership in Afghanistan and the

United Nations. The UN was demanding the deportation of Osama bin Laden to face charges of masterminding the bombing of two U.S. embassies in 1998.

I had seen videotape of bin Laden and his terrorist training camps in Afghanistan. I remembered the chilling scenes of the terrorists breaking into rooms and shooting mannequins with crosses and stars of David painted onto them. The Taliban had made international headlines earlier in the year when they destroyed two immense, 2,000-year-old images of Buddha carved into the side of an Afghan mountain. The *New York Times* speculated that bin Laden and the Taliban were responsible for the death of Massoud, the Northern Alliance military leader. *I wonder how this assassination will affect the United States,* I thought as I finished the article. Little did I realize bin Laden's master plan, of which this assassination was just a part.

As I looked out the window over the patchwork of farms scattered throughout America's heartland, I had no concept of the horror my fellow countrymen were facing at that very moment. When American Airlines Flight 11 hit the north tower of the World Trade Center at 8:45 A.M., I was casually chatting with Tim about upcoming strategies for CBN.com. At 9:03 A.M. when United Airlines Flight 175 slammed into the south tower at 500 miles an hour, I was marveling at the beautiful farmland laid out in neat blocks of various shades of green and gold below us. American Airlines Flight 77 crashed into the Pentagon at 9:40 A.M. just as we began our descent into Chicago.

We landed at Midway Airport with a tremendous jolt. The runways at this, the smaller of Chicago's airports, are shorter, and so as soon as we touched down the pilot reversed the engines and slammed on the brakes. As the airplane turned, I noticed the concrete wall at the end of the runway and realized why the pilot was so eager to stop the plane. Out of the corner of my eye I noticed a Chicago police car racing down an adjacent runway with its blue lights flashing. As we taxied toward the airport, I saw another police cruiser with its lights flashing sitting in front of a gate next to the road. My first thought was that perhaps this was a local drug bust or criminal sting of some sort. Out in the middle of the airfield our plane suddenly screeched to a halt. Within moments the pilot spoke over the intercom: "We will need to stay here on the tarmac for a moment as we wait for the airport to open a gate for us." I thought this was strange, and I wondered if it had anything to do with the police cars. A few seconds later the captain gave the passengers permission to use their cell phones and laptop computers.

At that moment it dawned on me that I had left my cell phone charging on the windowsill at home. Suddenly a voice from behind me spoke in a tone and volume that sounded like he was making an announcement: "Terrorists have hit the World Trade Center with an airplane." Throughout the plane, passengers were turning on their cell phones and receiving the news that was now being broadcast around the world. Instantly the aircraft was abuzz with conversation. "They also hit the second tower," someone cried out. "The Pentagon has been attacked," another voice said above the din of messages.

What is this obsession with the World Trade Center? I wondered as I thought back to the failed bombing attempt of the twin towers in 1993. The thought was immediate: *Radical Muslim terrorists.* The next thought was not far behind: *Osama bin Laden.* My mind spun, flashing back to major terrorist attacks in recent years: the bombing of the U.S.S. Cole, the embassy bombings in Kenya and Tanzania, the suspicious crash of an Egyptian Airlines plane in 1999, the explosion at the Khobar Towers in Dhahran, Saudi Arabia, killing nineteen American soldiers... I caught the eye of my boss as we shook our heads in disbelief.

One thing I knew for sure: The last place I wanted to be at that moment was sitting in an airplane on the middle of the tarmac! I needed to call home to let my family know I was all right. I needed to get to a television set to get some details. I needed to call CBN to see what was being done on the Web site! I mentally kicked myself for leaving my cell phone at home.

After a few minutes the plane eased forward, and we pulled into a hastily cleared gate. We were met at the door by an armed security guard who was allowing passengers off the plane and keeping others from getting back on. We hurried to the nearest television set and witnessed for the first time the images of the burning World Trade Center towers. "Look at that," I exclaimed out loud. "Can you believe it? They're both burning!" A woman standing in front of me turned and declared, "That is videotape that they're playing. The first tower has already collapsed."

I couldn't believe what I was seeing and hearing. Shaking my head I lifted up a silent prayer for the people in harm's way, for the families of the victims, for the President, and for America. Turning to my boss I declared, "Our lives have just changed forever. It will never be the same."

My prediction was accurate. The people of the world will never forget President George W. Bush as he stood on the rubble of what was once the World Trade Center, just days after the terrorist attack. He was surrounded by firefighters and rescue personnel who were working around the clock trying to find survivors. With bullhorn in hand he spoke words of encouragement to the legion of exhausted men and women.

From the midst of the crowd a man yelled out, "I can't hear you."

The president turned his bullhorn toward the man and responded, "I can hear you!" A raucous roar arose from the crowd. And then he continued: "I can hear you. The rest of the world hears you. And the people who knocked these buildings down will hear all of us soon!"

As we face the unknown difficulties that are before us, the world needs Christians who hear not just the president's voice, or the voice of any mere man, but God's voice. Even though those fear-filled days immediately following September 11 have passed, the need to seek — and find — God's voice and His direction in our lives remains as strong as ever. Over the years, I have discovered seven keys which God has given to help us hear and discern His voice:

1. The Bible;
2. The Holy Spirit's speaking directly to our spirit;
3. Godly counsel through mature Christian leaders;
4. The peace of God;
5. Personal prophecy;
6. Confirmation through multiple sources; and
7. Circumstances.

My prayer is that this study guide will not only inspire you to seek God's voice and direction, but also provide you with the tools you need to discern His voice in the midst of a chaotic world.

God Is Talking — Are You Listening?

DAY ONE   God Wants to Lead His Children

DAY TWO   God Is Love, and Love Communicates

DAY THREE   We Need to Hear God's Voice

DAY FOUR   God Loves You and Has a Wonderful Plan for Your Life

DAY FIVE   Seeking and Discerning God's Will

Years ago, when I was in college, I was fortunate to have an internship at a local public broadcasting station. I worked in the television production department creating promotional commercials for corporate sponsors. On the way to a particular video shoot the corporate donor representative was along for the ride. This young lady in her late twenties was sharing with my boss and I that she was thinking about purchasing a multi-unit apartment building, and she was not sure that she was making the right move. In her indecision she made a comment that I will never forget. "How can I know," she exclaimed, "that I am making the right choices in life? There are so many roads that I could go down. Which path is the right one?"

As mature Christians, how are we expected to discern God's will in major decisions? God has created us to be responsible individuals, and in most major decisions, He expects us to take an important measure of initiative, to make an effort to discover His will, and then to process the information and come to a decision on our own, yet with His leading. This week we will see that God wants to communicate with us and share His will for our lives. He is talking — are you listening?

Day One: God Wants to Lead His Children

Every person who has ever lived beyond childhood has wondered if they are making the right choices in life. For the person without God in their life, it is merely a question of survival and self-promotion. But for the believer, it is the cry of the heart to do what is pleasing in our heavenly Father's eyes.

Do you believe that God wants to lead you into His will for your life? Why or why not?

_____

_____

How have you heard God's voice in the past?

_____

_____

How do you feel about the extent to which God leads us in the small and big decisions? Does He have an opinion about the smaller everyday decisions that we make, or just the bigger life-altering ones?

_____

_____

_____

_____

We can be assured that God wants to lead His children. He created us to have intimate fellowship with Him. He wants to reveal Himself to us, and to communicate with us. When Corrie Ten Boom was in a Nazi concentration camp, she experienced doubt about God's willingness to direct her steps:

> I remember that once when I looked on the stars I said, "O Lord, all the stars are in Your guidance, but have You forgotten Your child?" I had my Bible with me and that was such a great joy. In the Bible I read that the hairs of our head are numbered, and God has all the universe in His hands. That means that God has a telescope and a microscope.[1]

God has His telescope in hand as He rules the universe, but He has His microscope focused on your concerns and the decisions you are facing. Jesus set the example for those of us who want to know God and do His will, when He declared, "I do only what the Father tells me to do" (see John 14:31). Even at His darkest hour, in the Garden of Gethsemane, as He faced the horror of crucifixion, He prayed, *O My Father, if it is possible, let this cup pass from Me; nevertheless, not as I will, but as You will* (Matthew 26:39).

Explain the concept of God's telescope and microscope. How do you see them in operation in your life?

_____

_____

_____

_____

More than ever before, the world needs the Prince of Peace — Jesus Christ. And the only way that they will see Jesus is through the demonstration of His power and love in the lives of Christians. People everywhere need to see the church rise up and take its rightful place of leadership in the earth today. This is not a time for timidity. This is a time for those who know their God to be strong, and to carry out great exploits in His name (see Daniel 11:32). This is a time for the Church to truly become all that the Bible declares us to be; the Bride of Christ; the Body of Christ; the Army of God; the Saints of the Most High.

The Bible makes clear what God has planned for His saints:

> *Let the high praises of God be in their mouth, and a two-edged sword in their hand, to execute vengeance on the nations, and punishments on the peoples; To bind their kings with chains, and their nobles with fetters of iron; To execute on them the written judgment — This honor have all His saints.*
>
> —Psalm 149:6–9

The weapons with which we fight are not laser-guided bombs or precision munitions. The apostle Paul declared that the believer operates in a different realm:

> *For though we walk in the flesh, we do not war according to the flesh. For the weapons of our warfare are not carnal but mighty in God for pulling down*

strongholds, casting down arguments and every high thing that exalts itself against the knowledge of God, bringing every thought into captivity to the obedience of Christ.

—2 Corinthians 10:3–5

So if this is the authority that God wants man to have, why are so few people experiencing it?

What do you think?

_____

_____

How does the ability to hear God's voice tie into the "exploits" we can do for Him?

_____

_____

_____

Sin has separated man from God, hindering us from hearing God's voice and walking in His perfect will for us. And it all started in the very beginning.

The Chinese have a symbol in their language to represent the concept of peace — it is a man and a woman walking in a garden with God. I'm convinced that this image has been passed down through generations of Chinese, originating with their ancestors Adam and Eve. Life, as God originally designed it, was absolute bliss. It was man and woman walking in a garden with God.

The writer of Genesis tells us that God walked with Adam and Eve in the cool of the day (see Genesis 3:8). They interacted face-to-face with God. Sin had not yet entered into this world. There was nothing that separated God and man. Nothing hindered full and complete communication.

Can you imagine what unhindered communication with God must have been like? Speculate for a moment, if you can.

Imagine what a glorious experience that must have been. Adam and Eve never wondered if God loved them. He demonstrated that love on a daily basis. There was no questioning of God's will. He communicated His desires to them face to face. There were no feelings of rejection, misunderstanding, bewilderment, or confusion. There was just perfect love, acceptance, and clarity of vision.

Why? Because God communicated with them every day, and they heard His voice.

"Good for them," you may be saying. And like the matchmaker Yentl in *Fiddler on the Roof*, you may add, "But this place is no Garden of Eden."[2]

You're right. Even though the man and the woman walked in perfect peace in the Garden of Eden, and communed with God without any hindrance whatsoever, when they were tempted by Satan to eat the forbidden fruit they could not resist and they fell. They flagrantly violated God's command concerning eating from the tree of the knowledge of good and evil, and they gave their allegiance over to the serpent, Lucifer, the enemy of God. When they did that sin entered this world, and from that moment forward, sinful man was separated from a holy God.

Sin still hinders our ears from hearing God's voice, and our eyes from seeing His face. Since the Fall, the race of man collectively has not wanted to be in fellowship with God. Though we are curious about our origins and the possibility of a personal God, we are far more interested in finding pleasure in our earthly existence.

How do you see the Fall of man and the lack of communication with God demonstrated in the world around you?

_____

_____

_____

But even in the midst of this sin, God reached out to man with a desire to communicate with him. God created us to hear His voice. Our ability to discern the voice of God is not based on our righteousness. We were made with the ability to hear God speaking to us.

Day Two: God Is Love, and Love Communicates

One of the clearest things that we see throughout Scripture is that God speaks to His people. He does it in many different ways, but the undeniable fact is that God does communicate with His people.

Because God is love, He desires communication with us. He created mankind in order to have a loving relationship with them. It was never God's intention that there be any separation between Himself and His creation.

The God of the Bible is a personal God who desires intimate fellowship with us as individuals. Communication is part of God's being. It is an integral part of who God is. Even under the Old Covenant God was communicating with mankind as His Spirit would come onto certain believers. King David declared the wonderful love of our heavenly Father toward each living human being:

> *How precious also are Your thoughts to me, O God! How great is the sum of them! If I should count them, they would be more in number than the sand; When I awake, I am still with You.*
>
> —Psalm 139:17–18

How does God's love affect His desire to communicate with us?

_____

_____

_____

How does God's love affect your desire to communicate with God?

_____

_____

_____

Because God is love, He created man with the freedom of choice. Only a loving God would give man the freedom to choose not to obey Him. It was sin that separated men and women from a holy God.

For He is our God, and we are the people of His pasture, and the sheep of His hand.
Today, if you will hear His voice: Do not harden your hearts.

—Psalm 95:7–8

Throughout the Old Testament we see numerous examples of God communicating with individuals:

- God communicated with Adam and Eve (Genesis 2:16–17; 3:9, 16–19).
- God communicated with Cain (Genesis 4:9–15).
- God communicated with Enoch (Genesis 5:24).
- God communicated with Noah (Genesis 6:13–21).
- God communicated with Abraham (Genesis 12:1–3; 15:1–21; 17:1–22; 22:1–2).
- God communicated with Hagar (Genesis 16:7–13).
- God communicated with Abraham and Sarah (Genesis 18:1–15).
- God communicated with Rebekah (Genesis 25:23).
- God communicated with Isaac (Genesis 26:2–5, 24).
- God communicated with Jacob (Genesis 28:13–15; 31:3).
- God communicated with Pharaoh (Genesis 41:28).
- God communicated with Joseph (Genesis 37:5–10).
- God communicated with Moses (Exodus 3:1–22; 4:1–17).
- God communicated with Balaam, even through a donkey (Numbers 22:12–35).
- God communicated with Joshua (Joshua 1:1–9; 5:13–15).
- God communicated with Deborah (Judges 4:6).
- God communicated with Samuel (1 Samuel 3:10–14).
- God communicated with David (1 Samuel 23:2).
- God communicated with Solomon (1 Kings 3:5–15).
- God communicated with Job (Job 38:1–41).
- God communicated with Elijah (1 Kings 19:11–18).
- God communicated with Elisha (2 Kings 6:8–12).
- God communicated with Isaiah (Isaiah 6:1–13).
- God communicated with Jeremiah (Jeremiah 1:4–10).

In His love, God communicated with the rest of the Old Testament prophets declaring that He would send a Messiah, a Savior who would take away their sins and restore communication between God and man — not just through the prophets, but God would make Himself available to every man, one on one.

Henry Blackaby says in his book, *Experiencing God*: "How God spoke in the Old Testament is not the most important factor. That He spoke is the crucial point."[3]

Describe God's communication with mankind in the Old Testament. How did this communication reflect His love for His people?

_____

_____

_____

The prophet Jeremiah was given a glimpse of what this glorious new covenant would be:

> *Behold, the days are coming, says the LORD, when I will make a new covenant with the house of Israel and with the house of Judah — not according to the covenant that I made with their fathers in the day that I took them by the hand to lead them out of the land of Egypt, My covenant which they broke, though I was a husband to them, says the LORD. But this is the covenant that I will make with the house of Israel after those days, says the LORD: I will put My law in their minds, and write it on their hearts; and I will be their God, and they shall be My people. No more shall every man teach his neighbor, and every man his brother, saying, "Know the Lord," for they all shall know Me, from the least of them to the greatest of them, says the LORD. For I will forgive their iniquity, and their sin I will remember no more.*
>
> —Jeremiah 31:31–34

You can almost feel the heart of God yearning for the day when there would be no barrier between Himself and sinful mankind. But until Jesus came, that chasm of sin remained.

God is holy, and He can have no sin in His presence. The Bible says that in His holiness, God is a consuming fire. I compare God's holiness to our sun, which is also a consuming fire. To help us understand the fact that there can be no sin in the presence of God's holiness, think of God's presence like the sun, and sinful man like a rocket that is launched toward it. When the rocket gets close enough to the intense heat of the sun, its molecules cannot stay intact. The incredible heat of the sun will melt the rocket, and so it will be vaporized and disappear completely in the consuming fire.

That is a crude picture of sin in the presence of a holy God. Because of God's love, and awesome wonder, He had to separate Himself from man, or man would be destroyed. We just could not endure the presence of a holy God.

Because God is love, He does not want to see His creation suffer such a fate.

Explain how sin prevents mankind from standing in the presence of a holy God.

_____

_____

_____

Look up the following verses. How does each describe the active love of God?
2 Peter 3:9

_____

_____

Romans 5:8

_____

_____

John 3:16

_____

_____

Through His plan of love, God reached down from heaven to reconcile sinful man to Himself, to restore relationship and communication. He loved the people of the world so much that He sent His Son to live a sinless life, to suffer the humiliation of the cross, to take sin upon Himself as the substitute for every person who will ever live, so that we could be reconciled back to Him. At the moment that sin came upon Jesus, the Bible tells us that the Father turned away from Him — sin cannot be in the presence of a holy God. During the time when Jesus was on the cross, the Father and the Son were separated by sin for the one and only time in eternity. That is why Jesus cried out, _"My God, my God, why have You forsaken Me?"_ (Matthew 27:46).

Jesus endured separation from His Father and the agony of the cross so that we could once again enjoy God's presence, and have the ability to hear His voice.

At the point of Jesus' death, He cried out, *"It is finished!"* (John 19:30). At that moment, the veil in the temple that separated the people from the Holy of Holies was torn in half. There would be no more separation between God and man. Our Abba Father sent His Son to build a bridge across the chasm of sin so that we could walk with Him in the cool of the day, and once again we could hear His voice.

Describe how Jesus' life, death, and resurrection restored the communication between God and man.

_____

_____

_____

_____

Jesus also promised that we will hear His own voice:

> *And when he brings out his own sheep, he goes before them; and the sheep follow him, for they know his voice. Yet they will by no means follow a stranger, but will flee from him, for they do not know the voice of strangers.*
>
> —John 10:4–5

> *My sheep hear My voice, and I know them, and they follow Me.*
>
> —John 10:27

The apostle Paul also assures us of God's leading in our lives:

> *For as many as are led by the Spirit of God, these are sons of God.*
>
> —Romans 8:14

There are numerous other examples in the New Testament of God communicating with individuals:

• God communicated with Joseph (Matthew 1:20–23).

• God communicated with the Wise Men (Matthew 2:12).

• God communicated with Zacharias (Luke 1:11–20).

• God communicated with Mary (Luke 1:28–38).

• God communicated with Simeon (Luke 2:25–32).

• God communicated with Pilate's wife (Matthew 27:19).

- God communicated with Philip (Acts 8:26–40).
- God communicated with Saul (Acts 9:1–9).
- God communicated with Ananias (Acts 9:10–16).
- God communicated with Cornelius (Acts 10:1–7).
- God communicated with Peter (Acts 10:9–16).
- God communicated with Paul (Acts 16:6–10).
- God communicated with Agabus (Acts 11:27–30; 21:10–14).
- God communicated with John (Revelation 1:1–2, 10–20).

Describe God's communication with man in the New Testament.

_____

_____

_____

There are other biblical examples of ways God has communicated with man.

Describe God's method of communication in each of the following passages.
Luke 1:19

_____

Genesis 15:1

_____

1 Kings 3:5

_____

Jeremiah 18:1–6

_____

1 Kings 19:11–13

_____

Exodus 8:20–25

_____

Jesus rebuked the Pharisees of His day declaring, *"He who belongs to God hears what God says. The reason you do not hear is that you do not belong to God"* (John 8:47 NIV).

If we belong to God, we are longing to hear His voice. As we walk with Him and talk to Him, we want to hear what He says to us.

What has the Lord said to you? Are you hearing His voice?

How does God speak to His people today? The answer to that question is: Anyway He wants to! He is God, and He can choose any method He wants to communicate with us whenever He wants to. Many people have too small a view of God. They put Him in a box and say that He can only speak in one particular way — and typically that is the way with which they are most comfortable. But the truth is that God can do whatever He chooses. He can communicate in any way that He desires.

Because God is love, He desires communication with us. God's speaking to us in our minds, and hearts, and through His Word is just as normal as one person talking to another. That is the way He is. That is the way He has always been. That is the way He will always be.

What kind of a God would He be if He created us, but couldn't talk to us? Without the ability to communicate, there would be an eternal chasm between God and man. Jesus died as a substitute for our sin so that chasm would be bridged, and we could have the freedom to come into God's presence and communicate with Him.

But we must make time in our daily walk with the Lord to spend time with Him and listen for His voice. The Lord promises to direct our steps as we spend time in fellowship with Him. In Psalm 16:11, David demonstrated his confidence in God's guidance: *You will show me the path of life; in Your presence is fullness of joy; at Your right hand are pleasures forevermore.*

Day Three: We Need to Hear God's Voice

I recently received this inspiring e-mail from a woman who was responding to one of our columns on CBN.com.

> I would like to share something unusually wonderful with you. My mother, Joan, grew closer to Jesus the last few years during my sister Gerri's illness. For the last few years before Gerri went home to heaven, she talked to our Mom a lot about the Lord.
>
> However, when Gerri passed on, my Mom got very discouraged and thought that God did not hear her prayers.
>
> That all changed recently! My mom had heard of the POW's and the MIA's from the 507th in Iraq. Like so many of us, she was sad for them and their families. The first evening she had learned of their plight she had an unusual occurrence. She went to bed and was suddenly struck with an extreme urgent need to pray for someone named Jessica. She didn't know why she felt so strongly for this one. She had never felt anything like it, she said. She began to pray and it was as if she could feel so much pain deep inside her heart for this girl. She cried a cry that only comes from deep within.
>
> She said she couldn't stop. She prayed, *God, if You never answer another prayer of mine, please answer this one! Please save Jessica!*
>
> When Jessica Lynch was rescued, my sister Debbie called my mom to tell her about it. My mom said she got chills up and down her whole body! She called me to tell me of the miracle. She said to me, "Now I know that God hears my prayers!"
>
> Not only did the miracle of Jessica's rescue happen, but the miracle of my mom's faith being rescued happened too!

This is the type of exciting walk that you and I can experience with the Lord if we will step out in faith to hear His voice.

Only God knows the path that lies before us as we press onward into this new millennium. Throughout the 1990s it seemed like the world had rid itself of many of the modern threats to civilization. The cold war came to a close with the fall of the Berlin Wall. Former communist nations threw off the shackles of that failed atheistic system and embraced freedom, and in many cases, the God of the Bible. Around the globe new democracies were being formed in formerly totalitarian states as people basked in the light of liberty.

But within the second year of the new millennium the September 11th terrorist attacks jarred us into a new reality. The war on terrorism rages in places known and unknown. In turn, attacks on Christians and Jews have increased. More Christians are being martyred around the world today than at any other time since the Roman era. Dangers seem to be mounting on every side.

At the same time, there are greater opportunities now than there have ever been for the preaching of the Gospel. More people are being won to Christ today than in the history of the world. This is truly the Church's finest hour.

As the darkness grows darker, the light grows brighter. In order to combat the forces of darkness, and to aid in taking the Gospel to hurting people in every nation, Christians must become equipped to hear the voice of God in this generation and obey God's leading in their lives. This is a critical time in the history of the church. If we miss this window of opportunity to see the Great Commission fulfilled, it may not open to us again for hundreds of years.

Describe how you have seen the darkness grow darker and the light grow brighter in your own world.

_____

_____

_____

On all levels, God's people need to be in tune with what the Spirit of God is saying to the church. Fathers and mothers need to be listening for God's leading in raising their children. Cell-group leaders need to be led by the Spirit in how to disciple those that God brings to them. Pastors need to be seeking divine guidance on how to best shepherd their congregation. Business leaders and inventors should have the spirit of Joseph and Daniel in creatively expanding their enterprises. Military planners must rely on the Spirit of the Lord to give them divine strategies for victory. Educators should seek the Lord for new and innovative ways to teach the young the necessary skills for succeeding in today's world. Government officials and lawyers must humbly seek the Lord in setting policy for their nations, and for the free world.

How do you need to hear the voice of the Lord in your own life?

_____

_____

We live in a natural, physical world that is controlled by certain natural laws — the law of gravity, the law of thermodynamics, and so on. But there is another realm in which we live that is just as real, though it is unseen — the world of the spirit. This unseen world is also controlled by certain spiritual laws, or principles, that are more powerful than most people can imagine. The authority to operate in this realm was opened to all Christians as a result of Jesus' death and resurrection.

> *All authority has been given to Me in heaven and on earth. Go therefore and make disciples of all nations.*
>
> —Matthew 28:18b–19a

When Jesus sent out His disciples to begin the work of evangelism that we continue today, He gave them authority over Satan.

Read Luke 9:1. What were the disciples given authority to do?

_____

Later Jesus extended that authority to the seventy when He sent them out to minister in His name.

> *"And heal the sick there, and say to them, 'The kingdom of God has come near to you.'" Then the seventy returned with joy, saying, "Lord, even the demons are subject to us in Your name." And He said to them, "I saw Satan fall like lightning from heaven. Behold, I give you the authority to trample on serpents and scorpions, and over all the power of the enemy, and nothing shall by any means hurt you."*
>
> —Luke 10:9, 17–19

Jesus gave all believers access to the spirit world so that we could be equipped to become all that He wants us to be, and to do all that He commands us to do.

Now we have received, not the spirit of the world, but the Spirit who is from God, that we might know the things freely given to us by God, which things we also speak, not in words taught by human wisdom, but in those taught by the Spirit, combining spiritual thoughts with spiritual words.

1 Corinthians 2:12–13 NASB

What spiritual laws influence our ability to hear God's voice?

_____

How does the Spirit of God help you in your daily life?

_____

Throughout His ministry on earth, Jesus spoke of the kingdom of God. He declared that the kingdom of heaven had come, and yet it had not arrived in its fullness. This is a spiritual kingdom that has immense power over the natural world. It was not yet a physical place (though it will be in the fullness of time), but rather a spiritual realm where the people of God submit themselves to the lordship of Jesus Christ. In return, God provides them with blessings and the keys to the kingdom — both in the physical world, and in the world to come.

Assuredly, I say to you, whatever you bind on earth will be bound in heaven, and whatever you loose on earth will be loosed in heaven. Again I say to you that if two of you agree on earth concerning anything that they ask, it will be done for them by My Father in heaven. For where two or three are gathered together in My name, I am there in the midst of them.

—Matthew 18:18–20

Jesus made it clear that access to this unseen kingdom was through salvation. Speaking to Nicodemus, a ruler of the Jews, Jesus declared:

"Most assuredly, I say to you, unless one is born again, he cannot see the kingdom of God." Nicodemus said to Him, "How can a man be born when he is old? Can he enter a second time into his mother's womb and be born?" Jesus answered, "Most assuredly, I say to you, unless one is born of water and the Spirit, he cannot enter the kingdom of God."

—John 3:3–5

Notice that the first time Jesus spoke of "seeing" the kingdom, and then he referred to the experience of "entering" the kingdom. Our initial rebirth as Christians is like "seeing" the kingdom of God. But there is a deeper, richer experience of walking in the Spirit — "entering" the kingdom.

How have you experienced "seeing" and "entering" the kingdom of God in your own life?

_____

_____

I like to compare "seeing" and "entering" the kingdom to the difference between the spectators in a stadium and the players on the field in a football game. The spectators are in the stands, and they are watching the action. They are identifying with the team, and they are excited about the game, but they are only "seeing" the action, they aren't really participating. The players, on the other hand, are out on the field getting dirty and making things happen. They are the ones working with the coach to execute the strategies that they prepared for this moment. When they score, it is as a result of working together as a team under the headship of the coach. When each player runs out onto the field they have "entered" the game and they are working together to win the game.

A person can be a believer and yet only taste the things of the kingdom — one who only "sees" the kingdom of God. But there is a life available to the believer where he or she walks in the fullness of all that God has for the saint of God — the fruit and manifestations of the Spirit operating in full measure to one who "enters" the kingdom of God.

There is more to our Christian walk than just salvation — as wonderful as this gift is. God has a plan, a personal destiny for each of us to fulfill. God wants to have a relationship with us, and part of that relationship is working with Him to see His kingdom established on this earth. As Jesus taught us in the Lord's Prayer, *"Your kingdom come. Your will be done on earth as it is in heaven"* (Matthew 6:10).

In order for the kingdom to be established in our lives, and in the earth, we must hear and obey the will of the King.

That is the purpose of this book — to learn to hear the voice of God as He speaks to you.

Day Four: God Loves You and Has a Wonderful Plan for Your Life

Many of us are familiar with this phrase made famous by Campus Crusade's *Four Spiritual Laws.* The four spiritual laws include: (1) God loves you and offers a wonderful plan for your life; (2) Man is sinful and separated from God. Therefore, he cannot know and experience God's love and plan for his life; (3) Jesus Christ is God's only provision for man's sin. Through Him you can know and experience God's love and plan for your life; and (4) We must individually receive Jesus Christ as Savior and Lord; then we can know and experience God's love and plan for our lives.[4] The great news is that these laws are true! God does love you, and He has an adventure prepared for you that is beyond your wildest dreams.

So why don't more people recognize these things about God?

What do you think?

_____

_____

For decades now, schools have been teaching our young people that they are accidental products of spontaneous evolution. There are generations today who are completely unaware of the truths of God and His universe. To these modern people, human beings are only one of the many evolving creatures on this planet — no more special than any other. There is nothing sacred about human life; no divine spark. If everything is merely a result of some distant "big bang" then it is all meaningless. If there is no God, there is no higher purpose in life. We should all just live for ourselves. Get as much out of this life as you can, because you only live once, and when you're dead, you're dead.

But for the person who is willing to think outside of the accepted scientific party line — to even consider the evidence that is shouting from the natural world, let alone the spiritual or metaphysical world, the universe displays overwhelming evidence of organization and intelligent design.

That's because a loving God created it and sustains it.

And the God who planned the universe has a wonderful plan for your life.

Did you know that you are the only person in the world who could be you? You are absolutely unique in all ways. Let's look at the math. From your mother's side, the chances that you would be born who you are were only 1 in 300,000. From your father's body came millions of potential human beings, no two had the same genetic heritage. When you multiply 1 in 300,000 times 1 million, then you have the odds that you would be born you, or I would be born me — and those odds are staggering.

What are some unique things about you?

_____

_____

_____

So many people are looking for ways to stand out from the crowd. The fact is that we all stand out from the crowd because none of us are alike.

And if you are a Christian, God wants to develop you into a believer who is unlike anyone else in the entire universe. That means that as you allow Jesus Christ to live through you — to be reflected in your personality and in your body, you will be different from the reflection of Christ through the personality of any of His other children.

God has a unique purpose for you to accomplish in your life to go along with that unique reflection of Christ. Only you can shine His love, and grace, and peace into this dark world the way that you are designed to do it. There are things that God wants you to do that no one else can do. There are places that God wants you to go so that He can use you uniquely. And there are people that you can reach out to that no one else would be able to touch.

When God made you, He broke the mold — but He did not jettison the plan for your life. It's there waiting to be discovered. But you've got to go for it.

The things of God are free, but they're not cheap. He wants to give them to you, but He also wants you to show that you really want them. The only way to discover God's plan for your life is to learn how to hear His voice.

"I buy that," you may be saying. "I want to live for God and do His will. That's why I'm reading this book. But I need some practical 'how-to's' to know if I'm actually hearing God's voice."

Fortunately, there is no formula that I can give you to help you to hear God.

"Fortunately? Then why am I reading this book?" you are probably asking.

I say "fortunately" because our walk with God is not a series of do's and don'ts, nor is it a recipe book that will give us the right ingredients to produce the desired results. No, being a Christian and hearing His voice come by being in relationship with a personal God. Learning to hear His loving voice is a process of trial and error — just like learning to obey our earthly parents is a process of trial and error.

Why do you think God hasn't provided us with a "formula" to be able to hear His voice and understand His will?

_____

_____

_____

The writer of Hebrews gives us a clue for learning to hear God's voice.

> *But solid food belongs to those who are of full age, that is, those who by reason of use have their senses exercised to discern both good and evil.*
>
> —Hebrews 5:14

What do you think this scripture is saying about learning to hear God's voice?

_____

_____

_____

_____

The Bible tells us that all things good come from God. The evil that is spoken of here refers to that which originates with Satan, with the world, or that which comes from our fleshly desires. There are four voices that compete for our attention — God, the devil, the world, and our own flesh. As we practice hearing God's voice — by learning the principles of the Bible and then applying them in a process of trial and error to the various messages that we are confronted with in life — we will begin to have our senses exercised to discern between the voice of God, the voice of the Evil One, the voice of the world, and the voice of our own carnal desires.

If you are reading this book, then you desire to hear God's voice. I encourage you to step out in faith and dare to believe that you can hear Him speaking to you.

The writer of Hebrews tells us this about our relationship with God:

> *But without faith it is impossible to please Him, for he who comes to God must believe that He is, and that He is a rewarder of those who diligently seek Him.*
>
> —Hebrews 11:6

What is necessary in order for us to please God?

_____

What happens to those who diligently seek after God?

_____

As we complete this lesson today, pray this prayer to the Lord and trust Him to reveal His will for your life.

> *Lord, I believe You exist, and that You are a rewarder of those who diligently seek You. I believe that You have a plan for my life, and that if I seek Your face, and obey Your commandments, You will reveal Your will to me by Your Spirit. So Father, I base my life on these truths. I trust in Your promise to guide my decisions. I believe that I can hear Your voice, and that You will lead me by Your Holy Spirit. I believe that it is Your desire that I understand Your will, and so You will show me how to discover it for my life. You are my heavenly Father, and as Your child, I want to know Your wishes and desires for my life. I ask You to teach me to hear Your voice. In Jesus' name, amen.*

Day Five: Seeking and Discerning God's Will

When you are diligent in your pursuit of God, and in your desire to know and do His will, God will allow opportunities to come to you where you will have to discern His voice in the situation. These opportunities will require you to examine the potential directions you could go. A business proposition or a potential relationship will come your way. These possible directions are either going to be in God's will for you, or they aren't. But because you desire to do God's will, when presented with this proposition, you're going to seek God's will in prayer. You will cry out to Him saying, *Heavenly Father, lead me. Show me the way to go. Make clear to me what Your will is in this choice that You have set before me.* God will answer this prayer! But He will likely do so in a manner that will force you to engage in an analysis of the seven keys to hearing His voice:

- The Scriptures;
- The Holy Spirit's speaking directly to your spirit;
- Godly counsel of mature Christian leaders;
- Peace or lack of peace in your spirit;
- Personal prophecy;
- Confirmation through multiple sources; and
- The circumstances surrounding the decision.

How has God led you through any one of these methods in your life to this point? Explain the situation and how you made your decision.

_____

_____

_____

Which of these areas have you never experienced? Why do you suppose that is?

_____

_____

_____

_____

When you walk in faith through this process, something is going to happen. Through the examination of these seven keys you will begin to hear God's voice. You will have an impression, a peace, deep inside you that a certain course of action is from God. You may receive advice from a friend, a mentor, or a trusted family member that helps point you in a certain direction. Circumstances may arise that give you a clear indication that your choice is either a good or a bad one. The door may even close altogether: The business deal or relationship you were considering may simply fall through.

However the leading comes, you will take action on the basis of what you believe God is speaking to you through the seven keys.

And then you will wait to see what happens. It may turn out to be a wonderful decision, with an unmistakable outpouring of God's blessing. Or it could be that there is no immediate outward indication that is either positive or negative, and so you press on until time makes it clear that this choice was or was not of God. In all of this, you're learning to discern the voice of your heavenly Father.

In every opportunity that is presented to us, we will discover one of two things. We may come to realize that we made a mistake. The guidance wasn't really of God, although we had thought that it was. In these cases, we must learn from the situation and keep following the Lord the best we know how.

Or we may discover that the direction we took truly was from God. When this happens we find that an assurance and a trust grows in our hearts that we really can hear God's voice. When this happens we will have just taken a giant step forward in our walk with God. Instead of being like a little baby, crawling on the floor, by faith we have stood up in Christ, and we have taken our first teetering steps as a child of God. The more we do this, the stronger our steps will become. Soon we will find ourselves walking, and then running in the exciting plans that God has for our lives.

Describe a time in your life when a decision you made turned out to be a mistake. What was the result?

_____

_____

Describe a time in your life when a decision you made turned out to be based on the leading of God. What was the result?

_____

_____

_____

You may think that it is impossible to hear God speaking to you. Rest assured, God created you with a measure of ability to hear His voice. That measure is multiplied when you accept Jesus Christ as your Lord and Savior, and then again when you are baptized in the Holy Spirit.

The question is, will you use the gift that God has already placed within you? This book is intended to give you seven keys, or as I call them, filters through which every possible inclination or leading can be weighed to tell whether it is a message from God, our flesh, the world, or a message from Satan. The Lord has given His church these key principles to use as a checklist when seeking His guidance. Jesus promised that His Spirit would guide us. These keys are like homing signals of the Holy Spirit to lead us in the Lord's will.

But in order to develop your ability to hear God's voice and receive guidance from the Lord, you must have a daily relationship with Him. You have to belong to Him. You have to submit to Him in every decision. Then you have to obey Him.

When you do these things, God will guide you, bless you, and even pour out His blessings on your life as you follow Him.

And when trials and tests come against you — because they come to all of us in this life — He will guide you through each one, and use the adversities in life to create His character in you in the midst of the struggle. He will bring you through to the other side, and into His best for your life.

> *And we know that all things work together for good to those who love God, to those who are the called according to His purpose.*
>
> —Romans 8:28

What does this verse mean to you?

_____

_____

I pray that this book will help you to better discern the voice of the Lord in your life, and through knowing His voice, you will grow to know and love Him more — because it's all about relationship.

Remember, the world needs what we've got.

"What do we have?" you may be asking.

As born-again believers, we have seen the kingdom of God. We have Christ in us, the hope of glory! Think of that. The world needs Jesus — Jesus lives in us — Jesus wants to use us to make Himself real to the world.

And Jesus makes Himself real to believers first through these seven keys to hearing His voice. Let's not just see the kingdom of God, but let's *enter* the kingdom of God by daring to hear His voice and obey His call on our lives.

The Question of the Ages — How Can I Know God's Will?

"I have no will but that of God."

— Brother Lawrence

One of my sister's favorite movies when we were kids was *The Sound of Music,* and since we only had one TV and VCR, I was forced to watch it more times than I would like to admit. I confess, I enjoy it now, but it took twenty years of not viewing it before I could come to that realization!

In one key scene, Maria has fled from her role as governess to the von Trapp family because she has fallen in love with their father, Captain von Trapp. As she is seeking the counsel of Mother Abbess, the leader of the convent of which Maria had been a member, the wise older woman asks her, "What is the most important lesson you have learned here?"

Maria answers, "To find the will of God and to do it."

Good answer! And it led her to where she needed to be: back with the von Trapp family.

What am I going to do with the rest of my life? Where should I go to school? Whom should I marry? Should I take this job, or is there something better on the horizon? Life is a never-ending series of choices. How can we know whether we are making the right decisions?

Should we consult our horoscope? Maybe we should call the psychic hotline. Should we go with what the experts are saying, or rely on our own gut feeling? Should we look to the stars — or should we seek the Maker of the stars?

When we surrender to the lordship of Jesus Christ, we quickly come to the conclusion that our lives are not our own. In fact, that is what it means to make Jesus the Lord of your life. Our very salvation depends on His lordship. The apostle Paul said:

> *If you confess with your mouth the Lord Jesus and believe in your heart that God has raised Him from the dead, you will be saved.*
>
> —Romans 10:9

It's all about following the Lord. And as I have already said, that comes from having a personal relationship with Him.

I recently received an e-mail in response to my article "The Harness of the Holy Spirit," in which a CBN.com reader makes these thought-provoking statements:

> Your article is typical of many books I have read. Everyone talks about doing what the Holy Spirit says, but you do not state how you "know" it is the voice of *God.* I have yet to read any book or article that can lay that out. It is easy to say *the Lord* told me to leave this or do that, and I was blessed down the road because of it. Anyone who can present a way one can actually know that the voice they are hearing is from *God,* not man or Satan, would change the world. That's probably why the world hasn't changed.

I have good news for my friend, and for you — God wants to speak to us, and yes, you can know that you hear His voice.

Day One: A Relationship with God

God wants to fellowship and communicate with us. That's two-way communication. Why? Because you can't really have a relationship unless there is true dialogue. How do we get to know a person? By communicating with them. By talking and listening.

It's the same with our relationship with God. He talks, we listen. We talk, He listens.

Consider a relationship you have with a spouse, friend, or family member. How important is two-way communication in that relationship? Describe how your relationship would be affected by a lack of communication.

_____

_____

_____

What can you learn about communication with God from your human relationships?

_____

_____

_____

God loves us so much that He sent Jesus to take our place and to die for us. He did this so that we could once again have fellowship with Him. The book of Hebrews tells us that we can have access to God's very presence:

> *And so, dear friends, we can boldly enter heaven's Most Holy Place because of the blood of Jesus. This is the new, life-giving way that Christ has opened up for us through the sacred curtain, by means of his death for us.*
> —Hebrews 10:19–20 NLT

What does this passage in Hebrews 10 tell you about God's desire to communicate with mankind?

_____

_____

Through what must we pass to enter the throne room of God? Why is this significant?

_____

_____

God wants us to be fulfilled, blessed, and successful in the plan that He has established for our lives — so that we can be a reflection of His love and blessing in the earth. In the Garden of Eden, Adam and Eve had perfect, unhindered fellowship with God: _They heard the sound of the LORD God walking in the garden in the cool of the day_ (Genesis 3:8). God wants to be this close, relate that intimately to us today. It is God's desire to walk with and to communicate with His children. He wants to talk to us. And He wants us to listen and talk to Him, too.

How does the intimate fellowship Adam and Eve had with their Creator in the Garden mirror the relationship God desires to have with His children today?

_____

_____

_____

How might you have experienced this intimacy with God in your own life?

_____

_____

There is more good news — we can hear His voice! The Bible, God's love letter to mankind, makes it clear that we were created to have two-way communication with Him. Jesus tells us in John 10:27, _"My sheep hear My voice, and I know them, and they follow Me."_

When I was in college, I did my internship in video production at a local public television station. One day my boss and I traveled to a video shoot with a young woman who worked in the donor relations department. Along the way she told us that, at the urging of her father, she had recently purchased a flat with two apartments. Still uncomfortable with the big step she had just taken, she thought out loud, "How do you know if you are making the right decisions in life?"

That's the question of the ages, isn't it?

Have you ever asked this question, the "question of the ages"? If so, to what decision(s) were you referring? Did you ever reach a satisfactory answer to the question? If so, what was it?

_____

_____

_____

_____

As children of God, we don't have to walk blindly through life, wondering about every decision that we make. We can have confidence that we will hear our Father's voice. The apostle Paul wrote in Romans 8:14: _For as many as are led by the Spirit of God, these are sons of God._ If we are God's children, if we are truly born again, the Holy Spirit will lead us through life.

We have further assurance of this promise in the psalms.

Write out Psalm 37:23–24.

_____

_____

_____

God will order our steps, and even when we "blow it," if we are truly seeking to do His will, He will pick us up from where we have fallen and give us a second chance.

The most difficult part of hearing God is the time it takes to learn to discern His voice from the many other voices that crowd our lives — and it takes a humble heart. Jeremiah 29:12–13 says:

> _Then you will call upon Me and go and pray to Me, and I will listen to you. And you will seek Me and find Me, when you search for Me with all your heart._

What does each of these passages have to teach us about hearing God's voice and discerning His will?
Romans 8:14

_____

_____

Psalm 37:23–24

_____

_____

Jeremiah 29:12–13

_____

_____

We can't make demands on almighty God. We can't shake our fist at the sky and say, *All right, God. Let me hear You!* and expect to receive an answer. But we can ask, seek, and knock, and the Bible promises that God will open the door. God will reveal Himself to those who humbly seek Him.

The writer of Proverbs describes how our thoughts and intentions will line up with God's will when we submit ourselves fully to the Lord:

> *Roll your works upon the Lord [commit and trust them wholly to Him; He will cause your thoughts to become agreeable to His will, and] so shall your plans be established and succeed.*
>
> —Proverbs 16:3 AMP

The Lord manifests Himself to us and through us as we humbly seek Him. Meditate on these words from Proverbs 3:

> *Trust in the LORD with all your heart, and lean not on your own understanding;*
> *In all your ways acknowledge Him, And He shall direct your paths.*
>
> —Verses 5–6

Day Two: Other Whispering Voices

In the e-mail I quoted in the introduction to this week's study, the reader had listed three different voices to which we may listen — and he was absolutely correct:

> Anyone who can present a way one can actually know that the voice they
> are hearing is from *God,* not man or Satan, would change the world.

By now, you should understand that you can hear God's voice, but you should also be alerted to the fact that other voices whisper into our ears as well: the voice of our own fleshly desires and the voice of the devil.

All of us have experienced the voice of our fleshly desires at some time in our lives. Describe a time when you have struggled to follow God's voice over the demands of temptation.

_____

_____

_____

_____

Jesus provides assurance for believers in John 10:4–5:

> *And the sheep follow him, for they know his voice. Yet they will by no means follow*
> *a stranger, but will flee from him, for they do not know the voice of strangers.*

What does "following the voice of the Good Shepherd" mean to you?

_____

_____

What are the benefits of being a "sheep" in this passage?

_____

What do those who belong to Christ do when they hear the voice of a stranger?

_____

What does this mean to your relationship with God and your ability to stand in the face of temptation?

_____

_____

We can train our ear to recognize the voice of God above all the noise of the other whispering voices:

> _Solid food belongs to those who are of full age, that is, those who by reason of use have their senses exercised to discern **both good and evil.**_
>
> —Hebrews 5:14, emphasis mine

What might "solid food" refer to in the context of our study?

_____

What might "discerning between good and evil" refer to in the context of our study?

_____

_____

How does the writer of Hebrews describe "those who are of full age" in this passage?

_____

_____

How have these people trained themselves to discern both good and evil?

_____

_____

It is by _practicing_, through _continual use,_ that we can discern whether what we are hearing is from God, our flesh, or the devil. What a comfort it is to know that — with practice — we _can_ discern what the voice of the Lord is saying:

> _Your ears shall hear a word behind you, saying, "This is the way, walk in it,"_
> _Whenever you turn to the right hand or whenever you turn to the left._
>
> —Isaiah 30:21

What a promise!

What does this verse mean to you?

_____

_____

Give an example of when your ears "heard a word behind you" and you knew exactly what God wanted you to do. What was the outcome?

_____

_____

_____

If you've never had such an experience, why might that be? What "other voices" might be making it difficult to hear the voice of God?

_____

_____

What would it take to confirm to you that you are hearing the voice of God, and not another?

_____

_____

God will speak, and you can hear His voice, but you must be careful — especially when you are a young Christian — that you objectively confirm that you are following the Holy Spirit and not another voice. Our own flesh can scream pretty loud (especially when we are under pressure, or we want something very badly). And the devil is the father of lies — he is the great deceiver.

Day Three: The Seven Keys — An Overview

How can we know whether we're hearing the voice of God and not another whispering voice? The Bible gives us seven basic keys or filters through which every possible leading should be judged. We are to carefully examine the thoughts and intentions of our hearts — and the words of godly people who may have influence on us — through the use of these keys. Today we will take a brief look at each.

1. Scripture

Every possible leading, every prophetic word, every voice that we hear or sermon from the pulpit must line up with God's Word. It must be the first and foremost "plumb line" for all that we do in life.

In Old Testament times, a *plumb line* was used in building construction; quite literally, it was a long piece of string, weighted at one end and when held from above would indicate a perfectly straight line. It was used for comparison in a building project to be certain the walls and structure were not leaning to one side or the other.[1]

With that understanding in mind, it is easy to see how Scripture is to be the ultimate "plumb line" in our lives, the measuring rod against which everything else must be lined up.

> *All Scripture is given by inspiration of God, and is profitable for doctrine, for reproof, for correction, for instruction in righteousness, that the man of God may be complete, thoroughly equipped for every good work.*
>
> —2 Timothy 3:16–17

God will never go against His Word — this is a great assurance to us as we seek His guidance for our lives.

Describe a time in your life when you either did or did not use Scripture as a basis for making an important decision. What was the result?

_____

_____

_____

_____

_____

_____

2. The Holy Spirit's Speaking to Our Heart

God speaks to His children, and we *can* hear His voice — it's part of the covenant that we walk in as New Testament Christians.

> FOR THIS IS THE COVENANT THAT I WILL MAKE WITH THE HOUSE OF ISRAEL, AFTER THOSE DAYS, SAYS THE LORD: I WILL PUT MY LAWS INTO THEIR MINDS. AND I WILL WRITE THEM UPON THEIR HEARTS. AND I WILL BE THEIR GOD. AND THEY SHALL BE MY PEOPLE. AND THEY SHALL NOT TEACH EVERY ONE HIS FELLOW CITIZEN, AND EVERY ONE HIS BROTHER, SAYING, "KNOW THE LORD," FOR ALL SHALL KNOW ME, FROM THE LEAST TO THE GREATEST OF THEM.
>
> —Hebrews 8:10–11 NASB

People who don't understand the ways of God might scoff and belittle the fact that you can hear His voice — but that doesn't make it any less true. Interestingly, however, those who would ridicule spirituality are quickly becoming the minority in our culture. The difficulty of the coming days will not be with modern thinkers who would deny the spiritual realm because they can't explain it in scientific terms. Instead, the challenge will be in confronting post-modern, "New Age" thinking that subscribes to "smorgasbord spirituality" — the idea that everyone can hear God, and each person can choose which god they prefer to listen to. "Best of all," proponents of these ideas say, "you can become a god yourself, while taking cues from the other gods of the universe."

Yikes! When we are only led by what we perceive to be the voice of God, we can fall into grave error. We must balance out any leading that we may be feeling from the Holy Spirit with the other six keys. But rest assured, if you are truly seeking almighty God — the God of the Bible — and are humble in your heart, He will direct your steps.

Jesus said:

> *I am the good shepherd; I know my sheep and my sheep know me — just as the Father knows me and I know the Father — and I lay down my life for the sheep.*

I have other sheep that are not of this sheep pen. I must bring them also. They too will listen to my voice, and there shall be one flock and one shepherd.

—John 10:14–16 NIV

Describe a time in your life when you either did or did not use the leading of the Holy Spirit as a basis for making an important decision. What was the result?

_____

_____

_____

_____

3. Godly counsel

Where there is no counsel, the people fall; But in the multitude of counselors there is safety (Proverbs 11:14). Thank God for the body of Christ!

But the manifestation of the Spirit is given to each one for the profit of all: But now indeed there are many members, yet one body. And the eye cannot say to the hand, "I have no need of you"; nor again the head to the feet, "I have no need of you."

—1 Corinthians 12:7, 20–21

We need each other. No one is able to fully comprehend the leading of God on their own because we all have our weaknesses. My father calls them "blind spots," and they affect many decisions that we make. These are the places where we are especially vulnerable to deception.

The writer of Hebrews encourages us to: *Remember those who led you, who spoke the word of God to you; and considering the result of their conduct, imitate their faith* (Hebrews 13:7 NASB).

The New King James translation says, *Remember those who rule over you.* Those to whom this verse is referring are people of faith with whom you have a trusting relationship. It is not wise to open the circle of our most intimate friendships too wide — but neither is it spiritually healthy to keep all things about our walk with the Lord to ourselves. We should seek out mature men and women of God who will act as sounding boards for the direction we believe we're hearing from the Lord. Such advisers could include your wife or your husband, your father or mother, your pastor or your priest, a cell-group leader, your brother or sister — anyone who is mature in the Lord and has demonstrated a proven track record of hearing God's voice. And they should have the genuine fruit of the Spirit operating on an ongoing basis in their lives.

Describe a time in your life when you either did or did not use the counsel of other godly people as a basis for making an important decision. What was the result?

_____

_____

_____

_____

4. The peace of God

Pat Robertson calls peace the "umpire" of our hearts — it tells us whether we are "safe" (in God's will), or "out" (on our own).[2]

> _Let the peace of Christ rule in your hearts, to which indeed you were called in one body; and be thankful._
>
> —Colossians 3:15 NASB

I have often said, "When God appoints, He anoints. When He calls, He equips. And what He orders, He pays for." Most of us want to know that it is God who is appointing, calling, and ordering the steps of our lives. Without God's appointment, there is no anointing. Apart from the call of God, there is no equipping. And if He doesn't order it, guess who gets to pay for it! I have paid some pretty expensive bills for things I went after that were not in God's plan. At other times I was ahead of God's timing — another expensive proposition.

One way to avoid missing God's direction is to check our "peace meter" when we are considering a decision — and make sure that we aren't just at peace because either we have finally made a choice or we have given in to our own fleshly desires. These situations can bring a false peace that will lead us away from the will of God. As with the other keys, peace is only one of seven, and it should be only one factor in our decision-making process.

Describe a time in your life when you either did or did not use the peace of God as a basis for making an important decision. What was the result?

_____

_____

_____

_____

5. Personal Prophecy (including a word of knowledge or wisdom)

Prophecy can be defined simply as God's communicating His thoughts and desires to man through other people. One of today's most respected prophetic voices is Dr. Bill Hamon of Christian International. He describes a personal prophecy as "God's revelation of His thoughts and intents to a particular person, family, or group of people. It is specific information coming from the mind of God for a specific situation, an inspired word directed to a certain audience."[3]

The Bible clearly tells us to be receptive to prophetic words: *Do not quench the Spirit; do not despise prophetic utterances* (1 Thessalonians 5:19–20 NASB). But the very next verse tells us to be cautious in our approach to the prophetic: *But examine everything carefully; hold fast to that which is good* (verse 21).

The apostle has said something both explicitly and implicitly in this passage. The explicit word to us is that we should welcome the gift of prophecy in our lives. It is there as a part of God's guidance, and we are to receive it with gladness. But the implicit message is that not every word that we receive through a prophecy will be good — all human beings are still sinful, and even the most well-intentioned person can allow what would be a pure word to be tainted. For that reason, Paul has exhorted us to "test every prophecy" and "hold on to what is good."

Dr. Hamon gives this caution about the prophetic: "Though personal prophecy can play an important role in helping Christians make decisions, it is by no means the only way the Holy Spirit uses to reveal God's will and way. Probably 90 percent of my decisions, major and minor, have been made without personal prophecy being the dominating or even motivating factor. But I have striven to make 100 percent of all my decisions based upon God's Word, will, and way."[4]

Prophetic words must be tested through the filter of the seven keys and through a list of safety guidelines for judging a prophetic word that we will examine in week seven.

Describe a time in your life when you either did or did not use a personal prophecy as a basis for making an important decision. What was the result?

_____

_____

_____

_____

6. Confirmation

BY THE MOUTH OF TWO OR THREE WITNESSES EVERY FACT MAY BE CONFIRMED (Matthew 18:16 NASB). Confirmation is reassurance from the Lord that, yes, we have heard from Him and that we are on the right track in following His guidance. Confirmation can come in a thousand different ways — that's up to the Lord. But He promises that He will confirm His word to us, and so, we should ask Him to do so for us — especially when we are facing major life decisions. Amazingly, these confirmations are often the most dramatic and faith-confirming aspects of our Christian walk! God is faithful, and He will make His plans known to you in ways that will astound you if you humbly seek His direction and then wait upon His timing.

Describe a time in your life when you either did or did not use confirmation from God as a basis for making an important decision. What was the result?

_____

_____

_____

_____

7. Circumstances/Timing

There is an interesting portion of Scripture that tells of the effect of circumstances on the life of the early church:

> *After these things he [Paul] left Athens and went to Corinth. And he found a certain Jew named Aquila, a native of Pontus, having recently come from Italy with his wife Priscilla, because Claudius had commanded all the Jews to leave Rome. He came to them, and because he was of the same trade, he stayed with them and they were working; for by trade they were tent-makers.*
>
> —Acts 18:1–3 NASB

This relationship between Paul, Aquila, and Priscilla — which was birthed as a result of life circumstances — became one of the most strategic partnerships in the book of Acts. Many Christians are on one extreme end of the spectrum or the other with regard to their view of the circumstances of life. Some newly-saved or less mature Christians are led entirely by circumstances and completely ignore the other six keys to God's guidance. But some "spooky spiritual" believers completely ignore the circumstances of life — because they claim to have heard the voice of God, they don't seem to care that there isn't enough money in their account to cover the "faith check" they just wrote.

It was circumstances that sent Priscilla and Aquila to Corinth. But because they were walking in the Spirit, the Lord was the One guiding their steps — and as a result they had a tremendous influence on the early church. If we will properly weigh circumstances — including the timing — along with the other keys of God's guidance, we can walk in the Spirit, obey the voice of the Lord, and have tremendous fruit as ministers of reconciliation.

Describe a time in your life when you either did or did not use circumstances or timing as a basis for making an important decision. What was the result?

_____

_____

_____

_____

Many times the Lord will confirm His direction to us through several of these keys — especially when we are in the process of making an important, life-changing decision. Above all, big decisions require big prayer! But as we humble ourselves before the Lord and seek His guidance in our lives, the Good Shepherd will be faithful to lead us, *in the paths of righteousness for His name's sake* (Psalm 23:3).

Day Four: W-GOD

As we discovered last week, because God is love, He is a communicator. In fact, God is always communicating with us. But are we tuned to His frequency? I like to think of His communication with man like a radio station — W-GOD.

Over the years I've been a disc jockey in various capacities. I remember taking the graveyard shift at the college radio station during my sophomore year. I had to set my alarm for 2 A.M., and then I spun the "platters that mattered" until the morning drive jock came in at 6. That was how we kept the station on the air — seven days a week, twenty-four hours a day.

It might astonish you to learn that God communicates with His people all day, every day — just like my college radio station did. But just as a radio has to be turned on and tuned in to the radio stations, we must be available and listening, our ears tuned to His frequency to catch the signals He sends.

How can we tune in to this "divine radio station": W-GOD?

In order to understand how God leads us today, a good place to start is to see how He has led his people — how He has revealed Himself — throughout recorded time. Theologians would say that we need a proper understanding of general revelation, special revelation, and subordinate revelation. Let's take a brief look at these three ways God has revealed Himself in the past, and how they might apply to our lives today.

General Revelation

God has chosen to reveal Himself to mankind because of His love for us. Any knowledge that we have of God and His ways comes as a result of His revealing it to us. God is the One who gives the revelation of Himself as He wills — when, where, why, how, and to whom He wills. As C. S. Lewis put it, "When you come to knowing God, the initiative lies on His side. If He does not show Himself, nothing you can do will enable you to find Him. And, in fact, He shows much more of Himself to some people than to others — not because He has favorites, but because it is impossible for Him to show Himself to a man whose whole mind and character are in the wrong condition. Just as sunlight, though it has no favorites, cannot be reflected in a dusty mirror as clearly as a clean one."[5]

There is an aspect of God which He has chosen to reveal to every human being in the world — this is referred to as general revelation, and it primarily comes through the amazing universe that God has created. Romans 1:20 says, *For since the creation of the world His invisible attributes are clearly seen, being understood by the things that are made, even His eternal power and Godhead, so that they are without excuse.*

Pat Robertson has said, "We can deduce clearly from all the created things that there has to be a Creator. As we see the sunsets, the regularity of the seasons, the laws of nature, we are drawn to the fact that there has to be an intelligence behind all of it."[6] Even still, some men will refuse to believe in God; man in his fallen state is evil and doesn't want to believe what he clearly sees.

The creation of the universe is not the only way in which God is revealed to all people. Since man is made in the image and likeness of God, he is himself a mirror, or reflection, of God. Dr. Robertson continues, "The law of God is written on the hearts of men. Through this moral sense, God also reveals Himself. Man is a being that worships, prays, builds churches, temples, shrines, and other places of worship, and seeks after the meaning of life and the existence of God. In all these things, God draws man to Himself."[7]

God is also revealed in the activities of man throughout history. Through the rise and fall of nations and peoples, God's hand can be seen over time. We recognize God's righteousness in the judgment or blessing of nations as they either reject or revere God.

How have you seen the general revelation of God in your own heart and life?

_____

_____

How has God been revealed to you in nature?

_____

_____

_____

In His creation of man?

_____

_____

Throughout history?

_____

_____

Special Revelation

God, in His love and grace, chose to reveal Himself to man through the people of the Bible — and primarily through His chosen people, the Jews. Theologian Dr. J. Rodman Williams writes, "God has come to be known through His dealings with the people of the Scriptures. This was an ongoing, unfolding, evolving revelation of God in biblical history. He was revealed as the same holy and loving God throughout — He is never changing. But mankind is growing in our understanding of who God is as He reveals more and more to us in each generation — with an ever deepening and enlarging declaration of both His holiness and His love."[8] This ongoing revelation of God through the Scriptures is called *special revelation.*

God's special revelation of Himself began through the holy men and women who prophesied in the Old Testament. These special people were spokespersons for God, personally appointed communicators of His special revelation. Under the Old Covenant the Holy Spirit did not indwell any person on a continual basis because mankind had not yet been redeemed from the Fall. So the Lord chose special individuals — primarily the prophets, priests, kings, and other rulers of Israel — and the Spirit of the Lord descended upon these people to reveal the love and grace of God to the world. The last of these Old Testament prophets was John the Baptist, who announced the coming of the Lamb of God who would take away the sins of the world.

The climax of God's personal revelation is Jesus Christ Himself. In Him *the Word became flesh and made his dwelling among us* (John 1:14 NIV). Jesus was God in the flesh, come to earth in fulfillment of two thousand years of Jewish history, precisely as foretold by the prophets. He came to earth and showed mankind what God is like, so that we could know Him better. In the person of Jesus Christ, God confronted people immediately and decisively. Jesus Himself declared in John 14:9, *"He who has seen Me has seen the Father."*

Jesus affirmed the full authority of the Old Testament as Scripture, but He made His own words and deeds equally authoritative. Before He returned to heaven, He promised the apostles that the Holy Spirit would remind them of His ministry and teach them its significance.

The New Testament apostles were the third venue of special revelation. The apostles provided a special witness, declaring the whole counsel of God from the New Covenant perspective. Through this apostolic witness, God's special revelation was canonized in the Bible in its ultimate dimension and final meaning.

In 393 A.D., the church fathers listed the twenty-seven books of the New Testament after a long, drawn-out debate. The five general questions that were asked before a New Testament book was added were: Is it authoritative? Is it prophetic? Is it authentic? Is it dynamic? and, Did the people of God use it? After reviewing the usage and authority of these books, the council concluded that these books were already recognized as having authority in the church, and so the canon was closed, giving us the New Testament Scriptures as we know them today. As Robert H. Gundry explains, "The closing of the Canon by limiting it to apostolic books arose out of the recognition that God's revelation in Christ needs no improvement."[9]

How has God revealed Himself to you through His Word, the Bible?

_____

_____

How was God revealed to mankind in the person of Jesus Christ?

_____

_____

How has Jesus Christ revealed Himself to you?

_____

_____

Subordinate Revelation

In the New Testament church today, God reveals Himself to the Christian community in a manner that is secondary to the Scriptures. This is done for the strengthening of the church — to equip the saints to take the Gospel to hurting people around the world. God has given the church ongoing revelation as a part of the new covenant. This revelation is given through the manifestation of the Holy Spirit — to our hearts and through the gifts of the Spirit.

As C. S. Lewis put it, "The one really adequate instrument for learning about God, is the whole Christian community, waiting for Him together. Christian brotherhood is, so to speak, the technical equipment for this science — the laboratory outfit."[10]

The coming of the Holy Spirit, the birth of the church, and the writing of the Bible did not eliminate the need for the prophetic voice of the Lord; in fact, it intensified that need. The apostle Paul emphasized this truth when he told the church at Corinth to *covet to prophesy* (1 Corinthians 14:39 KJV).

It must always be understood that prophets and prophecy are not on the same level as the Scriptures. Prophecy provides illumination and it gives specific direction to the believer for a specific situation — it does not, however, provide any further revelation than what the Bible has already given. The ideal means of communication is the Holy Spirit's speaking directly to each individual through the Scripture and by His Spirit. However, even this needs to be confirmed in the mouths of two or three — something that prophecy and the other keys of God's guidance can do.

Prophecy should never be a substitute for people's learning to hear God's voice for themselves. Yet many cannot or will not take time to listen for the voice of God. Some Christians don't even believe that God is speaking to His people today. Others are under so much emotional strain when faced with an important decision that they aren't sure if they're hearing the voice of the Lord or not. Personal prophecy, along with the word of knowledge and the word of wisdom, is a means for God to communicate with these people to bring edification, exhortation, and comfort (1 Corinthians 14:3).

Later we will more thoroughly examine the role that prophets and prophecy play in the life of a Christian. But for now it is good to note that God manifests the Spirit through each person for the good of the entire church (see 1 Corinthians 12:7). If you need to hear God's voice today, you are not alone. Make sure you're plugged into a good, Bible-believing local church where you can receive from other mature Christians. God is speaking today, but you must be tuned in to His frequency. To do that you must be walking in holiness, walking in forgiveness — and you must be a part of a local fellowship of believers.

How has God revealed Himself to you through a community of believers?

_____

_____

_____

Has His Word ever been confirmed to you through another Christian? Explain.

_____

_____

_____

Day Five: The Greatest Adventure

"This is one of the greatest adventures of my life!" my eight-year-old daughter, Margo, exclaimed almost breathlessly as we trekked along the narrow ledge of Wintergreen Gorge — one of Pennsylvania's awe-inspiring canyons.

Carved into the earth underneath the crushing, grinding weight of an ancient glacier, this lush valley is a spectacle of God's creativity and wonder. My breath is taken away when I stand at the base of the 100-foot sheer rock face cliffs, observing aeons of time reflected in the sedimentary layers that flow like tapestry across the canyon walls. I am filled with joy as I follow the delicate artistry of the channels in the bedrock where thousands of years of trickling water have eroded ribbons of limestone in varying shapes and depths. I am taken back to a simpler "Rockwellian" time as I watch my children frolic beneath a pristine waterfall. I remember my own childhood with sentimental satisfaction as I help my ten-year-old son, David, catch a salamander — and then I return to my role as a father as I urge him to set it free, because it would be happier here in the gorge.

Whenever we go home to visit my parents, I love to hike with my children through this living museum of natural curiosities. Of course, we never return to Virginia without several pounds of souvenir rocks, fossils, and sometimes even the living critters that I couldn't save from David's bug box.

The apostle Paul spoke of the wonder of nature in Romans 1, and how God reveals Himself to mankind through the beauty of the earth:

> *For since the creation of the world God's invisible qualities — his eternal power and divine nature — have been clearly seen, being understood from what has been made, so that men are without excuse.*
>
> —Romans 1:20 NIV

My thoughts are always sent heavenward when I experience nature — especially in places of grandeur like Wintergreen Gorge.

As we hiked along the valley floor we were constantly on the lookout for places to cross the meandering stream. While I was concerned about where I was placing my foot for the next step, working to keep from slipping into "the drink," I was also looking up from time to time to see where the best path would be ahead. I had to be vigilant so that we could continue along our pathway without getting stranded between the steep walls and the flowing creek. On occasion we found ourselves in a place that had no narrow crossing. We had no choice but to gather large boulders and build a bridge to the other side of the waterway.

This constant action of looking down at my feet and then up again at the trail ahead of me reminded me of the words of King David in the book of Psalms: *Your word is a lamp to my feet and a light to my path* (119:105).

As Christians, our walk with the Lord is similar to this hike through Wintergreen Gorge. We need God's Word to shine a light on the footsteps right before us — words of encouragement, comfort, wisdom, and sometimes, immediate direction for our safety, to keep us out of "the drink." But we also need to have God's Word to be a light for the path farther in front of us. These are words of direction by the Holy Spirit, spoken to our hearts, through the ministry of a trusted godly friend, or even, perhaps, through the utterance of a prophet of God.

How has God's Word been a lamp to your feet — the immediate decisions that you need to make?

_____

_____

How has it been a light for your path — the future direction for your life?

_____

_____

_____

As the children and I built one of our stone bridges to get across the deep water, I was reminded of a vision the Lord gave me during a time of decision in my life. I was facing some important choices and I felt the Lord leading me to fast and pray. During one of these prayer times, I saw a picture in my spirit.

I was standing on the banks of the Niagara River, only a few short feet away from the edge of the falls. Stretched out before me were several large, flat boulders that rose out of the water, creating a dry and relatively safe bridge across. The only difficulty in navigating this bridge was that the rocks were spaced two to three feet apart — just far enough that it required a slight leap to get from one rock to the next. Below me the mighty Niagara raged, lapping up on the sides of the great boulders, and then thundering over the edge, hundreds of feet to the gorge below. I knew in my heart that my task was to get to the other side of the river.

Although I was nervous about the rushing rapids, I was confident enough in my ability to leap from stone to stone. Gathering my courage, I leapt from the bank onto the first boulder, waving my arms as I landed to maintain my balance. The spray of the falls shot up in my face, and the thunder of the torrent rang in my ears, but I was safe for the moment on the first rock. Taking a minute to catch my breath and assess the situation, I determined that this would not be as difficult as I had first imagined. Bounding forward, I jumped to the next rock, and then to the next.

I was starting to get the hang of this, and suddenly I was feeling more confident than I should have. The pride of my accomplishment was crowding out the wisdom of caution that had earlier reigned in my heart. In that moment, I forgot about God's plan in this scenario as I was caught up in the excitement of the "extreme sport" of crossing Niagara Falls.

But at that moment, God did something that caught my attention. Just as I was reaching the middle of the river, poised to take my next jump, all of the daylight disappeared and I found myself standing there in the dead of night. I could still feel the spray of the water on my face, and now the roar of the waterfall echoed in my ears. I was overcome with the terror of my perilous circumstance. Suddenly I looked down and noticed that the stone I was standing on was lit, seemingly from within. The light shot up to my knees, and outward to illuminate the water rushing past me in an endless parade.

My thoughts turned to the Lord and I prayed, *Father, what are You showing me?*

He spoke gently to my soul: *My child, Jesus Christ is the Rock that you are standing on, and the Holy Spirit is giving you the light for the place where you are. As long as you stay in the light, standing on the Rock, you will be safe.*

But Lord, I inquired, *You've called me to the other side of the river. How am I going to get across? I can't see Your path before me.*

Again the Lord spoke to my heart: *Don't move from where you are until I light up the next stone. You cannot leap into the darkness, hoping to land on a solid place. If you try to move forward in your own strength you will miss the rock, fall into the river, and be carried over the falls to disaster. In My time I will provide the light for your path.*

I stood on that rock for a moment, listening to the torrents of water crashing onto the jagged boulders over the edge of the falls. But inside I finally had peace. I had the word of the Lord.

After a short time, the rock in front of me lit up. *Go forward,* the Lord spoke to my ear. With an easy leap I jumped onto that solid boulder, well above the raging river. As soon as I had landed safely on this new place, the glow from the former stone disappeared, and only the light at my foot remained. *This will be your life,* the Lord declared as the vision dissipated. *You will walk a difficult path. Danger will lap at your feet from beneath you. If you move out in your own strength, you will risk being swept over the falls. You must stand on the Rock, which is Jesus Christ. You must remain in fellowship with Me, and you must study and meditate on My Word. I will provide a lamp for your feet, and a light for your path. Trust Me completely, and only move forward when I light up the next stone.*

This vision from the Lord has come back to me many times since that day as I have gone to the Lord in prayer for direction in my life — sometimes seeking a lamp for my foot in a particular day or circumstance, and sometimes desiring a light for my path to receive direction for the future. And God has been faithful to His Word:

> *The steps of a good man are ordered by the LORD, and He delights in his way. Though he fall, he shall not be utterly cast down; For the LORD upholds him with His hand.*
>
> —Psalm 37:23–24

How has Jesus Christ been a Rock for you in your decision-making processes?

_____

_____

_____

In many ways my life has been like our hike through Wintergreen Gorge. I am constantly looking down at my feet, and then up again at the path ahead of me, all the time praying that God will direct my steps. But the Lord has always been faithful to guide me as I wait for His direction and timing.

The great church leader John Wesley said, "Do not hastily ascribe all things to God. Do not easily suppose dreams, voices, impressions, visions or revelations to be from God. They may be from Him, they may be from nature, and they may be from the devil. Therefore, believe not every spirit but try the spirits, whether they be from God."[11]

Hearing from God doesn't have to be a mystical, "spooky" thing. God gave us a brain and the ability to reason. He wants us to gather all the information that we can and then make a choice using our intellect. We gather that information through the seven keys that are presented in this study. The wonderful promise from Scripture is that if we are willing to submit to God, and we ask Him to lead our steps, He will be faithful to do it! And even if we miss it now and then, He will get us back on the right track as we humbly obey Him and follow His leading.

Dr. Richard Dobbins writes, "You need to see God's will as a stream. You can step into and out of a stream. I know many people who see the will of God as a road that comes to a fork. If you take the wrong path at the fork, they say you can never get back into the will of God. I would rather see God's will as a stream.

"At times you may step out and when you step out of it, you are going to miss the refreshing of that stream. The fact that you are out of it does not mean you cannot get back into it. Ask God to give you a fascination and an urge to go down the way that represents His will for you."[12]

How might viewing God's will as a stream affect the way you make future decisions?

_____

_____

_____

Has it changed your perspective on hearing His voice and following His plan for your life? If so, how?

_____

_____

_____

God's guidance comes step by step, incrementally in life. Taking the first step puts us in the position to take the next step after that. I agree with Margo's assessment of the journey, "This is one of the greatest adventures of my life!"

Are you passionate about obeying God's will for your life? Do you want to see God's kingdom established in the world? Do you want to learn how to hear the voice of God? Do you want to employ the seven keys of God's guidance in every decision in your life? Then read on.

The Scriptures — God Speaks Through His Inspired Word

As my children were growing up, we had a time of prayer together every morning before they left for school and I went off to work. The key element of that prayer was to put on the armor of God that the apostle Paul speaks of in Ephesians 6. As we prayed, each of us would take a turn with a different part of the armor. When it was time to take up the sword that person prayed, "We take up the sword of the Spirit, which is the Word of God, and we fight back against the enemy." And then they would ask in a loud voice, "And what do we say?" And the whole family would cry out, "It is written!"

Of course, the phrase "it is written" is taken from the gospel account of Jesus being tempted by Satan in the wilderness:

> *Then Jesus was led up by the Spirit into the wilderness to be tempted by the devil. And when He had fasted forty days and forty nights, afterward He was hungry. Now when the tempter came to Him, he said….*
>
> —Matthew 4:1–11

Every time Satan tempted Jesus, He answered the devil's lies by declaring, "It is written…" and then He quoted a relevant passage from the Law of Moses in the Old

Testament. He used the Word of God as His weapon to fight back against the temptation of the devil.

The writer of Hebrews speaks of the power of God's Word in our lives:

For the word of God is living and powerful, and sharper than any two-edged sword, piercing even to the division of soul and spirit, and of joints and marrow, and is a discerner of the thoughts and intents of the heart.

—Hebrews 4:12

Jesus made it clear in His earthly ministry that He spoke only what the Father wanted Him to speak (John 12:49). So when He quoted these Old Testament passages over Satan, Jesus was speaking from the authoritative Scriptures. In other words, Jesus was confirming that the Old Testament is God's holy Word.

Christians believe and teach that the Bible was inspired by the Holy Spirit — God spoke these words to men who faithfully wrote them down. The Scriptures are the final authority for our faith and life.

The only way that we can know anything about God and His ways is through what He reveals to us. Through the ages, Christians have held firm to the Holy Bible — both the Old and New Testaments — or as theologians would call it, the canon of Scripture, as the guiding truth for all believers.

Day One: Building Our Trust in God's Word

The apostle Paul spoke of the power of Scripture in his second letter to Timothy:

> *But you must continue in the things which you have learned and been assured of,*
> *knowing from whom you have learned them, and that from childhood you have known*
> *the Holy Scriptures, which are able to make you wise for salvation through faith*
> *which is in Christ Jesus. All Scripture is given by inspiration of God, and is*
> *profitable for doctrine, for reproof, for correction, for instruction in righteousness.*
> —2 Timothy 3:14–16

Of the seven keys of God's guidance, the Scriptures are paramount. It has been said that 95 percent of all the guidance we need as Christians can be found in the clearly understood principles of the Holy Bible. The Bible is the standard by which every doctrine can be judged. Any guidance that we receive must line up with the Word of God, or it must be rejected outright.

That is why a study of the seven keys to hearing God's voice must begin with a clear understanding that the Bible is God's infallible Word. There is no other holy book that can truly be called God's Word. The Scripture is our guide in life, and so we need to know how to properly read and interpret the Bible. Through His Word, God can and does speak to His people!

Non-Christians would respond, "Hey, why are you so narrow-minded? What makes your holy book more special than any other holy book? How is the Bible different than the Koran, or the Book of Mormon, or any other book that claims to be scripture?"

How would you respond?

_____

_____

The Christian view of the Bible is that it isn't just a holy book — we believe that it is the inspired Word of God. If it is truly the final word from God, then there can be no other book that could be God's Word.

The word *inspiration* in 2 Timothy 3:16 comes from the Greek word *theopneustos,* which literally means "God-breathed," as it is translated in the New International Version. Some theologians translate this word as "es-spired," or "breathed out." In other words, God breathed forth His Word to mankind. He didn't just stir the imaginations of the writers, who then wrote something that touches on God's leading, as some Bible critics have said. The God of the universe inspired the writers of Scripture in such a way that they wrote accurately and precisely what God wanted them to write.

Write out 2 Peter 1:20–21.

_____

_____

_____

How did the "holy men of God" speak?

_____

_____

While some things were "dictated" to the writers, like the Law of Moses and the Ten Commandments for example, in many other cases the Holy Spirit divinely superintended the choice of words they used. Dr. Jimmy Williams teaches that, "for the most part, the Spirit simply superintended the writing so that the writer, using his own words, wrote what the Spirit wanted written."[1]

What does it mean to you that Scripture is God-breathed?

_____

_____

_____

Evidence from the Old Testament

The Old Testament explicitly states 3,808 times that it is conveying God's very words.[2] Throughout the Old Testament, we see that God is interested in communicating with His people. The prophet Isaiah declared that his writing was inspired by God.

Write out Isaiah 45:23.

_____

_____

The Jews in Bible times considered the Law to be the true Word of God. They felt such awe and respect toward Scripture that they worked with almost fanatical discipline to preserve the unblemished accuracy of the documents. In ancient times, no printing presses existed. Instead, professional people known as scribes were trained to meticulously copy documents. These devout Jewish scribes believed they were entrusted with the authentic Word of God, and so they approached their duties with extreme discipline and precision.

All of the earliest copies of the Hebrew text are in remarkable agreement. Comparisons of various texts have revealed that great care was taken in copying and that little deviation occurred during the thousand years from 100 B.C. to A.D. 900. But until recently, there was no way of knowing how what was written in 100 B.C. compared with the original texts.

Then a discovery of monumental proportions happened by accident in 1947. A young Bedouin goatherd was exploring some hot, dry caves near the valley of the Dead Sea when he stumbled upon some ancient clay jars. Inside these jars were scrolls on papyrus, leather, and copper — the now famous Dead Sea Scrolls.

The Dead Sea Scrolls were found in eleven different caves from 1947 to 1956. The discoveries include a complete copy of the book of Isaiah; a fragmented copy of Isaiah, which contains much of Isaiah 38–66; and references to every book in the Old Testament except Esther. The majority of the fragments are from Isaiah and the Pentateuch (Genesis, Exodus, Leviticus, Numbers, and Deuteronomy). Fragments of the books of Samuel were found along with two complete chapters of the book of Habakkuk. There is universal agreement among scholars that these materials were written during the last centuries of the second temple, from 200 B.C. to A.D. 100.

As scholars have examined the Dead Sea Scrolls and compared them to the texts copied a thousand years later, they have made an amazing discovery. A comparison of the Qumran scroll of Isaiah with the earlier texts revealed them to be *virtually identical!*

R. Laird Harris writes in his book *Can I Trust My Bible?*, "We can now be sure that copyists worked with great care and accuracy on the Old Testament, even back to 225 B.C. Indeed, it would be rash skepticism that would now deny that we have our Old Testament in a form very close to that used by Ezra when he taught the word of the Lord to those who had returned from the Babylonian captivity."[3]

Jesus Christ Himself called the Jewish Law the Scripture.

Read Matthew 5:17–19. How does this passage demonstrate Jesus' opinion of the Old Testament?

_____

_____

Jesus quoted Moses, Isaiah, David, and Daniel in His teachings. He also referred to Genesis, Exodus, Leviticus, Numbers, Deuteronomy, the Psalms, and five of the prophets.[4] It is obvious that Jesus considered the Old Testament to be the inspired Word of God.

How does the accuracy of the Old Testament manuscripts affect your view of Scripture?

_____

_____

Evidence from the New Testament

The writers of the New Testament also verified the validity of the Bible as the Word of God. The apostles had been sent forth by Jesus as His chosen messengers to carry on His work in the earth after He had ascended to heaven. The apostle Paul wrote that His teachings came to Him as a direct revelation from Christ. Peter taught that the Scriptures were the very words of God, and did not originate in the minds of the prophets.

Read 2 Peter 3:2. In addition to the _words...spoken before by the holy prophets,_ of what else did Peter tell his readers to be mindful?

_____

_____

Read 2 Peter 3:15–16. According to what did Peter say Paul had written his letters? Why is this significant?

_____

_____

_____

Jimmy Williams in his book _Evidence, Answers, and Christian Faith_ writes that the Greek word _graphe_ in the New Testament refers only to sacred Scriptures. _Graphe_ was used in 1 Timothy 5:18 and 2 Peter 3:16 to refer to the writings of the apostles.[5]

How does this evidence from the New Testament increase your trust in God's Word?

Archaeological and Literary Evidence

"All right," you may say, "but it's not like the church had the Bible on a compact disc and copied it flawlessly from generation to generation. There must have been mistakes made through the centuries. People probably inserted or deleted words, or added their own ideas. How do we know that the Bible we have today is anything like the original message of the writers?"

Many exciting archaeological breakthroughs have happened in the twentieth century that confirm the authenticity of the New Testament. The unearthing of early papyri manuscripts, including the John Ryland manuscript, A.D. 130; the Chester Beatty Papyri, ca. A.D. 155; and the Bodmer Papyri II, A.D. 200, bridged the gap between the time of Jesus and existing manuscripts from a later date.

Yale scholar Millar Burrows explained the significance of these discoveries. "Another result of comparing New Testament Greek with the language of the papyri [discoveries] is an increase of confidence in the accurate transmission of the text of the New Testament itself."[6]

Today, archaeologists have unearthed more than three thousand different, ancient Greek manuscripts containing all or portions of the New Testament. In the twentieth century, the remains of many ancient manuscripts of all kinds were found, especially in the dry climate of North Africa and the Middle East.

Biblical scholars of all persuasions around the world have come to an increased confidence in the reliability of the Bible based on these exciting archaeological discoveries.

Has the archaeological evidence increased your trust in and reliance upon the Word of God? If so, how?

_____

_____

_____

Now that we know that we can trust the authenticity of the Bible, let's take a look at how we can best read it, interpret it, and apply the truths of God's Word to our lives.

Day Two: The Bible Is HIStory — The Story of Jesus

The Bible was written over the span of some 1,500 years by forty different writers. These men and women lived centuries apart, in different areas of the ancient Middle East. The background of these people varied greatly from shepherds and fishermen, to doctors, lawyers, and kings. Parts of the Bible were written in three different languages; Hebrew, Greek, and Aramaic. There was no way for these people to gather and discuss what was being added to the Bible — it had to have been compiled under the divine direction of the Holy Spirit.

Even though they wrote in different languages, at different times, in different places, often having no knowledge of what the other had written, the message they wrote was unified under the guidance of God's Spirit. These sixty-six books are each colorful strands in a magnificent tapestry that we call the Bible. Only God could orchestrate such a book — and what a magnificent book it is.

The Bible consists of sixty-six different books with one message: man's need for a savior, and God's provision of that Savior, Jesus Christ. Billy Graham has said, "Jesus Christ is the true theme of the Old and New Testaments."[8]

The apostle John tells us that Jesus is the Word made flesh (John 1:14). He is the same yesterday, today, and forever (Hebrews 13:8). Because He is unchanging and complete, His Word, the Holy Scriptures, the Old and New Testaments, are unchanging and complete. Jesus and the Bible are mirror reflections of each other. When you see the Bible, you are seeing Jesus. God will never guide us in a way that is contrary to His Word. The Bible gives us clear direction for moral decisions — areas of conduct, repeated behaviors, and universal principles where God has clearly stated His will. These are moral concepts that are explicitly stated in Scripture, which are the same for all people at all time. The Ten Commandments are a good example of the moral law.

It is easy to make a decision about whether or not to lie, or to steal, or to murder someone — the Bible make these things clear. But it is not so easy to find help from the Bible in making personal decisions — unique, individual choices that may or may not involve moral principles. Even though moral values may be a part of making a decision, no moral principle of Scripture once and for all tells me what God's will is regarding the choice that is set before me.

For this reason, the Bible is an important barometer to help me determine if a choice falls in line with the moral principles of God's Word but it is not sufficient in helping me to make personal decisions about the choices that confront me in my day-to-day life. That is why God has given us seven keys to hearing His voice — and the Bible is the first, and most important key for finding the will of the Lord for our lives.

Describe a situation in your life in which the Bible clearly told you what decision you should make. What did you do? How did the situation turn out?

_____

_____

_____

Describe a situation in which the Scriptures were not as clear. What did you do? How did the situation turn out?

_____

_____

_____

The Wisdom of God Is Foolishness to Man

The philosophy of man is ever-changing. There was a time when the common belief was that the world was flat. We now know that's not true. There was a time when doctors would "bleed" their patients because they thought it would cure them of diseases. Scientists used to think that the earth was the center of the universe, and everything revolved around it. We know today that this is not true. Today, the so-called wise teachers of science declare emphatically that man evolved from apes, and before that from microbes in the ocean. But this assertion contradicts the very science that these people hold to religiously — there is simply no evidence on which to base such a claim.

So much for man's wisdom.

The textbooks that we used in science class when I was in elementary school would be laughed at today because we have discovered so many new things that we didn't understand then. Imagine what children in fifty years will say about the things that "wise" men hold as fact today. The truth is that God has created such a complex universe, and there are so many new discoveries today that scientists are coming to the realization that man's understanding of the world around him is imperfect, and will always be so.

And yet sinful man continues in his own prideful thinking, considering himself wise.

But there is one thing in this world that is never changing, and that is God's Word. And yet to the man or woman who has not come to the saving knowledge of Christ, the Scriptures are incomprehensible.

Read 1 Corinthians 3:18–21. How does God see the wisdom of this world?

_____

_____

Read 1 Corinthians 2:6–16. How are the things of God revealed to us?

_____

_____

Whose mind do we have which enables us to understand the things of God?

_____

_____

It is the truly wise person who builds his life on the rock of God's Word, and not on the sand of worldly wisdom. Every decision we make, every choice we are confronted with in life, must be judged against the principles found in the Bible. The serious Christian will include in his or her daily schedule regular time for prayer and reading the Word of God — taking time to listen for God speaking through the Scriptures.

God's will is expressly revealed in His Word. Hundreds of thousands of people have suffered, sacrificed, been imprisoned, and even died to make sure that you and I received a copy of the Holy Bible. It is actually foolish to neglect the Scriptures when such a high price has been paid to ensure that we have access to them. No guidance from any of the other six keys will ever contradict scriptural principles, if the guidance is from God. A systematic study of the Bible will teach us what God expects from us and desires for us in our daily lives.

It is not enough to merely know about God — you must know Him. Remember, it's all about relationship, and that relationship is built in daily times of prayer, meditation, worship, and Bible study.

Why would people die for a lie? Have you ever considered how many early Christians gave up their lives for the sake of the Gospel? Why would the early disciples suffer martyrdom if they knew that Jesus didn't really rise from the dead? Write down your thoughts on this subject.

_____

_____

_____

_____

_____

WEEK THREE
Day Three: How to Read God's Word

In order to accurately judge the other keys of God's guidance against the Scriptures we must first learn how to properly read and interpret the Scriptures for ourselves.

Every believer should make it their goal to eventually read through the whole Bible. But if you are just starting out, you may want to approach the Scripture like a library of sixty-six mini-books. Start your reading with the Gospel of John, because the writer was one of the closest people to Jesus on the earth, and the book is written with many intimate details. Next read the book of Acts, which tells us how the disciples lived in the power of God's Holy Spirit. When you have finished, read the book of Romans, which clearly describes the great doctrines that Paul taught. Then read the letters of John, and Paul's epistle to the Philippians. Then go on to read the Old Testament stories of key people in the book of Genesis. After that, turn to the Psalms to learn what it means to worship God and pour out your inner feelings to Him. You can continue from there until you have read the whole Bible, word for word.

How much of the Scriptures have you read? Have you ever read the Bible entirely through?

_____

One of the biggest mistakes that many Christians make is to ascribe to Bible passages meaning that the original text never intended. The best way to approach Bible study is with a goal of discovering first what the biblical texts meant to the people for whom they were originally written. In other words, in order to apply meaning from the Scriptures for ourselves today, we must first discover what the meaning was for the readers then.

Have you ever known someone who took Scripture out of context in order to make it fit what they wanted it to say? What was the situation?

_____

_____

_____

_____

_____

How can we be sure that we are reading the Bible "correctly"?

_____

_____

When studying the Bible we have two tasks: First, to find out what the text originally meant — this is called *exegesis*. Second, we must learn to hear that same meaning in the variety of new or different contexts of our own day — this is called *hermeneutics*. Many of the difficulties in the church today are as a result of the basic struggle with bridging the hermeneutical gap — moving from the "then and there" of the original text to the "here and now" of our own life settings.

What do you see is the distinction between "exegesis" and "hermeneutics"? Why is this distinction important to maintain?

_____

_____

_____

One leading Christian who was involved in a very public scandal some years ago confessed later that many of his problems rose out of improper interpretation of the Scriptures. In this man's case it wasn't just he and his family who suffered as a result of poor exegesis, but it was also thousands of people who followed his ministry.

In their book, *How to Read the Bible for All Its Worth,* Gordon Fee and Douglas Stuart state, "The aim of good interpretation is simple: to get at the 'plain meaning of the text.'"[7]

They continue: "The first reason one needs to learn how to interpret is that, whether one likes it or not, every reader is at the same time an interpreter. That is, most of us assume as we read that we also understand what we read. We also tend to think that our understanding is the same thing as the Holy Spirit's or human author's intent. However, we invariably bring to the text all that we are, with all our experiences, culture, and prior understandings of words and ideas. Sometimes what we bring to the text, unintentionally to be sure, leads us astray, or else causes us to read all kinds of foreign ideas into the text."[8]

How does your life experience and culture affect the way you interpret the Bible?

_____

_____

_____

When approaching any Bible passage, it is important to be able to ask the right questions to find out the original meaning of the text. For example:

• What is the historical context of the book, including the time and culture of the author and the readers, as well as the geographical, topographical, and political factors that are relevant to the author's setting?

• What was the occasion of the book, letter, psalm, prophetic oracle, or other genre: What prompted its writing?

• What is the overall purpose of the biblical book?

• What is the literary context of the wording? Most biblical sentences only have meaning in relation to the preceding and succeeding sentences.

• What is the "point" that the author is trying to make in each sentence and paragraph?

• What is the author saying, and why does he or she say it at that particular point in the text?

• What is the meaning of the words that have been chosen?

• What are the grammatical relationships in the sentences? When translations differ, what did the original text say?

After these basic questions have been answered, you can begin the task of hermeneutics: seeking the contemporary relevance of the ancient texts. When finding a modern application, it is important to be careful of pride and super-spirituality. The aim of interpretation is not uniqueness — you are not trying to discover what no one else has ever seen before.

Why is it important to have some sort of objective control when interpreting the Bible?

_____

_____

How does the original intent of the biblical author affect our interpretation of what is in the Bible?

_____

_____

This kind of inductive Bible study is not intended to take the joy from daily devotional reading of the Bible. In time, serious Bible study will actually enhance devotional reading because the principles and insights gained from this exercise will open up new and exciting understanding of the biblical text that will deepen and broaden your time in communication with your heavenly Father.

It can be helpful to read the Bible in various translations. The King James Version of A.D. 1611 continues to be useful; however, there is need for supplementation by more recent translations, for example, the New King James Version (NKJV), Revised Standard Version (RSV), New American Standard Bible (NASB), and the New International Version (NIV). The New Living Translation (NLT) is a wonderful modern language edition that provides valuable insights to the Christian reader. It is important to make use of more than one translation so as to gain as much perception as possible of the original text of Scripture.

What Bible translations do you use on a regular basis? Why do you prefer these translations over the others?

_____

_____

In order to fully comprehend the Scriptures, we need the help that can only come from other Christians. From the earliest days of the church, believers were strengthened in their faith by the teaching of fellow Christians. The first thing said about the believers on the day of Pentecost was that _they devoted themselves to the apostles' teaching_ (Acts 2:42 NIV). Even though these believers had received the Holy Spirit, the Spirit of truth, they also needed the teaching of the apostles to give them fuller understanding.

One of the ministries that Christ has given to certain persons in the church is the ministry of teaching: *He Himself gave some to be apostles, some prophets, some evangelists, and some pastors and teachers* (Ephesians 4:11). The teachers, along with other gifted ministries, function *for the equipping of the saints...till we all come to the unity of the faith...that we should no longer be children, tossed to and fro and carried about with every wind of doctrine* (verses 12–14).

We do have the truths of the Scriptures, but we still need others who, building on that teaching, give further help in understanding. Without such teaching, people can easily get carried away into error.

Faithful attendance in a Bible-believing church to receive anointed preaching and teaching, study of God's Word together in Sunday school and home fellowships, the reading of good Bible commentaries, inductive Bible study — these are just some of the ways we can grow in our knowledge of God's written Word. Though the Holy Spirit often does illuminate the Word for a believer in his own reading and prayer, the Spirit may — and often does — use the teaching of others to provide insight and understanding.

It doesn't matter how long we have walked in the things of God, all of us need the help of others in understanding God's Holy Word. The Holy Spirit is not simply given to the individual so that he may understand, but the Spirit is also given to the community of Christians and to those who are especially anointed as teachers. We need one another. God may illuminate a passage of Scripture through another brother or sister as we meet together, or He may speak through one who is gifted to be a teacher.

Why do you think it is important to learn the truth of the Bible from other Christians?

_____

_____

_____

What should you do if someone claims to have a "new revelation" from the Scriptures? How should you respond to that teaching?

_____

_____

_____

Our primary goal in hearing the voice of God through Scripture — or through any of the seven keys to hearing God's voice — is to be the kind of person who can receive this spiritual illumination. A Christian who is still largely carnal can only go so far. He or she cannot really get into "solid food," the meatier stuff of Scripture. Progress in the Word can only occur when we purpose to grow up — to turn away from sin and the world and turn toward the things of God with all our heart.

It is mind-boggling what God will reveal in His Word to those who make this commitment to receive. Jesus promised that when the Holy Spirit comes, *He will teach you all things* (John 14:26). Even so, the Holy Spirit through God's Word will lead into all truth — you will hear God's voice through the Scriptures.

Day Four: *Logos* or *Rhema*

The great eighteenth-century church leader John Wesley said, "We sought counsel from the oracles of God."[9] That's the way they sought to hear God's voice. They looked at God's Word, the *Logos,* and desired to receive a personal word, a *rhema,* from it.

The term *Logos* refers in part to the Bible, the written Word of God. The apostle John also used the term *Logos* in relationship to Jesus Christ as the Word made flesh (John 1:1, 14). The written word is a revelation of the living Word.

The Logos has been given to all men — it is God's revelation to the world. But people must act upon the Logos in order to receive all from the Scriptures that God intended for them.

There are millions of people who own a Bible, and many may even read it. But until a person acts on the directive of God in Romans 10:9, to *confess with your mouth the Lord Jesus and believe in your heart that God has raised Him from the dead,* there is no salvation. God has brought the promise of eternal life to their door through His grace, but unless they open the door by an act of their faith, there is no salvation. The next verse makes this clear: *For with the heart one believes unto righteousness, and with the mouth confession is made unto salvation.*

This is true of every promise of the Scriptures. God has given us amazing promises in His Word, but unless we step out in faith to receive them as our own, they will be just like the lifeless family Bibles that sit unread on many people's shelves.

Just as John Wesley received direction from the oracles of God, we can also have the Word come alive for us as we read and study the Scriptures. The Lord will often speak to us out of the Scriptures by what is known as a *rhema* word — a Holy Spirit-inspired word that brings life, power, and faith to perform and fulfill that word.

When God illuminates a personal word for you from the general Word, that is a *rhema* word from God. As you are seeking the Lord by reading His Word, specific things may leap off the page and come to life. God will bring something to your heart. The Holy

Spirit will quicken it to you — this is one of the ways that God leads us through His Word.

Explain the difference between the *Logos* and a *rhema* word from God. How are the two interrelated?

_____

_____

_____

Describe a situation when you have been led of God through the Word of God (Scripture).

_____

_____

_____

Apart from your salvation experience, what was another time that the Lord revealed a rhema word to you from the Bible?

_____

_____

_____

Describe a situation in which a rhema word from God led you to make a decision.

_____

_____

_____

_____

Just as we stressed yesterday in our lesson on Bible study, a *rhema* word must be evaluated by both the Spirit and the context of the *Logos.* It must not only agree with the letter of the Word, but with the spirit of the Word as well. The *rhema* word is dependent upon the *Logos* just as a branch is dependent upon a vine.

When we believe God has revealed a *rhema* word to us from the Bible, we must evaluate it against the other seven keys. You can stake your life, your future, your marriage, your health, your hope — everything — on God's Word!

The Word of God will be a mirror, showing you your need for God. It will break your own will, and lead you to desire only God's will for your life.

Do you have a daily time set aside to spend with God and His Word? If not, ask the Lord to show you what a good time would be for you. Write it down here, and ask the Holy Spirit to help you keep this appointment with your heavenly Father.

_____

_____

_____

_____

_____

_____

Being Led Through the Scriptures

There is an unhealthy practice in seeking direction through the Scriptures that is sometimes called "Bible bingo." This occurs when someone who wants guidance from the Lord through the Scripture lets the Bible fall open and then points his finger at a verse, trusting that this will be the "word of the Lord" for them. The old joke that is told about this practice is that a person first pointed at the verse that reads, *"Judas went out and hung himself."* Under the impression that God wanted to say more, this person pointed at another verse, which said, *"Go out and do likewise"*!

Seeking direction through Bible bingo, casting lots, or setting out "fleeces" are dangerous gambles with God's direction and should be avoided by the New Testament Christian. In the Old Testament, God sometimes told His people to cast lots or set out fleeces to establish His will, but today God leads His people through His Word and by His Spirit.

Have you or someone you know ever used Bible bingo or the practice of laying out fleeces in an attempt to determine the will of God? How did the situation turn out? Why are these practices no longer valid for Christians today?

_____

_____

_____

_____

_____

There is a valid way of being led through the Scriptures that is different from Bible bingo, and that occurs when the Holy Spirit plants a verse in your heart or causes a portion of Scripture to jump off the page at you. The Lord has often spoken amazing things to me through this method of Holy Spirit-inspired direction through His Word.

How does Holy Spirit-inspired direction through the Word differ from Bible bingo?

_____

_____

Provide an example in your own life when God has spoken to you through a verse of Scripture that He brought to your attention.

_____

_____

_____

_____

_____

God used this means of communicating with a friend of mine who was in a grueling time of seeking direction for his life. Over the years the Lord had birthed a genuine burden in his heart for the Chinese people to come to Christ. He had enrolled in seminary with the goal of being trained as a missionary to China. He had a tremendous desire to evangelize the Chinese people. For six years he studied, working full-time and going to school part-time. Throughout all this time, his wife was willing to support him in his training, but she never had a passion to leave the United States and move to China. She loved the Chinese people, but unlike her husband, she did not have a burden for China.

My friend was obviously conflicted in this situation, and he asked the Lord, _What is the deal? Why do I have a desire to go to China and my wife does not?_ The Lord did not give him a reply, and so he just kept following step by step and trusting God to bring them into agreement.

After six challenging years in seminary, he finally graduated. That summer an opportunity came for the family to take a long vacation visiting relatives in Colorado. My friend chose to use that time to seek God for clear direction on what He wanted him to do in ministry. He prayed, _Lord, either open the doors for China, and confirm it in my wife's heart, and we'll step out in faith, trusting You for whatever needs we have to go do that. Or give me a clear word that You don't want us to go to China at this time._

One morning my friend traveled to the base of the highest mountain in that area, Long's Peak, which is more than 14,000 feet high. He had never done any climbing before, but he brought a backpack with water, sandwiches, and a rain poncho. Despite his inexperience, he was determined to climb that mountain. He also brought his Bible with him, and he purposed to be by himself to listen to the Lord — to hear from Him, no matter how long he had to wait.

He climbed up a couple of different trails and made it to one level below the summit, a beautiful spot called the keyhole. By the time he got to this point it was getting too late to climb to the peak, so he decided to stop and head back down the mountain. To get to the keyhole there is a boulder field that you have to navigate. He had crossed it without any difficulty on the way up, but on the way down he took a false step and injured his knees as he jumped from one boulder to another. When he was finally past the field, he decided to stop and take a rest. But when he sat down his knees froze up on him, causing excruciating pain.

Until that point he had been praying throughout the day and reading different portions of Scripture, but he had not heard a clear answer from God. Now in the midst of his pain he cried out to God, *Lord, I've been here all day, reading Your Word, and listening for Your voice. I need to know Your plan for my life. What is it?* He opened his Bible at that moment, and the Lord drew his eye to Acts 16:7 which says, *But the Spirit did not permit them* [Paul and Timothy] *to go to Asia.*

At that moment the Lord brought the entire scenario of the apostle Paul's experience to light.

> *Now when they had gone through Phrygia and the region of Galatia, they were forbidden by the Holy Spirit to preach the word in Asia. After they had come to Mysia, they tried to go into Bithynia, but the Spirit did not permit them. So passing by Mysia, they came down to Troas. And a vision appeared to Paul in the night. A man of Macedonia stood and pleaded with him, saying, "Come over to Macedonia and help us." Now after he had seen the vision, immediately we sought to go to Macedonia, concluding that the Lord had called us to preach the gospel to them.*
>
> —Acts 16:6–10

Paul had been trying to go to Asia, and he believed that was the Lord's will for his ministry. He was pressing in that direction for an untold length of time. Who knows how long it was that Paul had wanted to head in that direction — it could have been years. But he finally discerned that God did not want him to go to Asia. Soon after that, Paul had a dream of the man from Macedonia. As a result, Paul was led into Europe where the Gospel flourished.

Immediately the Lord spoke to my friend declaring, *Do not go to Asia, and quit asking.* God didn't tell my friend where to go or what to do. He just made it clear that he was not to go to Asia. After meditating on these things for some time, he stood up, still in a great deal of pain, and still needing to descend 13,000 feet. Needless to say, it took him some time to get to the bottom. But on the way down, the Lord began confirming His Word to him. He started seeing how in one thing after another God was leading his steps. He had wanted him to be in seminary. He wanted him to learn the principles of missions. He wanted him to interact with all the people he met along the way. So He allowed that desire to stay in his heart, and He even fostered it a little bit, so that he could become the minister that He wanted him to be. But the ultimate goal in the mind of the Lord was not China — the ultimate goal was my friend's personal development and a greater relationship with God.

My friend wrestled with God that day, just like Jacob did. And just like Jacob, this man of God walked with a limp after that day. But the limp that my friend has is one of humility — recognizing that it is not just our desires that help us determine the will of God. We also have to consider the input of key people around us — wives, parents, pastors, and trusted godly friends — even if we don't at first understand it. This is especially true of married couples. God calls spouses together, and they must be in agreement to move forward in His direction for their lives. The Lord ordained families before He ordained ministries.

Have you ever felt God leading you in a direction that was different from what the people in your life (parent, spouse, friends) thought was His will? Explain the situation. What did you do? How was it resolved?

_____

_____

_____

_____

We are not an island unto ourselves nearly as much as we think we are. We must recognize that God speaks to us through His Body, and through all of the other keys to hearing God's voice.

If you are married, is there any way that your "ministry" or service to the Lord has come before your relationship with your spouse? List the order of your priorities, along with Scriptures to support your position.

_____

_____

_____

_____

_____

What lessons can be learned from the story of my friend who wanted to go to China? Have you ever thought the Lord was leading you in a certain direction only to find out later that you were mistaken, or that you didn't have the full picture of where and why God was taking you down a certain path? Explain.

_____

_____

_____

_____

_____

_____

_____

_____

_____

_____

Day Five: Study to Show Yourself Approved

As Christians it is our responsibility and privilege to know the Word of God for ourselves. We can't rely on someone else's concept of Christianity to guide us. The Lord has made His Word available to us. And to whom much is given, much is required. You must study to know the Scriptures for yourself.

Write out Hosea 4:6.

_____

_____

_____

Great heroes of the faith have struggled, fought, and even died so that you and I could read the Bible. The Scriptures were not always so readily available. In the Middle Ages, only the priest and the religious elite could read and have access to the Holy Scriptures. But through the courageous stand of many great men who gave their lives for the Gospel, the Bible was made available to the common man in the common tongue.

You have a wonderful privilege that others in history only dreamed of — you have total access to the Word of God and can read and study it every day. Make it a priority in your life.

According to 2 Timothy 2:15, how are we to divide the word of truth? How can we go about doing this?

_____

_____

_____

_____

According to James 1:22–25, how might we deceive ourselves with regard to God's Word? What are we to do instead?

_____

_____

_____

_____

As we study and meditate on God's Word, we can store away God's principles that we glean in our daily walk with God. These can be drawn upon later when we are looking for specific guidance for our lives.

God loved us so much that He made sure that His Word was made available to us. He protected and passed it from generation to generation so that we could have it as a guide in our lives. Remember, God will never lead us contrary to His Word. We need to be serious students of the Bible — God blesses the person who makes the Bible a priority in their life.

Read Psalm 1:1-3. In what does a "blessed" person delight? What does he or she do with the law of the Lord? What is the result?

_____

_____

_____

_____

God will keep you in the center of His plan as you meditate on His Word on a daily basis. To meditate is to think often about the things of God — of His teachings, principles, and the example of Jesus Christ on the earth — and to apply them to the circumstances of your life. As I read the Bible on a daily basis, I endeavor to apply the principles to all the situations that I encounter in that day. I am open to the influence of what I have read, and seek to be Christ-like in all I do. If this is my lifestyle, then my life will be opened in a dramatic way to the Lord's guidance in all that I do.

Studying Scripture increases my consciousness of God in my life and circumstances. The Spirit and the Word work together to draw me closer to the Lord. The closer my relationship is with God, the more I desire to do His will. Through prayer and devotion to God, I open my life to His influence in all the affairs of my life.

As I study and meditate on the Word of God, I grow to understand His principles. When I put those principles to use in my life, I receive the blessings of the kingdom of God as a result of my obedience. As God's blessings increase in my life, I am drawn closer to the Lord, and I desire an ever-deeper relationship with Him. And as my relationship grows deeper, I learn to hear and discern His voice, and He leads me on in His will for me.

And so the progression of God's adventure of faith goes in the life of a believer.

If you want guidance from the Lord, and if you want to recognize the voice of God, then get to know the Word of God through reading and meditating on the Scriptures. God is faithful to all His promises, and He will never contradict Himself. Knowledge of the Bible will keep you from falling into deception and error.

List some ways that you can study the Bible that will make your time with the Lord more fruitful.

_____

_____

_____

_____

_____

_____

_____

Spirit to Spirit — Learning to Recognize God's Still, Small Voice

The great revivalist preacher Charles Finney had this to say about guidance:

> When the signs of the times or the providence of God indicate that a particular blessing is about to be bestowed, we are bound to believe it. The Lord Jesus Christ blamed the Jews and called them hypocrites because they did not understand the indications of Providence. They could understand the signs of the weather and see when it was about to rain and when it would be fair weather, but they could not see from the signs of the times that the time had come for the Messiah to appear and build up the house of God.
>
> There are many professors of religion who are always stumbling and hanging back whenever anything is proposed to be done. They always say, 'The time has not come,' when there are others who pay attention to the signs of the times and who have spiritual discernment to understand them. These pray in faith for the blessing, and it comes.

The Apostle refers to these desires inspired by the Spirit in his epistle to the Romans, where he says, "In the same way, the Spirit helps us in our weakness. We do not know what we ought to pray for, but the Spirit himself intercedes for us with groans that words cannot express. And he who searches our hearts knows the mind of the Spirit, because the Spirit intercedes for the saints in accordance with God's will" (Romans 8:26–27 NIV).

If, then, you find yourself strongly drawn to desire a certain blessing, you are to understand it as an intimation that God is willing to bestow that particular blessing, and so you are bound to believe it. God does not trifle with His children. He does not put within them a desire for something to turn them off with something else. But He incites the very desires He is willing to gratify. And when they feel such desires, people are bound to follow them through until they get the blessing.

When the Spirit of God is upon you and inspires strong desires for a particular blessing, you are bound to pray for it in faith. You are bound to infer from the fact that you find yourself drawn to desire such a thing that these desires are the work of the Spirit. Unless motivated by the Spirit of God, people are not apt to want the right kinds of things.[1]

By His Spirit, the Lord will use our sanctified desires to lead us into the fullness of His will for our lives!

Day One: New Testament Christians Hear God's Voice

God wants to lead His people. And because God is Spirit, He leads His people by His Spirit. Throughout the New Testament we see the Holy Spirit speaking to and directing the saints.

Read Acts 8:29.

Did you ever wonder how the Holy Spirit spoke to Philip? Was it an audible voice? Did it sound like Philip's own voice inside his head, but somehow he knew it was God? Was it merely a feeling or an impression? We aren't told how the Spirit spoke, but He did. And because Philip knew that it was God communicating with him, he obeyed. History tells us that this Ethiopian eunuch received the Gospel from Philip and then carried it with him to his home country. There is still a Christian church in Ethiopia to this day that can be traced back to this man and his amazing conversion.

The New Testament church described in the book of Acts was a Spirit-led church. In Acts 1, Jesus set the stage for the tumultuous events that were to take place in and through the infant church: *"But you shall receive power when the Holy Spirit has come upon you; and you shall be My witnesses both in Jerusalem, and in all Judea and Samaria, and even to the remotest part of the earth"* (verse 8 NASB).

It is interesting to note that before the Holy Spirit descended on the disciples, an important decision was made.

Read Acts 1:16–26.

In obedience to Jesus' command, the disciples returned to the Upper Room in Jerusalem. They were devoting themselves to prayer and waiting for the promised Holy Spirit. At that time, Peter decided that the place of Judas, one of the original twelve disciples, needed to be filled.

How was the decision made?

_____

_____

While drawing lots was a common practice in the Old Testament, it is interesting to note that it was never practiced again by the New Testament Christians after the day of Pentecost.

Why do you suppose this is significant?

_____

_____

In Acts 2 Jesus' promise to send the Holy Spirit was dramatically fulfilled.

Read Acts 2.

After the Holy Spirit came upon them, the disciples went out and did marvelous things in the name of the Lord Jesus Christ. There are numerous examples of their following the leading of the Holy Spirit. When the time came to send out the first missionaries from Antioch — a vibrant New Testament church — the leadership did not resort to drawing straws or rolling dice.

Read Acts 13:1–4. How was the decision made to set apart Barnabas and Saul?

_____

_____

According to verse four, how was Saul sent out?

_____

_____

This was the beginning of Saul's missionary work — and it was the result of a direct word from the Holy Spirit. Later, Saul would become Paul, and he would write to the church in Rome, exhorting them to walk "in the Spirit" and not in the flesh.

Throughout the book of Acts, the disciples went out into the world as the Spirit led them. It is vital that we as Christians submit ourselves to the same leading today. If we want New Testament results, then we need to use New Testament methods — and the most important thing we can do is walk in the Spirit.

Recently a young lady named Jennie shared this story of how God spoke to her through the seven keys — and primarily directly to her heart — about a key decision in her life.

Shortly after I became a Christian, I had a summer job working with a theater group in West Virginia. I didn't have a regular church to attend that summer, but visited various area churches with friends. No matter where I happened to be on Sunday, I had that wonderful new sense that God was speaking directly to me at each service, as though the pastor knew my thoughts and exactly what I needed to hear at the moment. I looked forward to every Sunday service and was glued to the speaker, eager to hear what God would say to me through him.

However, on one particular Sunday, I had trouble listening. My mind wandered endlessly, and I pulled myself back to the speaker again and again only to find myself distracted a few seconds later. After wrestling through a few rounds of this concentration match, I thought of the story of Samuel. I recalled that he didn't recognize God's voice the first few times he heard it. I wondered if God was trying to get my attention.

I quit fighting my "distraction" for a moment, and shut out the speaker voluntarily. "God," I asked, "Is there something you want to tell me?"

Immediately, the words *Fort Wayne Bible College* were emblazoned across the front of my mind's eye. It was as if they were burning on the inside of my forehead and I could see them against the background of the front of the sanctuary. Instantly, I knew I was to attend that college.

Now, I was presently an honors student at a large university in Ohio. I knew nothing about this tiny Indiana college, except that an acquaintance from high school was attending there. But I was so sure that I had heard God's voice that I went home and told my mother that I would be attending FWBC. I was seized with a kind of energy and excitement that I just couldn't explain. I knew God wanted me to go to school there.

It was fortunate that I had this energy to sustain me.

My conservative mother was afraid I was joining a cult, and called the school to make sure I wasn't being taken advantage of. The school passed inspection, and I did indeed go, although my parents had their doubts.

During my two years at the Bible College, I discovered a church where most of my growth in the Lord took place, a church that built the foundation for me eventually to move into leadership as a pastor's wife and worship leader. I met my husband, who eventually became the worship pastor with whom I partner. We attended a small group that is still like family to us today. The close relationships I formed at that school and in the Fort Wayne community are still dear to me, and the college radio station has interviewed me more than once to help support the ministry of the children's books I now write.

I have no doubt that God wanted my attention in that church service. The move to the Bible College changed my life and gave me direction for the ministry that is now such a joy to me. And after years of listening to God's voice, I find that it is still my favorite 'sound' in the whole world!

As the result of hearing the voice of the Spirit in that fateful service, Jennie's life was radically changed, leading her to the vital ministry she serves in today!

We see a dramatic biblical example of the life in the Spirit from Paul himself, beginning in Acts 20. The impression is given that the apostle is rushing to Jerusalem — and the reason is revealed beginning in verse 22. Meeting with the elders in the church at Ephesus, Paul encourages them and then declares:

> *And now, behold, bound in spirit, I am on my way to Jerusalem, not knowing what will happen to me there, except that the Holy Spirit solemnly testifies to me in every city, saying that bonds and afflictions await me. But I do not consider my life of any account as dear to myself, in order that I may finish my course, and the ministry which I received from the Lord Jesus, to testify solemnly of the gospel of the grace of God. And now, behold, I know that all of you, among whom I went about preaching the kingdom, will see my face no more.*
>
> —Acts 20:22–25 NASB

The Bible says that Paul knew that he would never see them again. But how did he know? Because he was living a dynamic Christian life, walking in the Spirit by faith.

You and I can enjoy that same walk today! Jesus is the same yesterday, today, and forever — and the kingdom of God is among us. We just need to take a step of faith to leave our safe, comfortable, spiritually-unproductive life in the flesh, and enter the unsure, uncomfortable, fruit-bearing life in the Spirit.

What "step of faith" might you need to take to reach a place in which you "live in the Spirit"?

_____

_____

_____

In verses 37–38 (NIV), the Bible says that the other believers _began to weep aloud and embraced Paul, and repeatedly kissed him, grieving especially over the word which he had spoken, that they should see his face no more._

These early Christians were so confident in the leading of the Holy Spirit that when Paul said he would see them no more, they believed him — and it brought them to tears.

The story continues in chapter 21 as Paul pressed on toward Jerusalem. Stopping along the way in Tyre, he located the disciples and stayed with them for seven days. During his time with them, the disciples continued to tell Paul through the Spirit not to set foot in Jerusalem. Now we already know, thanks to the book of Acts, that the Lord Himself had spoken directly to Paul that he would be bound when he arrived in Jerusalem. Paul was unmovable. When his time in Tyre was over, he thanked the disciples for their hospitality and boarded another ship for his final voyage to Jerusalem.

Before entering Jerusalem, Paul stopped at the house of Philip the evangelist. This man had four virgin daughters who were prophetesses. After they had stayed in the house for several days, a prophet named Agabus came down from Judea. Luke was making it quite clear that there were several people in the house who walked in the Spirit and heard the voice of God. In verse 11, Agabus physically demonstrated the prophetic word that he had received from the Lord.

According to Acts 21:11, what did Agabus prophesy?

_____

_____

There it was again — the same word that the disciples in Tyre had had! Now remember, Agabus was no slouch. He was a respected prophet with a proven track record. Luke had even mentioned one of his prophecies earlier in chapter 11.

What was the prophecy given by Agabus in Acts 11:28? How did this prophecy increase his credibility?

_____

_____

_____

The proven prophet had validated the previous word that had come to Paul. And when Luke and the others heard this, they began to beg Paul not to go to Jerusalem. Paul had to make a decision at that point. Would he trust in the leading that he had received from the Spirit, or would he listen to the impassioned pleas of the other disciples? It may seem to us as if the word that he had heard directly from the Lord contradicted the words from the other disciples — but that wasn't really the case. The contradiction was not in the word of the Lord, but in the different interpretations of that word.

In this instance, how might the word of the Lord to Paul actually have been the same, but sounded different due to different interpretations?

_____

_____

_____

This is why considering all seven keys is vital. There are times in our Christian life when we are at the point of decision, and it may seem like a thousand voices are all clamoring at once to be heard. You may hear the voice of the Lord speaking to your heart, giving you specific direction for your life, but then in the midst of seeking confirmation and God's timing on the matter (two of the seven keys), other words that come from godly counsel or prophetic ministry (two more keys) can cloud the issue. Suddenly you don't have peace (another key). What do you do?

What should you do?

_____

_____

The answer is to consider _all_ of the keys, not just one or two.

One of the primary ways we can discern between the voice of God and any other voice is if we sense the peace of God in the midst of us. The voice that is accompanied with peace is usually the voice of God. The voice that is harried, hurried, and fearful is either the voice of Satan, or it comes from your own human nature.

A key point to remember is that God leads, Satan pushes. If you are feeling pushed, wait for the leading, and wait for the peace.

One of the most important lessons that can be learned in following the leading of the Holy Spirit is found in Hebrews 5:14.

Read Hebrews 5:14. According to this verse, how do we learn to discern the voice of God in a situation?

_____

_____

_____

How have you heard the voice of the Spirit in your heart? Does God's voice sound different from your own inner voice?

_____

_____

_____

How can you tell the difference between being led and being pushed?

_____

_____

_____

What are some practical ways that you can walk in the Spirit, instead of walking in the flesh?

_____

_____

_____

_____

Day Two: The Spirit Guides Us into Ministry

A friend recently told me her story of growing in faith to hear God's voice.

"No, you're wrong, Lord. I've already scoured Kmart," Stephanie said aloud. "I've been to Kmart, Wal-Mart, Target, Academy, Sears, and Dillard's searching for the boots."

Stephanie Blackstone, the founder of the "Treasures of the Heart" ministry, had provided aid to six orphanages in Russia in the last two years. But none prepared her for what she saw at Borskoe Gorodische. She was shocked.

Now it was April, and she could not shake the images of the children and their shoes from her mind.

Driving to the orphanage from Moscow had been uneventful. Crops were growing in the wide-open fields. It reminded her of Kansas. A turn down a country road that had no road signs led past a few wooden frame cottages. Nestled in the corner as the road turned again stood the 300-year-old building, once a Russian Orthodox Church. A wide path next to the church wound down the slope to a picture-perfect river.

In spite of the beautiful scenery, the pear trees blooming in summer, and the river flowing nearby, the facilities inside the orphanage were horrible. The building had been left in disrepair to a few adults who were committed to care for these abandoned children. Alex, the director, had an agreement with the government that if they would pay his workers he would find a way to feed the children. They came faithfully every day even though they had not been paid for the last eight months.

They were living on the edge of survival when Stephanie arrived. Raw and rugged conditions existed within the thick concrete walls. Live electrical wires dangled from the wall sockets exposing children to one more danger. Hot water was nonexistent. The limited heat in deep winter didn't even cut the bitter chill. Hand-me-downs were layered on for the only insulation between the Russian winter and their weather-beaten figures.

The kitchen was bare except for a few persistent flies nibbling on a stale piece of bread. The wooden floor had rotted and collapsed into the dirt below. And the ninety-nine youngsters who lived there needed more than walls and food. Their feet had outgrown the already pre-worn and worn-out shoes. Bare feet during the brief summer months were acceptable, but the bitter cold of twenty degrees below zero was sure to come.

Growing toes were peeking out of the holes in the well-worn shoes they were wearing. Some were dress shoes, while others were sandals. Most would not have been appropriate for children even when new, but those shoes were all they had. The deteriorated leather had broken in layers and was matted with manure fragments from the pastures where the children played make-believe among the milk cows. Stephanie knew those shoes wouldn't make it through a harsh winter.

How would they fare without proper shoes in the filth and raw ice? Stephanie wondered.

Once back in Texas, Stephanie sought funds to buy the children shoes. A number of people were sensitive to the need and donated money. Due to the harsh Russian weather, she decided to purchase boots that would last longer than regular shoes. The money donated, however, allowed only $12 for each child.

Stephanie suffers with severe idiopathic edema which causes swelling. She usually reclines on Mondays to recover after Sunday activities. This particular Monday she shrugged off the still, small voice urging her to look for boots at the local Kmart.

No store in our warm climate has boots, certainly not in early spring. People seldom, if ever, needed winter boots in southeast Texas.
Still the spiritual messenger insisted, "Go to Kmart now."

"Okay, okay. I'll go," she relented.

She entered Kmart and made her way straight to the shoe department, certain that there were no leather boots in this Texas store in the spring.

A well-dressed gentleman approached her. "May I help you?" he asked her deliberately, as if he knew he was supposed to appear at just this moment.

A little surprised, Stephanie chuckled. "Only if you have heavy duty winter boots. I need ninety-nine pairs in children's sizes!" she said, almost challenging him to respond.

Wondering what this distinguished gentleman was doing here, she asked curiously, "Who are you?"

"I happen to be the buyer for the shoe department at this Kmart," he said with a smile. "What sizes do you need?" he asked.
Still joking, Stephanie said flatly, "Every size."

"Funny thing," he said, his voice sounding puzzled but intrigued. "I just received a shipment of boots that weren't ordered for this store, and I didn't know why."

Astonished, Stephanie allowed him to show her the "miraculous" merchandise. She then explained the situation to him. As if he were appointed, he went to work, sorting and stacking. He loaded box after box of boots onto a large shopping cart. Many were already marked as sale merchandise. He marked the others half price. There were boots for boys, girls, and teenagers, a wide selection of sizes for kids, seven to seventeen years of age.

"I don't know how many pairs there are, but I hope these help," he said after he had the cart piled high with an assortment of boots.

Astounded by the surprise shopping spree, Stephanie replied, "I am amazed by this. Thank you ever so much for your kind generosity."

Her van was brimming with boots. She thanked God, in awe of how He had provided for the orphans in such a specific way. Stephanie offered up a prayer of gratitude that she had responded to the spiritual messenger. The total bill averaged out to $12 a pair, and there were exactly ninety-nine pairs of boots. Each child would have a pair for the winter!

They were shipped in a cargo container to England in July, caravanned through Belgium, Germany, Poland, and Belarus before they were delivered on what was Russia's Christmas Day, just before the temperatures dipped twenty degrees below freezing.

Pray and Obey

Dr. Paul Yonggi Cho, the leader of the largest church in the world, was once asked the secret of his success, and he answered unwaveringly, "I pray, and I obey."[2]

What do you think Paul Yonggi Cho meant when he said, "I pray, and I obey?"

_____

_____

How can you apply this concept as you seek guidance from God for your life?

_____

_____

_____

Hearing God's voice is all about a relationship with the Father, humility before the Lord, and obedience when we receive direction from the Holy Spirit.

Let's return to the story of Paul and Agabus. The apostle Paul had walked with the Lord for many years. He recognized the voice of God. When the respected prophet Agabus declared the word of the Lord, Paul instantly ran it through the filters:

• The Scripture;
• The leading of the Holy Spirit;
• The prophetic word;
• Godly counsel;
• Confirmation;
• Peace; and
• Circumstances.

In the end, Paul took the words as confirmation of what the Lord was already speaking to his heart — he just differed in the interpretation of the word (a key point that we'll deal with later in detail).

How did Paul respond in Acts 21:13?

_____

_____

How did the disciples respond in verse 14?

_____

_____

The prophet's words were exactly what happened. A few days later, Paul was seized in the temple. From that point on in the book of Acts, Paul was a prisoner — but some of his most dramatic ministry came as a result of his obedience to the voice of the Lord, even while in danger of death. He spoke before Jewish leaders and Roman rulers, declaring boldly the gospel of grace. Finally, he stood before Caesar himself.

So, did Agabus give a false word? I don't think so. Paul was bound and delivered to the Gentiles, even though it was the Jews' intention to kill him. The actions that the Jews took against Paul caused the Roman guard to send out his men to quell the riot. Though Agabus may have given his own interpretation of the vision that he saw, his word to Paul did come to pass. The apostle Paul was mature enough in his faith to receive and consider what the disciples and Agabus had declared, and to continue to follow the leading of the Holy Spirit.

How could a word from God be interpreted in different ways?

_____

_____

_____

Have you ever heard from the Lord, but added your own interpretation to what was said? What were the results? What did you learn from this experience?

_____

_____

_____

How can we prevent wrong interpretations in our lives?

_____

_____

_____

I received this e-mail from a woman named Laverne who read my article about hearing God's voice on CBN.com. She wanted to encourage me in how God had led her steps in making a difficult decision.

> The last week of December I felt that the Lord was prompting me to start double tithing. I wrestled with this thought for two weeks until I got my first paycheck of the year on January 15th. The impression in my heart would not leave, and so I knew then what I was supposed to do. As part of my double tithing I called CBN and doubled the amount that I had previously been giving.
>
> The following week, on January 20th, I was laid off from my job. I started questioning whether I had really heard from God. But I was quickly reassured. A short time later, on February 18th, I started a new job with a 20 percent increase in pay. This new position had a generous benefits plan, and I ended up paying 40 percent less for insurance coverage. To God be the glory!

If we want New Testament fruit in our lives we need to live by New Testament principles — and that includes the seven keys to hearing God's voice. God is speaking in all of these ways today to His church — are you listening?

Day Three: Changed into "Another Man"

A dramatic example of God's Spirit moving dramatically in the life of a typical person is found in the story of Israel's first king, Saul. This physically strong man was emotionally weak. After the Lord revealed to the prophet Samuel that Saul was to be king, Samuel relayed the message to Saul. The young man's response to the Old Testament prophet was, *"Am I not a Benjamite, of the smallest of the tribes of Israel, and my family the least of all the families of the tribe of Benjamin? Why then do you speak like this to me?"* (1 Samuel 9:21). Samuel wasn't moved by his response, because the Lord had already made it plain that this would be the new king.

The next day Samuel took a flask of oil, poured it on Saul's head, kissed him, and said, *"Has not the Lord anointed you a ruler over His inheritance?"* (1 Samuel 10:1 NASB). Then he began to foretell the events that would unfold during the coming day. After giving him many details of his coming journey, Samuel declared to Saul:

> *"After that you shall come to the hill of God where the Philistine garrison is. And it will happen, when you have come there to the city, that you will meet a group of prophets coming down from the high place with a stringed instrument, a tambourine, a flute, and a harp before them; and they will be prophesying.*
> *"Then the Spirit of the LORD will come upon you, and you will prophesy with them and be turned into another man.*
> *"And let it be, when these signs come to you, that you do as the occasion demands; for God is with you.*
> *"You shall go down before me to Gilgal; and surely I will come down to you to offer burnt offerings and make sacrifices of peace offerings. Seven days you shall wait, till I come to you and show you what you should do."*
> *So it was, when he had turned his back to go from Samuel, that God gave him another heart; and all those signs came to pass that day.*
> *When they came there to the hill, there was a group of prophets to meet him; then the Spirit of God came upon him, and he prophesied among them.*
> *And it happened, when all who knew him formerly saw that he indeed prophesied among the prophets, that the people said to one another, "What is this that has come upon the son of Kish? Is Saul also among the prophets?"*
>
> —1 Samuel 10:5–11, emphasis mine

When we yield to the Spirit of God in our lives, we are truly changed, just as Saul was. We become the kingdom Christians that God intends for us to be. We stop just observing the kingdom from the outside, and we begin to enter the kingdom and participate in it. We're no longer just spectators in the stands; we're players on the field, following the direction of the coach, and scoring big points for the team!

Throughout the Old Testament, the Spirit of the Lord came upon men and women, and they declared the word of the Lord. This was primarily true of the prophets. In the foreword to Cindy Jacobs' book *The Voice of God,* Jack Hayford writes:

> That God *today* talks with His people is so basic to the Bible's promise and so abounding in the healthy and healing evidence of its fruit among believers, it should never be doubted or rejected. But it is. It is denied by those who fear that an uncontrolled access to or an un-patrolled wall against such a warm, interactive relationship with God might surrender the subject of "divine revelation" to unlimited, hopelessly subjective definition. They fear, in short, that if anyone can say, "God told me," then anyone can usurp the role of God, either through intentional deception or innocent ignorance of His true Word.
>
> That is not an unjustified fear. The history of mankind is littered with the carcasses of multitudes who have fallen prey to such deception. From the time of the Fall of man until the most recent headlines describing the destruction of a band of cultists, either emotionally damaged or physically dead by reason of the influence of an erratic "voice," the danger of deceptive "revelations" has continued.
>
> Still, the Lord Jesus Christ gave pointed instructions encouraging our expecting to know an ongoing personal communion with God. Even more than an "allowance" of this blessedness in intimacy and confidential communication between the Father and His redeemed children, Jesus promised it! And He gave the specific terms around which such interaction of a human with the Almighty may be founded.
>
> *He who has My commandments and keeps them, it is he who loves Me. And he who loves Me will be loved by My Father, and I will love him and manifest Myself to him* (John 14:21).[3]

In my own life, I have seen some of the extremes that Pastor Hayford is talking about. My parents came to Christ in the late 1960s and became a part of a Catholic charismatic community. As a child in a Christian school, I was able to do really "cool" things like witnessing in the park and marching in parades declaring "Jesus is Lord." But I also experienced some of the "weirdness" of the time. There was an exclusivity that abounded — an attitude that said, *We have the truth, and other churches aren't as mature or spiritually "with it" as we are.* As the 1970s progressed, certain out-of-balance teachings began influencing the leaders of this community. And part of the manipulative aspect of the time included some "flaky" personal prophecy.

There were some people who would speak "a word" to another person, telling them to do thus and thus, go here or there, marry this person or that — and there was not much mature spiritual oversight or proper judgment over what was happening. As a result, some people made unwise decisions based on these "parking-lot prophecies," and they suffered some serious consequences. Sadly, some people abandoned personal prophecy altogether, which is a shame, because under proper guidelines it is a wonderful gift from the Lord. Others were so hurt that they suffered shipwreck in their spiritual lives and have yet to recover.

It must be understood that not all of this was done out of improper motives. Much of it happened out of sheer ignorance. Many of the leaders of this community were not much older in the Lord than the people they were supposed to be leading. Their understanding of proper biblical oversight, shepherding, and leadership was in its infancy. Many of these people had come out of mainstream churches where the Bible was looked upon merely as a collection of inspirational stories. Others had come out of the drug culture of free love and free expression.

On the other hand, there were some who were looking to control other people in order to stroke their own ego. There will always be wolves among the sheep. Unfortunately, some of them came to the party dressed like shepherds. Over time their true colors were revealed, but not before several people suffered the shipwreck of their faith. But others, like my parents, learned to forgive and to go on to find genuine, godly leadership. When it became apparent that the leaders of the community had become too controlling, my parents left and started searching for a church home. After spending a few years at a Pentecostal Holiness church, and a few more at an Assembly of God church, we finally landed at an independent charismatic church that was strong in the word of faith movement. While there was freedom in the spirit at this church, there was not a strong set of guidelines for the proper flow of the Spirit in the life of the Christians there.

Then one of the men in the church gave the pastor Dr. Bill Hamon's book, *Prophets and Personal Prophecy.* What he discovered in this book would revolutionize his life and the life of the church. While there had been charismatic ministry in the church, there was not a systematic structure to it. The pastor began teaching on the proper procedures for both giving and receiving personal prophecy in the local church. He taught on the different ways that we receive prophetic ministry in the church. We learned about prophetic terminology, the timing of God, the word, will, and way of God's guidance, and much more. We learned to properly "test all things, and hold on to that which is good" (see 1 Thessalonians 5:21).

In the 1980s and 90s, God was about a work of restoring the church to a proper understanding of the role of prophets and prophetic ministry in the church. In the new millennium, I believe that God is raising up a generation of believers who will incorporate all seven keys to God's guidance in their walk with the Lord.

Read John 3:1–21.

Jesus told Nicodemus that we must be born again in order to see and enter the kingdom of God. In his groundbreaking book, *The Secret Kingdom,* Pat Robertson examines this important meeting between Jesus and the Jewish leader.

> The Lord skipped small talk and went to the heart of Nicodemus' concern, preserving for all generations an understanding of the indispensable initial step toward life in an invisible world that governs all else.... The natural eye cannot see this domain, and Jesus quickly explained that. He probably spoke softly, but distinctly. "Unless one is born again, he cannot *see* the kingdom of God."
>
> Nicodemus was startled.... "How can a man be born when he is old? He cannot enter a second time into his mother's womb and be born, can he?" The poor man wanted to glimpse the invisible world and had been told how, but it went right by him, as it probably would have most of us. But Jesus really had told him how to peer into the throne room of God, from which the universe is directed. It should be noted, however, that He referred first to "seeing" the kingdom. Next, He took it a step further: "...unless one is born of water and the Spirit, he cannot *enter* the kingdom of God."

God is spirit. Those who would know Him — who would worship Him — must do so in spirit. Since the Fall left man spiritually dead, we must be reborn. Flesh begets flesh and spirit begets spirit, so this rebirth must be accomplished by God the Holy Spirit. After that, being children of God, we are able to engage in communion and fellowship with Him, as Adam did in the original kingdom in the Garden of Eden.[4]

That is walking in the Spirit and not in the flesh. It's all about the kingdom. God reveals Himself and His ways to those who are willing to press in to the things of His kingdom, by His Spirit. That's why Jesus taught us to pray, *"Your kingdom come. Your will be done on earth as it is in heaven"* (Luke 11:2).

You could replace a few of those words to personalize it: "Your kingdom come. Your will be done, in my life as it is in heaven." I believe that this is the kind of prayer that moves the heart of God, because ultimately, God's plan is to reconcile this fallen world to Himself. God's heart beats for lost souls.

The Bible reminds us again and again that God is a *personal* God — not some faraway distant "force," but the Supreme Person, who actually enjoys the fellowship of His people. Unlike the cold, stern gods of some religions, our God is approachable. He wants to be near us, and He wants our devotion and love. The good news is that we don't have to wait to get to heaven to enjoy this. Fellowship with God can begin now, and it will continue forever and ever without end.

Read Leviticus 26:12; Revelation 3:20; and Revelation 21:3–4. What do these verses have in common?

_____

_____

_____

Sometimes God uses spectacular methods to reveal His will, such as the cloud by day and the pillar of fire by night for the Israelites in the wilderness (see Exodus 13:21–22). At other times it is a "still small voice" like the one that Elijah heard (see 1 Kings 19:12). But no matter what method God chooses to unfold His will, the life lived following God is truly a great adventure.

Jesus gave us this promise regarding our relationship with Him: *"He who has My commandments and keeps them, it is he who loves Me. And he who loves Me will be loved by My Father, and I will love him and manifest Myself to him"* (John 14:21). How do you know what commandments you need to keep in order for the Lord to manifest Himself to you?

_____

_____

_____

_____

_____

How does knowing that the God of the Bible is approachable affect your daily time with the Lord?

_____

_____

_____

_____

In Romans 8, Paul exhorted us to walk in the Spirit and not in the flesh. Jesus was our example of being led by the Spirit. He prayed, and then He did what the Father led Him to do. Spending time in God's presence is key to knowing His will. In our pride we may think we know what is best — even better than God sometimes. But when we come into His presence, He shows us our weakness and reveals His strength. He shows us our inadequacy and reveals His sufficiency. He shows us our need for direction and reveals His wisdom.

How do we discern the voice of God? How can we distinguish God's voice from the voice of the devil, from our own fleshly desires, or from the many other voices that cry out to us from this world?

Read John 10:27. What does this verse tell you about hearing the voice of God?

_____

_____

_____

A shepherd has both compassion and a firm hand. God will lead us in love and fatherly concern, and He will go out of His way to keep us in His will if we submit completely to Him. If we approach the Lord with a heart to know and obey His will, then we can trust that God will lead us in our decision-making process.

Such was the case for Tamma Westman.

I wondered if I was reaching anyone at all. A Christian writer with a column in a secular paper (Minnesota's *Chaska Herald*), I longed to live up to Matthew 5:16 and be a light to my world. I knew that sometimes believers are the only reflection of Christ the world sees, and my articles motivated, encouraged, and expounded the virtues of our community. But was I *really* making a difference?

One day my editor asked me to cover the story of a local teenager giving a talk on organ donation to his high-school leadership training class. I was surprised when the boy's mother — a short, bubbly burst of energy — showed up a few minutes early, only to leave before her son began his presentation. She hugged the shy teen and seemed proud of what he was about to do — but then she was gone. *I would have stayed,* I thought to myself. *What could be so important as to pull her away from her son's special moment?*

His ball cap pulled low to shade eyes that brimmed easily with tears, the sixteen-year-old walked fellow students through the day his father died of a brain aneurysm. And while his message promoted organ donation, the message I received was quite different: *Call his mother.* The words repeated in my head all day long. Finally obeying, the next morning I phoned her.

She told me the bank had called to offer condolences just two days after her husband's funeral and then asked when she would be out of her house.

"Excuse me?" she had replied in amazement.

"Your house was sold in a sheriff's sale two months ago. Surely you knew?"

She had no idea. And now her family was in serious trouble. She couldn't stay to hear her son's speech — she had work to do.

After I hung up, God spoke again to my heart. He showed me that I could make a difference right here, right now, with this woman and her family. Reaching out through my writing would be a way for me to demonstrate God's love. I wrote one column about the son's presentation.

And then I wrote a follow-up column — alerting the community to this family in need among us.

That column seized the very heart of our town, and my editor was inundated with phone calls: "How can I help?" "What do they need?" Food items and casseroles filled the freezers of neighbors up and down the family's block as people pitched in to feed a widow and four hungry boys. Then, due to the outpouring of our town's goodwill, the local Housing Authority went to bat for the family and reversed the sheriff's sale — an unheard-of feat.

But the crisis was not over yet. They still needed nearly $20,000 in order to keep their home. Donations accumulated in a memorial fund set up at the bank, and in a matter of weeks, they had $32,000. "Thank You, Chaska! You Saved My House!" was the banner headline in that week's newspaper.

God showed me through this situation how my writing could impact my community for Christ — person by person, family by family. *Oh, that You would bless me indeed, and enlarge my territory,* says the prayer of Jabez. God had blessed indeed and enlarged my territory. And although I was only its bearer — like a modern-day Nineveh, our town was prepared for the message I delivered. Had I not obeyed the Father's call on my heart, I might have forestalled the blessings He bestowed on this family, my community, and me. We all might have missed seeing Christ among us.

The Spirit of God will speak to us directly, like He did with Tamma — directly to our spirit; through journaling; through visions; through dreams; and even through the desires He places in our hearts.

Day Four: Desires, Dreams, and Visions

Hearing God's Voice Through Desires

"I am led by the Holy Spirit and this burning fire in my soul — for Africa," said Reinhart Bonnke. Often the Lord will place a burning desire or passion to do a certain thing into you that will be a driving force to accomplish His will, as He did for Reinhart Bonnke. This little-known German evangelist could not shake his passion to see souls won for Christ on the continent of Africa. Today, millions of people are Christians because this brave man refused to be stopped from seeing God's purposes fulfilled in his life.

Follow the fire of desire that God places within you.

T. L. Osborne says, "Desire is the window into God's call for your life. Your talents and abilities are connected to your desire, which is connected to your calling." What do you think about. day and night? What are you passionate about? What possibilities thrill your heart when you think or hear about them? These could well be the call of God on your life. Pay attention to your desires, and ask the Lord to confirm them through the other keys to His guidance.

Will God give you any desire of your heart? What do you think?

_____

_____

_____

What is a desire He might not grant to His children?

_____

_____

_____

What are some desires that you feel God may have planted in your heart?

_____

_____

_____

What would it take to fulfill those desires? How will you determine if they are "from God"?

_____

_____

_____

Hearing God's Voice Through Dreams

Through His Spirit, God speaks to people in dreams.

Read Job 33:14–16. What does this passage have to say about God's speaking through dreams?

_____

_____

_____

The apostle Peter, speaking on the Day of Pentecost in Acts 2, quoted from the book of Joel declaring, *"And it shall come to pass in the last days, says God, That I will pour out of My Spirit on all flesh; Your sons and your daughters shall prophesy, Your young men shall see visions, Your old men shall dream dreams"* (verse 17).

Write out Numbers 12:6.

_____

_____

Joseph was one person in the Bible who had amazing dreams from the Lord, but when he shared them with his family they made fun of him. Years later, after he had been sold into slavery, God delivered him from prison, and he became an interpreter of dreams. Before he knew it, he was in charge of all of Egypt under Pharaoh. After that, his family wasn't laughing at him anymore — they were bowing down before him, just as God had revealed in the dream.

God has a long history of speaking to people in dreams. Nebuchadnezzar had a dream and brought it to Daniel. God gave him an interpretation of the dream, laying out before him all the things that the dream predicted. We are still seeing this dream unfold prophetically today!

According to John and Paula Sandford, one of the reasons that God chooses to speak to us through dreams is that in one fast-moving reel, God may speak with minimum conscious interference.[5] The Bible clearly links dreams, visions, and prophetic utterances, and it is not uncommon for God to speak to His people through dreams. I keep a journal next to my bed so that if the Lord reveals something to me in a dream, I can write it down immediately when I awake. Sadly, many people wait to write out their dreams, and they often forget some or many of the important details. Others ignore their dreams altogether, thinking they are merely a part of their imagination.

Dreams from the Lord can be:
• Warnings of danger;
• Proclamations of events or announcements;
• Used to give direction;
• Used to give comfort;
• Used by God to bring emotional healing; or
• Used by God to call His people into intercession.

If you believe you have received a dream from the Lord, but are unsure what it means, ask the Holy Spirit to give you the interpretation of what God is trying to say to you. It is also good to share the dream with a trusted pastor, mentor, or parent. But don't share it with just anyone. Some people cannot keep a confidence, and others are not spiritually mature enough to have insight into what God is saying. Ask the Lord to guide you to the right people to talk to about your dream.

If the dream remains a mystery, but you sense it is from the Lord, don't be too hasty to throw it away. It may be that the interpretation will come in time. Some dreams, like some prophecies, take years to come to pass.

Cindy Jacobs warns, "If the dream seems to indicate a change in life's direction, seek guidance from those in spiritual authority to confirm what you believe God is saying to you. The dream may be for someone else. Ask the Lord if and/or when you should share it with the person. It may be something you need to pray about yourself, thus allowing the Lord to avert the situation without worrying the other person."[6]

Like all the other ways God will guide us, a dream should be tested against the other keys of guidance. If it is of the Lord it will be scriptural, and you will have an enduring peace that the Spirit is leading you through it. You may be disturbed by the dream at first, and that uncomfortable feeling may linger, but if it is from the Lord, He will give you an assurance that He is speaking to you, even if it is unsettling for a time.

Dreams can be a part of God's guidance, but be cautious; many dreams have no meaning whatsoever, they are merely a function of our brain on autopilot while we sleep. Dreams can come from the subconscious, or they can be brought on by indigestion, emotional pressures, fear, or anxiety. Like all other potential direction, test any dream against the seven keys of God's guidance, and hold on to that which is good.

Has God ever spoken to you through a dream? What was the result of His leading in this way?

_____

_____

_____

Hearing God's Voice Through Visions

A vision is direct communication from God in which He illuminates His purposes in such a clear way that they are unmistakable. A vision can be open — so real that the person senses that what he or she is seeing is actually happening right in front of them. Or a vision can be in our mind's eye, or as some would say, our sanctified imagination. John and Paula Sandford describe visions as "the picture language of God." The important difference between dreams and visions is that when we receive a vision, we are awake, so visions are much more subject to our control.

God spoke to Paul in a vision, calling him into Europe.

Read Acts 16:9–10.

Twice before Paul had tried to preach the word of God in Asia, but the Holy Spirit had forbidden it. It was God's intention that they break into Europe with the Good News.

Why did the Lord use such a dramatic means of guidance? It may be that the Lord had been speaking to Paul to move into Europe, and for some reason he hadn't gotten the message. Or it could be that the Lord needed to provide unmistakable direction on which Paul could look back when persecution arose. The Lord will often speak to us in direct proportion to the challenges that we will face in the future.

As a matter of fact, not long after entering Europe and preaching the gospel in Philippi, Paul and Silas were severely beaten and thrown into prison. Had they not been certain that it was the Lord who led them to Macedonia, they may have concluded that the beating was a result of their disobedience.

Just as the Lord directed Paul and Silas into a new area of ministry through a vision, he also used a vision to break Peter away from his traditional religious moorings.

Read Acts 10:9-48. How did this vision change the course of the preaching of the gospel?

_____

_____

As a result of this encounter, the gospel was preached to the Gentiles and they were born again and baptized in the Holy Spirit. Later, when some of the more legalistic believers in Jerusalem questioned why Peter would do this, Peter told them the vision and how it was confirmed through Cornelius. He also recounted how the Holy Spirit came upon the Gentiles as He had come on the Day of Pentecost. The dramatic way that the Lord confirmed the vision silenced the critics, and the Good News began to be taken beyond the Jews to the rest of the world.

One of the most powerful instances of supernatural guidance happened to Saul on the road to Damascus. Saul had an open vision of a tremendous light, and he heard an audible voice. In Damascus, the Lord also appeared to Ananias in a vision, telling him to go and pray that Saul's sight be restored. Why did God resort to such a dramatic form of guidance with Saul? For one, Jesus told Saul, *"I am Jesus, whom you are persecuting. It is hard for you to kick against the goads"* (Acts 9:5). Another translation says, "It is hard for thee to kick against the pricks"(KJV). I believe the Holy Spirit had been working on Saul's heart for some time — perhaps since the stoning of Stephen, who gave such a tremendous witness for the Lord. The spirit of conviction must have been burning in his heart. But Saul was a zealous Pharisee who thought he was diligently serving God by harassing the Christians. It would take a dramatic event to get his attention — and God did just that!

I have met people who have said, "How I would love to have an open vision, or see an angel, or hear the audible voice of God." But they neglect to take into account that the Lord will often require much, in both service and suffering, from those to whom He reveals Himself in such a dynamic way. The Lord spoke to Saul in direct proportion to the challenges and persecution that he would face as the apostle Paul — he needed such a dynamic display to sustain him and keep him moving forward in Christ amid the great difficulties that would confront him. Thank God that Paul didn't back down from this daunting assignment. In his defense before King Agrippa he referred back to this amazing encounter with the Lord Jesus Christ:

> *"Therefore, King Agrippa, I was not disobedient to the heavenly vision, but declared first to those in Damascus and in Jerusalem...and then to the Gentiles, that they should repent, turn to God, and do works befitting repentance."*
>
> —Acts 26:19–20

In the midst of the trials and persecution, Paul was able to persevere and overcome, in part because of this tremendous revelation from God.

God, who knows everything, who knows the end from the beginning, can indeed reveal His will to people through dreams and visions. They are a revelation from God at a particular point of time. God speaks in visions. God speaks in dreams. God speaks in a still, small voice. He speaks from the Bible, and He speaks from circumstances — and it is all by His Spirit to your spirit.

What do you think of the statement, "The Lord will often speak to us in direct proportion to the challenge that we will face in the future"?

_____

_____

_____

_____

Think about the times when the Lord gave you clear direction. Did you find that it was in direct proportion to the challenges that you later faced?

_____

_____

_____

_____

Day Five: Discerning the Voice of God

God speaks to us through our new created spirit. The Holy Spirit is dwelling in us, speaking only what He hears the Father say. We must train ourselves to hear and respond to that first, by recognizing that it is, in fact, God speaking. And then we must act on it.

We recognize the voice of God by learning about Him through His Word and receiving instruction through other mature believers. It is so important to continue to grow in Christ and in the knowledge of God's Word. We can't live on yesterday's manna. Examine yourself. Are you teachable? Are you seeking to learn more? Or do you feel that what you have learned about God and His ways is sufficient? Attending Christian school, Sunday school, Bible college, cell groups, Sunday morning services, conferences, and seminars are all important. But these are just foundations, not the end of our learning experience. We must commune with God on a daily basis.

As we grow in our relationship with God, and begin to know His Word, we will begin to discern His voice. And as we act on that leading, we will grow more in our confidence as we trust what we are hearing in the big decisions. As we are faithful in little, God will increase in what He tells us.

Hearing God Through Prayer

Prayer is communion with God — it is talking to Him and then listening for Him to talk to you. It is the closest, most intimate relationship with the Creator you can have on this earth. *Deep calls unto deep,* the Bible says in Psalm 42:7. In prayer the depths of your spirit are in communion with the depths of the Spirit of God. Out of this you can begin to discern the heart of God as He gives you instruction, guidance, or a burden to pray for certain things.

Believers should build into their schedules daily quiet time alone with God in prayer and Bible study. But Christians should always be in an attitude of communion with God, ready to pray at any moment. Prayer can take place in any circumstance. Throughout the day, as events pass by, I may find myself talking to the Lord, wanting to know something, asking for advice and counsel, or for favor and blessing. The Christian's life should be filled with prayer.

As we pray, we must remember that prayer is rooted in forgiveness. Jesus taught in the Lord's Prayer that we are to pray, *"Forgive us our sins, for we also forgive everyone who is indebted to us"* (Luke 11:4). The relationship of God's people to Him comes about because of continuous forgiveness — He forgives us, and we forgive others. In fact, Jesus said that unless we forgive, God will not hear our prayers at all — and that is a pretty sobering thought.

Is there anyone that you need to forgive? Could the lack of forgiveness be hindering your prayers? Right now, write down a list of anyone that you need to forgive. Ask the Lord to give you the grace and strength to release them from their trespasses against you.

_____

_____

_____

_____

_____

Be Careful of False Guidance

People want to hear from God. You only have to look in the yellow pages under "astrology" to see how hungry people are for God's voice. But astrologers are merely a cheap, and dangerous, counterfeit of how God wants to communicate with people.

Another false source of divine communication is through seances, as can be seen on the popular television program "Crossing Over." These supernatural encounters seem real, especially when you see the reactions of the family members who respond to the purported communication given. But the Bible makes it clear that God will only communicate with man by His Spirit, and not through some astrologer, soothsayer, or medium. In fact, to seek guidance through such means is an abomination to the Lord.

Read Deuteronomy 18:9–14; Leviticus 19:31; Isaiah 8:11, 19; Isaiah 2:6; and Micah 5:12. What do these scriptures say about consulting with mediums or astrologers? How strong are the warnings?

_____

_____

_____

It is clear that the consequences for seeking guidance outside the biblical pattern are severe — it could even affect your eternal salvation. Stay within the biblical guidelines of the seven keys to hearing God's voice and you will walk in safety and in the blessing of God. There is a difference between hearing God's voice in a biblical manner by the Holy Spirit, and seeking God through New Age guidance. It is easy to be deceived. That's why we need to know the Word of God and use it as a guide to truth in this life.

Rejoicing in Relationship

You should not feel inferior when you hear stories of supernatural guidance or revelation from the Lord to other Christians if you yourself have not had these types of experiences. God leads us as individuals. He will speak to us and lead our footsteps in the way that He chooses. I have never seen a physical vision, and I have never heard the audible voice of God. There are other spiritual experiences that others have had that are biblical, and that I'd actually like to experience some day, but God has not chosen to do that yet in my life. It's not about a supernatural *experience,* it's about our *relationship* with Him.

When Jesus sent out the seventy disciples in His name, they returned with excitement about their new ability to cast out demons and heal the sick.

According to Luke 10:18–20, how did Jesus respond?

_____

_____

Even though God may not yet have chosen to lead us in some of these supernatural ways, we should always remain open to the possibility of His directing us supernaturally. We should also guard against having a cynical response to reports of supernatural guidance or events in the life of another believer. Our carnal reaction is often to assume that these reports are merely an illusion or an exaggeration on the part of the person reporting it. The Bible makes it clear that God will guide His people supernaturally, and we should extend our faith to believe for such guidance in our lives. That is what it means to "walk in the Spirit," and to enter the kingdom of God.

Dr. James Dobson rightly warns, however, that determining the will of God exclusively by the means of feelings or impressions can lead you away from God's plan for your life. He experienced what he called a "phony impression" on the day that he completed his

Ph.D. studies at the University of Southern California.

I had the prize I sought so diligently. Driving home that day, I expressed my appreciation to God for His obvious blessing on my life, and I asked Him to use me in any way He chose. The presence of the Lord seemed very near at that moment.

Then, as I turned a corner, I was seized by a strong impression that conveyed this unmistakable message: *You are going to lose someone very close to you within the next twelve months. A member of your immediate family will die, but when it happens, don't be dismayed. Just continue trusting and depending on me.*

I had not been thinking about death and was greatly alarmed by the threatening thought. My heart thumped a little harder as I contemplated who might die. When I reached my home, I told no one about the experience.

One month passed without a tragedy. Two and three months sped by, and still death failed to visit my family. Finally, the anniversary of my morbid impression came and went without consequence. The impression had been invalid.

Through my counseling experiences, I have learned that my phony impression was not unique. Similar experiences are common, particularly among those who have not adjusted well to the challenge of living.[7]

We can hear God's voice, and as Christians we are led by the Spirit. But we must be very careful when interpreting what we are sensing in our feelings. That is why the leading of the Spirit in our own heart is only one of the seven keys to hearing God. What we sense in our heart must be weighed against the other keys.

• Does the impression in your heart line up with the Scripture? If you're not sure, you should do a thorough Bible study on the topic. You should seek confirmation and assurance that what you are sensing lines up with the Word of God. You may want to get further advice from other mature Christians, asking them what they think.

• Does the impression line up with other things that you believe the Lord has spoken to your heart? In this you must be careful, especially when you are a younger Christian. Sometimes it is difficult to discern if what we are sensing is of the Lord, of the devil, of our own fleshly desires, or a message that we have picked up from the world. In the multitude of counselors there is safety, and the peace of God should rule in your heart.

• Does the leading line up with any prophetic insight that you have received through a personal prophecy, word of wisdom, or word of knowledge? Remember the admonition of the apostle Paul from 1 Thessalonians 5:19–21: *Do not quench the Spirit. Do not despise prophecies. Test all things; hold fast what is good.*

• Has the Lord confirmed the impression that you have received through the mouth of two or three witnesses? I personally do not take what I sense in my spirit or in my mind as a part of confirmation. I believe that these impressions must be confirmed outside of my own feelings or thoughts. And God is well able to confirm what He has spoken to you in a number of ways. Don't be afraid to speak with several mature believers about your decision. The more important the decision, the more vital it is that you seek a multitude of godly counsel.

• Do you have peace about this leading in your heart? You may have peace about one aspect of the counsel, but not all of it. Or, you may not have peace about it at all. Wait until you have peace about your decision before moving forward. *Let the peace of God rule in your heart* (Colossians 3:15).

• Does the impression jive with the circumstances of your life? It may be a great idea. It may line up with the Bible, with what God has said to you in the past, with prophetic words that you have received, with what other godly leaders have said to you, and with the peace in your heart. But if the circumstances are not lining up, it may be that the timing to move forward on this direction is not right, or that it is just not God's will for your life. God gave us an intellect to help us determine what is the right thing to do. Part of the process of seeking God's will for your life includes asking yourself, "Does this make sense?" God won't have you do something that is foolish.

As you look forward, are you viewing the future with fear — or with faith? As believers, we should move forward with confidence, based on the eternal truth of God's Word. Take your cue from Joshua. After forty years in the wilderness, the Israelites were finally poised to enter the Promised Land when Moses died. God told Joshua, *"You must lead My people across the Jordan River into the land I am giving them.... Everywhere you go, you will be on land I have given you…. For I will be with you…. I will not fail you or abandon you* (Joshua 1:2b, 3b, 5b NLT).

God had promised His people a land flowing with milk and honey, filled with vineyards they didn't plant and cities they didn't build. It was theirs for the taking. But first they would have to fight!

So God fortified Joshua for battle by exhorting him three times, *Be strong and courageous* (Joshua 1:6, 7, 9 NIV). In faith, Joshua led the Israelites across the Jordan to a miraculous triumph over Jericho…and then to victory after victory throughout the land! This was only possible because Joshua and his warriors sought the Lord's direction, and then took God at His word.

Today, God is still speaking to His people, declaring, "I will be with you! Be strong and courageous!" As He leads you by His Spirit, move forward with boldness and know that God is on your side, and that He is directing and protecting your steps.

What should we do with impressions that we sense are from God?

_____

_____

Why is it dangerous to be led by our feelings alone?

_____

_____

How is faith an important element in hearing God's voice?

_____

_____

List some of the ways that people seek guidance outside of the biblical pattern. Then list corresponding Scripture verses that warn against such practices.

_____

_____

_____

_____

_____

Godly Counsel — Relying on the Wisdom and Experience of Others

DAY ONE   Read the Book!

DAY TWO   Considering Godly Counsel

DAY THREE   Biblical Examples

DAY FOUR   Checks and Balances

DAY FIVE   The Sticky Issue of "Spiritual Abuse"

Plans are established by counsel; By wise counsel wage war.

—Proverbs 20:18

It shouldn't have happened.

"Bob Slosser's writing class is the most popular one we have," the faculty secretary told me. "He sets a limit of twenty students in the class, and there is always a waiting list of our communication students. Since you're a student in the Divinity School, it is doubtful that there will be an opening. But if you like we can put you on the list...."

She didn't hold out much hope, but I insisted that I be placed on that precious list. I had been an admirer of Bob Slosser for many years. Bob was still the president of Regent University when I first attended in the late 1980s. Although a job opened up for me and I moved away from Virginia after only two semesters, I continued to be impressed by the writings of Dr. Slosser. Bob retired while I was away, taking the title of President Emeritus, and remaining a writer-in-residence in the College of Communication. I had always enjoyed reading his work. In my estimation, he was one of the great Christian writers of our time.

I've always had a passion for writing, and I hold in high esteem those who can meld their craft with their ministry: people like Jamie Buckingham, Ken Gire, Max Lucado, and Bob Slosser.

Years later, when I returned to Regent as a student in the Divinity School, I had hoped to take elective writing classes in the College of Communication. A friend who was a joint degree student in both schools told me that I should take Bob Slosser's class, "The Craft of Good Writing" — that is, if I could get in.

I checked back with the faculty secretary, hoping for a miracle. "I can't explain it," she told me, shrugging her shoulders. "Only fifteen students have signed up for this class. I guess you're in."

I found out later that there had been a glitch, and a class that was required for graduation was scheduled at the same time as Bob's course. All the second-year communication students who wanted to graduate that year were forced to forego "The Craft of Good Writing." By God's grace I received my first opportunity to get to know this godly man. Throughout the semester, Bob encouraged us to look at writing as a ministry. "Make your words white-hot, hard-hitting, passionate," he declared.

The class was tough — brutal at times. Bob didn't pull any punches with his students. Like many aspiring writers, I had romantic notions concerning the life of a wordsmith. Without apology, he smashed those naïve assumptions to pieces. "Writing is painful," he declared, his face wrenched to mirror the statement. "It is just plain hard work. If you are to be a good writer, you will have to toil for countless hours to hone the craft."

For me it was sweet agony. Bob was painfully honest. But it made me better. It made me think. It made me stretch. It made me grow. I was sitting at the feet of a master writer — and I knew I might never have this opportunity again. I wanted to make the most of it. But my professor was also a mature disciple of the Lord Jesus Christ. Bob didn't just talk about ministry — he did ministry, even in the classroom. Every class was opened with prayer, and the needs of the students were lifted before the throne of grace. If one of the students was not feeling well, or requested prayer for a physical ailment, this elder in the Episcopal Church would pull a vial of oil from his pocket, and would anoint the head of the student as he prayed for their recovery.

On one occasion one of my fellow classmates was facing a troubling circumstance with her health. Like always, Bob anointed her head with oil and prayed for her recovery. But on this day, led by the Holy Spirit, Bob knelt down in front of this young lady and placed both hands on her head. Looking up to heaven he implored God on her behalf, praying with fervency and genuine concern — not something you are likely to witness in most of America's institutions of higher learning.

As the semester commenced, Bob's words about making writing a ministry burned ever deeper into my soul. One day in the Dean's office, I was informed that a new program had begun that year in the Journalism School called religious journalism. This study course was designed for students who wanted to integrate writing with ministry by spending a year in the Divinity School and a year and a half in the Journalism School. I prayed about making the move, and decided to seek godly counsel. Among other mature Christians that I talked to, I set up a meeting with Dr. Slosser.

Although he didn't say the words "thus saith the Lord" to me in his reply, I knew that he was prophesying as he spoke. His words shot through me like a laser beam: "There are a lot of 'right-thinking' pastors, Bible teachers, and missionaries out there, Craig. But there aren't a lot of 'right-thinking' writers and communicators. If you believe this is what the Lord is saying to you, I am in absolute agreement."

I transferred into the journalism program the next day, and from there the Lord has opened tremendous doors for me to minister through the media at the Christian Broadcasting Network and in several other ministries.

The writer of Proverbs declares: *In the multitude of counselors there is safety* (11:14). This week we will examine this third key to hearing God's voice: the wisdom of godly counsel.

Day One: Read the Book!

When I was in high school, my father gave me some advice that I will never forget. He said, "Read books and learn from them. All of the achievements and mistakes that a person makes in a lifetime can be learned by reading their book." Dad also said, "Learn from the mistakes of others, you don't have time in your life to make them all yourself."

Seeking godly counsel is like reading a portion of the book of someone's life.

No one is an island to themselves in Christ. We all need to seek out and listen to the wisdom and experience of godly men and women who have walked farther with the Lord in life than we have. There are a number of people who would qualify to give us godly counsel: Christian parents, a pastor, a cell group leader, a professional Christian counselor, a youth group leader, a Sunday school teacher, another mature leader in a church, or a trusted and mature Christian friend.

Have you ever sought counsel from a godly person in your life? If so, what was it about? What did they tell you to do?

_____

_____

_____

_____

When seeking godly counsel, it is important that we maintain an attitude of humility. James says, *God resists the proud, but gives grace to the humble* (4:6). As believers, no matter how long we have walked with God, we must remain open to the input of others. One of my former pastors used the metaphor of a ladder when speaking of godly counsel: "You may be on the fifth rung of the ladder in your life, and this man or woman of God is twenty rungs up above you. They have felt and experienced those twenty rungs, and they can give you advice based on that valuable experience."[1]

The apostle Peter gives us an excellent blueprint for how relationships are supposed to work between spiritual leaders and their followers:

> *The elders who are among you I exhort.... Shepherd the flock of God which is among you, serving as overseers, not by compulsion but willingly, not for dishonest gain but eagerly; nor as being lords over those entrusted to you, but being examples*

to the flock; and when the Chief Shepherd appears, you will receive the crown of glory that does not fade away.

Likewise you younger people, submit yourselves to your elders. Yes, all of you be submissive to one another, and be clothed with humility, for "God resists the proud, But gives grace to the humble." Therefore humble yourselves under the mighty hand of God, that He may exalt you in due time.

—1 Peter 5:1–6

Peter uses a metaphor from his day and culture in this passage. To what occupation is he comparing the job of spiritual elders?

_____

Now read John 13:16–38 and 21:15–17. Do you see any similarities in Jesus' command to Peter and his later writings in 1 Peter?

_____

_____

_____

The term *shepherd* that is used in 1 Peter is the metaphor that Jesus chose when He restored Peter to apostleship after he betrayed Him. This term must have been burned into Peter's psyche, because Jesus used it three times after asking him if he loved Him — once for every time that Peter had denied knowing Christ. "Feed my sheep," Jesus said, and later Peter passed this command on to the elders of the church.

Earlier, Jesus had given the disciples the example of the shepherd's heart when He washed their feet. In ancient times washing the feet was the role of the lowliest servant, and Peter protested. But Jesus answered:

"If I do not wash you, you have no part with Me." Simon Peter said to Him, "Lord, not my feet only, but also my hands and my head!" So when He had washed their feet, taken His garments, and sat down again, He said to them, "Do you know what I have done to you? You call Me Teacher and Lord, and you say well, for so I am. If I then, your Lord and Teacher, have washed your feet, you also ought to wash one another's feet. For I have given you an example, that you should do as I have done to you."

—John 13:8–9, 12–15

Peter's blueprint for spiritual leadership flowed from the relationship he had with Christ. Peter was a shepherd to the early church, and he passed Jesus' instructions on to others, including the admonition for young people to properly submit themselves to the godly leaders placed in their lives.

The apostle Paul spoke of the need for spiritual fathers and mothers when he wrote, *Though you might have ten thousand instructors in Christ, yet you do not have many fathers* (1 Corinthians 4:15). There is a difference in relationship between an instructor and a father. A father can be an instructor, but an instructor is not a father. A father cares deeply for the overall well-being of the spiritual child, not just that the child has learned the lesson.

This is the kind of person that a Christian should seek when looking for godly counsel — a spiritual mother or father in the Lord.

Do you have a "spiritual" mother or father? If not, how might you go about finding one?

_____

_____

The writer of Hebrews adds this advice:

> *Remember those who rule over you, who have spoken the word of God to you, whose faith follow, considering the outcome of their conduct. Obey those who rule over you, and be submissive, for they watch out for your souls, as those who must give account.*
> —Hebrews 13:7, 17

The New Testament is filled with exhortations to respect authority, submit to godly leadership, maintain discipline in the church and in our individual lives. We need to be accountable to some kind of godly headship — a pastor, a mature Christian friend, a cell group leader, or a youth leader.

List any persons to whom you are accountable. In what ways are you accountable? How does this accountability help you in living out the Christian life?

_____

_____

_____

_____

_____

_____

_____

Day Two: Considering Godly Counsel

How should you choose godly counselors? You should align yourself with those who are humble, walking closely with the Lord. Look for a leader who lives out what he or she preaches. Are they guiding their own lives according to the Scriptures? This should be a person of prayer — someone who prays publicly in church services, but also encourages people to have a strong life of prayer and devotion.

You should feel confident that this person truly cares about you. They should have your best interest at heart. They should continually encourage your relationship with the Lord through practical disciplines, like reading your Bible and praying every day, staying in fellowship with other believers, and walking in holiness. This person should want the best for you for the sake of the kingdom of God, for the church, and for you as an individual.

You should carefully consider the advice and counsel of godly leadership, remembering it is only one of the seven keys of God's guidance. Spiritual input from a pastor, mentor, parent, counselor, or mature Christian friend should be weighed against the other seven keys.

Ask yourself these important questions:
• Does the counsel that you are receiving line up with Scripture? If you're not sure, begin to read through your Bible, seeking assurance that what the person is saying lines up with the Word of God. You may want to get further advice from other mature Christians, asking them what they think of the counsel that you receive, although you should be careful that you are not pitting one believer against another if their counsel doesn't agree. (You don't have to tell the other person to whom you have been talking specifically. Just share that you were given some advice and see what the other person thinks.)

• Does the counsel you receive line up with what you believe the Lord has spoken to your heart?

• Does the counsel line up with any prophetic insight that you have received through a personal prophecy, word of wisdom, or word of knowledge?

• Has the Lord confirmed the counsel in the mouth of two or three witnesses? Perhaps the counsel is one of the confirming words to let you know whether this direction is of God. Don't be afraid to speak with several mature believers about your decision.

• Do you have peace about the advice?

• Does the counsel "jive" with the circumstances of your life?
How do you know how to stand firm in what God is saying to you when others around you are advising you to go in another direction?

What do you think?

_____

_____

_____

Have you ever experienced a time when you felt that God was telling you to do something, but your family and friends disagreed?

_____

_____

_____

What was the situation?

_____

_____

_____

What choice did you ultimately make?

_____

_____

What was the result?

_____

_____

Day Three: Biblical Examples

Throughout the Bible, we can see many examples of people who sought the wisdom of godly men and women when facing important decisions. In the Old Testament, Moses received input from his father-in-law, Jethro, in organizing the tribes of Israel.

Read Exodus 18:13–27.

What was the problem that Moses faced?

_____

_____

What did his father-in-law tell him to do?

_____

_____

What was the result?

_____

_____

Moses wisely listened to his father-in-law's counsel. By doing so he was blessed, the nation of Israel was blessed, and the leaders who were chosen were able to do the thing that God had called and equipped them to do.

The New Testament provides another example of the use of godly counsel in the book of Acts. A controversy arose in the early church concerning whether or not converted Gentiles should take on all of the customs of the Jews. The apostles convened a meeting at Jerusalem where the matter could be discussed and a decision could be made.

Read Acts 15:1–29.

What was the problem that was causing division in the church?

_____

_____

_____

What did the apostles and elders do to solve the problem?

_____

_____

What was the result?

_____

_____

Sometimes a divisive issue in the church has to be settled in a meeting of the elders, as was the case in the Jerusalem council. I thank God that salvation through grace won that day in Jerusalem. Can you imagine what our lives would be like had this collective decision gone the other way? While this is not an example of an individual seeking godly counsel, it does have wonderful lessons to teach about coming together in the name of Jesus to make a decision on a vitally important issue.

Another interesting example of godly counsel is seen in the story of Paul's choosing Timothy as one of his traveling companions.

Read Acts 16:1–5. What caused Paul to choose Timothy as a traveling companion?

_____

_____

It is interesting to see that nothing is said in this passage of a dramatic revelation from God concerning Paul's choice of Timothy. There was no vision. There was no dream. There was no prophetic utterance. Paul seems to follow the advice that he gave to other churches for choosing leadership in the church. In his letters, Paul encouraged the church to make sound, practical choices, carefully examining the candidates' gifts, personality, and qualifications for the role.

In Acts 16, Timothy is described as _well spoken of by the brethren_ (verse 2). From this phrase we can deduce that Paul sought the advice of others as he considered Timothy's qualifications. He sought counsel, and he got references. He saw that Timothy had a godly heritage. His father was a Greek, a quality that might come in handy in Paul's ministry to the Gentiles. Luke also tells us that Timothy was a disciple — he was a follower of Christ who was willing to do God's will.

The Scripture also says that Paul wanted Timothy to join him in the ministry. There was some sort of inner leading, a desire on Paul's part to have Timothy come along on this missionary endeavor. We don't know if the Lord directly spoke to him concerning Timothy, but somehow a desire to bring Timothy along was placed in Paul's heart.

After Paul considered all of these things, he came to the determination that Timothy would be right for the job. This decision proved to be a good one, as the churches were strengthened in the faith and increased in number daily. Later, Timothy would become a great leader in the early church, and his personal ministry to Paul would last until the great apostle's final days.

What do these examples from Scripture tell you about seeking godly counsel when making decisions?

_____

_____

_____

How might they change the way you seek godly counsel in your own life?

_____

_____

_____

Day Four: Checks and Balances

Tim and Jeff had both felt led to start a street-level evangelism project in their city. One area of town was populated with X-rated bookstores, prostitutes, and teenage runaways, and they wanted to reach these lost and forgotten souls with the gospel. Their hearts had been impressed with the scripture, *Go out into the highways and hedges, and compel them to come in* (Luke 14:23). They knew that Jesus hadn't spent much of His time with the healthy, but with the sick and lost sheep of Israel. So Jeff and Tim spent three months preparing. Once they spent an entire day interceding for their city. They met in the early morning and asked God to go before them, to help them start something neither of them had ever done before, but most importantly, to bring souls into His kingdom.

They set an arbitrary date. As October 15, 1986 approached, Jeff and Tim made appointments with their pastors to relay what they were planning and to submit to their counsel. They went to different churches, so their pastors had no contact with each other. Nonetheless, both Jeff and Tim discovered that both of their pastors had given the same admonition: The two were not ready and needed three more months of preparation. Despite their disappointment, Jeff and Tim submitted to their pastors' guidance.

Three more months of weekly early-morning-prayer times passed like a summer breeze. As the third month drew to a close, Jeff and Tim were given the opportunity to go to a street-level evangelism outreach at the Mardi Gras festival in New Orleans. Each year, hundreds of evangelical Christians gather in New Orleans and fill the city's streets with Christian drama, preaching, and music during one of the world's most vulgar public parties. Jeff and Tim learned the skills they needed for this particular outreach and headed to New Orleans. They won many souls for God's kingdom during their week of "guerilla evangelism." And when they returned home, they started a street ministry that lasted for four years.

During those years, they saw many lost lambs come back into God's fold. Through many frozen nights during those four Michigan winters, Jeff, Tim, and a handful of believers walked through the streets praying for God to redeem the people there. They prayed and claimed the bars and adult stores for God's kingdom and for His glory. And dancers from the adult theaters, gay men, runaways, and backslidden Christians who had gotten re-entangled in the world, all found that Jesus was calling their names. To this day, the area of town that was targeted by Jeff and Tim has been reclaimed and contains wholesome entertainment, clean restaurants, and even a family-focused minor league baseball stadium. God answered the prayers of Tim and Jeff through the lives that were changed and the positive businesses that have replaced the decadence that once lined the streets.

In this example, how did God provide a check and balance to the leading He was giving Tim and Jeff? What was the result?

_____

_____

_____

_____

As in the case of Jeff and Tim and the counsel of their pastors, sometimes God uses key people in your life as a check-and-balance system to keep you seeking Him for direction. It is wise to use the doubts of godly counselors as a means of double-checking whether or not what you are sensing is really from the Lord. If people whom you trust are throwing up caution flags, it may be wise to slow down for a time of introspection. Check your motivation for making the decision. Are you really being led by the Spirit, or are you just trying to escape a difficult situation?

On the other hand, we must always test the counsel that we receive against the other six keys. Blaine Smith tells the story of the famous missionary William Carey who sensed an overwhelming call from God to the mission field. When he shared it with trusted leaders around him, one man chastised him saying, "If God wants to save the heathen, He can do it without your help." Although this was a godly man, and the others who discouraged him from going were also believers, Carey ignored their counsel. William Carey knew that God had called him. He knew it in his heart, and through confirmation in the Scriptures. He went out on his own, and the missionary movement of the nineteenth century was birthed. Today many of the countries that received missionaries through Carey's efforts are now sending missionaries of their own to other parts of the world.[2]

Sometimes when the people we trust as counselors have a check in their spirit about the guidance we are sensing, it is an indication to wait until the Lord has made His will more clear to us. We may sense that God is saying to go one way, while our parents or pastor are sensing that we should go another way. In the end we may find that neither way was God's plan, but that there was a third alternative that we were to follow. By waiting we allow God to reveal His perfect will to us at the right time. And God is honored by our willingness to trust Him and humble ourselves while we wait for Him to open the right door.

Have you ever waited on making a decision, only to find out that God had an entirely different plan for the situation? What happened?

_____

_____

_____

_____

_____

_____

Mistakes of the Past

Many sincere Christians have made mistakes while seeking godly counsel. Trying to find the Lord's will for our lives can be a tricky business. Disappointments in guidance do happen, especially when people step out erroneously, basing their decision on a vision, dream, or prophecy without receiving the input of others.

Some people reject godly counsel altogether, saying, "I can hear God perfectly well by myself." They willingly walk away from the safety that is only found in the multitude of counselors.

This is dangerous ground. It is very easy to fall into self-deception. Because we are emotional beings, our feelings can sometimes interfere with our reason. God gave us a mind to help us to make rational decisions. Sometimes we want something so badly that we ignore what makes sense just to fulfill our fleshly desires. At other times we are so emotionally involved in a situation that we can't come to a rational decision. One day our heart is saying one thing, and the next day it is saying something else. At these times we need the help of others to sort through our feelings to find God's plan for our lives.

Write out Proverbs 20:18.

_____

_____

Another word of admonition: Don't seek counsel from someone who is in the middle of a similar struggle! For example, a person who has been hurt by other people in the church probably can't give you good counsel on finding a church of your own, at least until they have sorted through and resolved their own issues.

Another mistake that some Christians make in seeking counsel is giving in to what I call "manipulative personal prophecy." As we said earlier, the apostle Paul tells us to _"not despise prophecies,"_ but to _"test all things and hold fast what is good"_ (1 Thessalonians 5:20–21). This statement implies that not all things are good when it comes to personal prophecy! Some people allow their own interpretations of what they are seeing in the Spirit to influence how they deliver a personal prophecy. The Christian, particularly the new believer, needs to be on their guard when receiving a word of prophecy — especially when it comes from someone who knows and understands their circumstances. It can be very easy for a person to move from sharing a word from the Lord into sharing his or her opinion on a situation "in the name of the Lord."

Sometimes this can simply be the result of an immature believer's giving the personal prophecy, someone who hasn't learned to separate the leading of the Holy Spirit from their own interpretation of the word. At other times, however, the motive can be more sinister. There are those in the church who have used personal prophecy as a manipulative device, simply to get other people to do what they want. That is why it is important that a person not rely solely on personal prophecy in making decisions. Again, a word of prophecy is only one of the seven keys of God's guidance, and should be tested and weighed against the other keys in the process of making any major decision.

There are also immature leaders out there who may have been in church their whole lives but are still babes when it comes to the things of the Lord. A person's title does not necessarily indicate their level of maturity in Christ. You don't want to seek advice from a counselor whose pride will be puffed up because they are giving you advice. Be careful to make sure that the counselor you seek doesn't have some hidden agenda. Some people get their ego stroked by advising other people, or even being considered an elder in the church. Again, the Lord will give you peace when you are in the presence of a godly counselor, and you will have a check in your spirit if you are not.

A final warning in the area of counsel is to be on guard for manipulative leaders. Be careful to avoid the pastor or spiritual leader who is caught up in what is called spiritual abuse, which will be discussed further in tomorrow's study.

While the Bible makes it clear that we are to properly submit ourselves to the leadership in the church, dictatorial leadership is never condoned by this command. Only Jesus Christ is Lord over our lives. No man or woman should assume that role.

There is clearly a biblical call for proper spiritual authority in the church, in the community, and in the life of a believer. We need the input of other believers in our lives. We need to seek the counsel of mature godly believers, especially in major decisions. But as believers we have access to God's throne through a personal relationship with Jesus Christ. There is no need for a priest or minister to take the place of Jesus as Lord over our lives. We look to Him for guidance in our decisions, and then we seek confirmation and clarity from other brothers and sisters on what we sense the Lord is saying — we don't seek their permission.

Read John 16:13. Who is the One who is to guide us into all truth?

_____

How can this passage relate to your own life?

_____

_____

_____

_____

Day Five: The Sticky Issue of "Spiritual Abuse"

Today we will look at the subtle but dangerous issue of spiritual abuse.

Spiritual abuse can be difficult to detect at first if you have never encountered it. In a manipulative church, the pastor or senior leaders have positioned themselves to take the place of the Holy Spirit in people's lives. They may try to put undue influence on the choices that people in their congregation are making. They might try to sway someone's decision in a matter to keep them under their control, or to keep them from leaving the church. People in a controlling church are often told they cannot leave the church with God's blessing unless the pastor approves the decision. They are warned that if they don't follow the pastor's guidance, not only will God not bless them, but they will also bring a curse upon themselves or their family. Leaving the "covering" of the church and the controlling pastor will result in some sort of calamity.

When a pastor tells his congregation that those who leave his church or disobey his authority are in danger of God's wrath, you can be sure this man is operating in a spirit of control. He is attempting to sow fear as a carnal means of keeping people in his church.

"If you leave this church," he may warn, "the blessing of God will be lifted from your life, and you will miss God's will. You will be in rebellion, and you will open yourself up to all kinds of calamity. The devil will have freedom to attack you because you have walked away from God's protection," that "protection" being the one true church that he happens to pastor.

Fear is the motivation behind such comments — not love. You can be sure that this type of reasoning is not from God. Jesus never motivated people out of fear. Fear is a form of manipulation, which the Bible calls witchcraft. Manipulation is sin. Instead of motivating people through love and a call to serve the body of Christ and reach the lost, a spiritually abusive minister will try to motivate through manipulation.

The apostle John is called the apostle of love because he wrote so much about our call as Christians to walk in love. *There is no fear in love; but perfect love casts out fear,* he wrote in 1 John 4:18.

How can 1 John 4:18 help us to detect the presence of spiritual abuse?

_____

_____

By keeping people in fear, controlling spiritual leaders work to get good Christian people to build their religious kingdoms — by telling them that they are building the kingdom of God. We see this kind of prophet and priest in the book of Jeremiah. The controlling leaders are focused on their own needs being met, and the needs of the people are ignored.

Read Jeremiah 6:13–14. How were the prophets and priests disobeying God?

_____

_____

Jesus was more critical of the religious leaders of His day than He was of the sinners, and for good reason. The Jewish leaders put false religious burdens on the people for the sake of their own prosperity.

Read Matthew 23:4. What did Jesus have to say about the Pharisees?

_____

_____

In this case, as it is in controlling churches today, the people were burdened with rules and regulations that needed to be performed to gain the acceptance of the religious leaders — in that day the Pharisees. Today, it is the manipulative spiritual leader. Many Christians today find themselves bearing the heavy load of the religious baggage in an abusive system. Around the world, hurting churchgoers struggle to earn the favor and approval of a modern-day Pharisee, all the while thinking they are earning the favor of God.

What examples of spiritual abuse have you seen? It may have been in your church or another, by a pastor or a lay person.

_____

_____

_____

_____

How was your experience similar or dissimilar to the description of the Pharisees in the Bible?

_____

_____

_____

The good news is that if you are in Christ, you already have God's favor! And no amount of work for a spiritually abusive pastor will give you more acceptance than you already have.

Jesus recognized the burden that was being placed on sincere believers in His time, who just wanted to do what is right. He saw them as sheep without a shepherd, even though they were involved in the religious rituals in the temple and synagogues.

> _They were bewildered (harassed and distressed and dejected and helpless), like sheep without a shepherd._
>
> —Matthew 9:36 AMP

In his book, _Warning Signs of Spiritual Abuse,_ Mike Fehlauer points out that Jesus saw these dear people as harassed: "This word conveys the idea of some outside force pressing upon the people, causing them to feel weary, distressed and downcast. This outside force was the religious system that placed its emphasis on outward appearances. It was a system that promised peace based on one's ability to follow the prescribed rules and regulations. If one failed, then there was judgment."[3]

"Not having a shepherd didn't mean that the people lacked for those who told them what to do," he continues. "There were plenty of Pharisees willing to do that. It meant they had no one to lead them to spiritual green pastures. A shepherd doesn't drive his sheep as cattlemen drive their cattle. A shepherd leads his sheep to a safe place where food is plentiful and where they can find rest."[4]

The term _shepherd_ is an Old Testament metaphor as well. Ezekiel 34 contains an exhortation in which the Lord holds the leaders of Israel responsible for failing to care for the flock:

Son of man, prophesy against the shepherds of Israel, prophesy and say to them,
"Thus says the Lord GOD to the shepherds: 'Woe to the shepherds of Israel who feed
themselves! Should not the shepherds feed the flocks? You eat the fat and clothe
yourselves with the wool; you slaughter the fatlings, but you do not feed the flock.
The weak you have not strengthened, nor have you healed those who were sick, nor
bound up the broken, nor brought back what was driven away, nor sought what
was lost; but with force and cruelty you have ruled them. So they were scattered
because there was no shepherd.'"

—Ezekiel 34:2–5

I wonder if these modern-day Pharisees realize that God considers their congregations as sheep without shepherds. Perhaps if they recognized how God viewed the situation, they would change their ways.

The Christian seeking guidance from a spiritual leader must also be on the lookout for the dangerous trap of spiritual elitism that can produce an "us-and-them," or a "fortress" mentality. This is a telltale sign of spiritual abuse. A church or pastor with an elitist attitude teaches, if ever so subtly, that no other church or ministry is preaching the pure gospel — or at least, no one is preaching it the way they should, in other words, the way that he is preaching it. An elitist leader will discourage members from visiting other churches or receiving counsel from anyone who doesn't attend their church. If anyone breaks this rule, he or she is viewed as rebellious.

We see a biblical example of this in 3 John 9–10:

I wrote to the church, but Diotrephes, who loves to have the preeminence among them,
does not receive us. Therefore, if I come, I will call to mind his deeds which he does,
prating against us with malicious words. And not content with that, he himself
does not receive the brethren, and forbids those who wish to, putting them out of the
church.

How does this verse reflect a spiritual "elitism" in the church at that time?

_____

_____

_____

Spiritual elitism is not a new thing in the church, but the apostle John rightly called it "evil."

A healthy spiritual leader, on the other hand, respects and encourages the other churches and ministries in a community, recognizing that there are several different expressions of the body of Christ. A spiritually free pastor realizes that no one denomination or local church can represent the love of Jesus to a city. A healthy church will promote revival in the entire Christian community. It will not promote the idea that it has some kind of doctrinal or spiritual superiority.

In a healthy relationship, a spiritual mentor will provide godly counsel from selfless motives. He or she will want God's will for your life. If that means that you will need to leave the church or ministry, then they will rejoice that you are being sent out to be a blessing in another place.

A healthy pastoral relationship should produce peace in the life of the believer — another one of the seven keys of God's guidance. If the godly counsel that you receive is not giving you peace or rest in your soul, it may not be from the Lord.

Remember, godly counsel is only one of the seven keys of God's guidance. You should never rely solely on the advice or input from another human being in determining God's will for you life — regardless of how long they have been walking with the Lord.

Because man is a sinner, building healthy spiritual relationships will always be a challenge. Someone once said, "the perfect church stopped being perfect the minute I walked in the door." God's intention all along has been for the local church to be healthy, life-giving, serving, encouraging, and Christ-centered. But because He has chosen to use sinful men and women to lead His church, there will always be the possibility that a local congregation can fall into deception or unhealthy spiritual patterns.

There must be a balance between humbly seeking guidance from a person of spiritual authority, and subjecting yourself to the manipulative practice of spiritual abuse. Finding that balance is an ongoing process in life. But it is a necessary struggle that will prevent you from becoming weary and worn on one hand, trying to jump through religious hoops that promise God's acceptance and love — and on the other hand, from becoming an island unto yourself, determining what is right in your eyes alone. Both sides of this spiritual spectrum are dangerous, and should be avoided. Ask God to give you the grace and guidance to walk in the tension of these truths — opening yourself to the input of mature Christian leaders, while avoiding spiritual control.

If you find yourself striving to gain the acceptance of spiritual leaders, or if your church constantly requires more and more of your life with no end in sight — and little encouragement along the way — then you may want to re-examine the church you are attending.

What Can I Do About It?

How should you respond if your church displays one or more of these unhealthy traits? Mike Fehlauer gives this advice:

• Talk with your pastor or someone else in leadership about your concerns, keeping in mind that if he is truly motivated by a spirit of control you may encounter some manipulation during the conversation. Stay in a humble attitude rather than getting angry or defensive.

• A controlling church leader will discourage you from speaking with anyone else about your concerns. As we have already pointed out, the Bible says that *in the multitude of counselors there is safety* (Proverbs 11:14). Seek counsel from a mature, objective leader in another church or another mature Christian. It is possible that what you have perceived as a controlling attitude may be genuine concern — so pray for discernment.

• If after receiving counsel you are convinced that your church is practicing spiritual abuse, then you are free to leave. You are not responsible for anyone else who is still loyal to the church, so don't try to rescue them. Pray for those people to discern the situation.

• At first you may feel that you can't trust another pastor again, but resist those thoughts and find a healthy church where the life of God is flowing, where the Bible is preached without compromise and where love is evident.

Every believer can hear God's voice. And the more you walk with the Lord — the more you act on God's leading and then see Him bless your obedience — the less you will need to rely on the input of others. This is what the New Covenant is all about, God's Spirit residing in you.

> *But this is the covenant that I will make with the house of Israel after those days, says the LORD: I will put My law in their minds, and write it on their hearts; and I will be their God, and they shall be My people. No more shall every man teach his neighbor, and every man his brother, saying, "Know the LORD," for they shall all know Me.*
>
> —Jeremiah 31:33–34

There is safety in the seven keys to God's guidance. Godly counsel is an important part of the seven keys, but it is only one part. By filtering direction through all of the seven keys, you can avoid some of the pitfalls that others have succumbed to — in this case, rejecting a spiritually abusive relationship.

Remember, hearing God's voice is all about your personal relationship with Him.

How can a personal relationship with God protect a believer from spiritual abuse?

_____

_____

_____

_____

How should receiving godly counsel be balanced with the other six keys to hearing God's voice?

_____

_____

_____

_____

How can you begin to put these truths into practice in your own life?

_____

_____

_____

_____

WEEK SIX

Peace —
Reaping the Fruit of
Hearing God's Voice

> *For the kingdom of God is... righteousness and peace and joy in the Holy Spirit.*
> —Romans 14:17

When you are born again — when you have made Jesus Christ the Lord of your life and you have entered the kingdom of God — then the fruit of that relationship will be righteousness (which comes as a result of salvation), peace, and joy. You can expect peace and joy to become a part of your daily life when you are a Christian — but just like all the other benefits of the kingdom of God, these attributes come at a price.

During the darkest days of the Revolutionary War, as George Washington tried to regroup during the winter of 1776, the great English writer, Thomas Paine, wrote a stirring essay on a drumhead that encapsulated the monumental struggle of that conflict. It was called "The American Crisis," and it so moved George Washington that he ordered his officers to read it to every soldier in the Continental Army, hoping that it would inspire them not to give up hope.

> These are the times that try men's souls. The summer soldier and the sunshine patriot will in this crisis shrink from the service of their country.

But they that stand it now, deserve the love and thanks of men and women. Tyranny, like hell, is not easily conquered. But the harder the conflict, the more glorious the triumph. Heaven knows how to put a proper price on its goods. It would be strange indeed if so celestial an article as freedom should not be highly rated.[1]

It is the same with the other "celestial articles," like peace and joy, and the other fruits and gifts of the Spirit. Things of great value, both natural and spiritual, come at a great price. In response to an article I wrote on God's guidance for CBN.com, I received this e-mail question:

> Years of making choices from voices that I thought were from God ended up causing me misery, grief, and heartache. Through years of experience, I realized that the voice I heard ended up just being from my own mind. Why does God make it so difficult for us to find Him or understand Him or to know we are hearing His voice?

Being a disciple of Jesus Christ is not easy. God's salvation may be free, but discipleship is costly. The gifts of the Spirit may also be freely given, but they are not cheap. In some ways, it is easier to be in the world. Our preparation for God's eternal purpose is as rigorous spiritually, as an Olympic athlete's training is, naturally — even more so, because the outcome of our training has eternal ramifications. Learning to hear God's voice is a lifelong process. God's preparation in our lives is part of His eternal design — and *only He* knows what that purpose will be.

There is a scene in the movie *A League of Their Own* in which Gina Davis' character wants to quit the women's baseball team to be with her husband who has returned wounded from World War II. Tom Hanks, who plays the manager of the team, travels to her house to try to talk this star player into coming back for the remainder of the season. She begins to cry at the thought of returning to the road with the baseball team, and she protests that "…it is just so hard." Tom Hanks' character gets right in her face and spouts back at her, "Of course it's hard. That's what makes it great."

Our walk with the Lord is hard. There are some, like the writer of this e-mail, who find that it is so difficult that they want to give up and go back to the pleasures of the sinful life. But Jesus said, *No one, having put his hand to the plow, and looking back, is fit for the kingdom of God* (Luke 9:62). We can't look back. We must press on in this walk with Christ — we must learn to hear His voice and obey His commands. Only then will we experience His joy and peace — and only then will we be the effective ministers of reconciliation that He wants us to be, and that the world needs us to be.

WEEK SIX
Day One: Being Led Forth in Peace

Without great trials, we would have no great victories. The Lord reveals Himself in the difficulties of life as our Deliverer, our Sufficiency, and our Lord. The psalmist tells us, *Many are the afflictions of the righteous, but the LORD delivers* [us] *out of them all* (Psalm 34:19).

If you are really serious about walking with God, He will teach you, and guide you, and comfort you, and yes, you will know His peace in your life. In fact, as you mature in your walk with the Lord, peace and joy will be multiplied to you. It is an interesting paradox that our heavenly Father orchestrates in our lives. On the one hand, our trials increase as we grow stronger in the Lord. On the other hand, the fruit of the Spirit — including peace and joy — develop to the point that we are given grace to weather the trials, and the rest of our lives are filled with harmonious fellowship with God.

We should expect to experience God's peace in our lives. If you are not walking in peace, it may be as a result of several different scenarios. It may be that you are in the midst of a particular test or trial sent from God. Or you may be under attack from the devil. Or you may have an area of your life that you have not yet surrendered completely to God. The Lord intends for you to have peace. If you are not experiencing God's peace on an ongoing basis, you may need to ask the Holy Spirit to show you:
• if you are experiencing a test that should be submitted to;
• if you are under an attack that you should resist; or
• if there is an area of continual sin, unforgiveness, anger, or some other hindrance that should be renounced and repented of.

Why do you think that God places such a high price on His goods? How is that price paid?

_____

_____

What does the saying, "Without great trials, we would have no great victories," mean for you?

_____

_____

Most pastors will teach that when you are seeking to find God's will, you can identify the leading of the Holy Spirit when you sense God's peace about a matter. I agree, and I believe that is absolutely true. The peace of God is one of the key indicators of God's guidance. Colossians 3:15 tells us to *let the peace of God rule in* [our] *hearts*. Peace is the umpire of our heart, telling us if we are "safe" in God's will, or "out," following our own path or the deception of the devil.

The prophet Isaiah wrote, *For you shall go out with joy, and be led out with peace* (Isaiah 55:12). God's best for our lives is that we will be led forth in peace and joy. Have you ever heard someone say, "I'm not going to allow these circumstances to rob my joy?" In making this declaration they are being absolutely biblical — peace and joy are our possessions when we are born again. The only way that you will walk in unrest as a mature believer is if you allow circumstances or the devil to rob you of your joy.

Larry Tomczak says, "You are the only being in the universe that can cause defeat in your life."[2]

You may say, "The devil robbed my joy." The truth of the statement is that the devil attempted to rob you of your joy — but he only succeeded if you allowed him to. The life of the Christian is one of peace and joy.

• That is why Paul and Silas could sing praises to God in the Philippian jail (Acts 16:25).

• That is why the apostles praised the Lord after being beaten by the teachers of the law, rejoicing that they were counted worthy to suffer shame in Christ's name (Acts 5:40–41).

• That is why Stephen could praise the God of heaven as he was being stoned for his bold witness (Acts 7:55–60).

• That is why the apostle Peter wrote, *But rejoice to the extent that you partake of Christ's sufferings, that when His glory is revealed, you may also be glad with exceeding joy* (1 Peter 4:13).

• That is why the apostle Paul, at the eve of his martyrdom, could write, *I have fought the good fight, I have finished the race, I have kept the faith* (2 Timothy 4:7).

You will keep him in perfect peace, whose mind is stayed on You, because he trusts in You (Isaiah 26:3).

You'll notice that the promise of peace carries with it a condition — to trust in God. Once again we come back to the necessity of living a lifestyle of faith. Paul wrote to the Romans, *For to be carnally minded is death, but to be spiritually minded is life and peace* (Romans

8:6). A carnally minded person is one who is self-interested, self-indulgent, and self-sufficient. There is no peace in the selfish life. The spiritually-minded person puts God in the center of their life. They are interested in doing the will of Christ. They are motivated by the Lord to minister to others. They recognize that they are nothing outside of Christ — He is their sufficiency. It is from this attitude of surrender to the lordship and headship of Jesus Christ that peace comes into our lives.

How do you see the relationship between trust in God and peace in your life?

_____

_____

_____

There are times, when we are seeking the will of God and we reach the point of decision, that we experience supernatural peace. This is an important aspect of discerning between good and evil, and it comes by reason of use (Hebrews 5:14). The peace of God is like a compass for our souls, leading us in the direction that the Holy Spirit intends for our lives. We can take great comfort in knowing that the sovereign God is so involved in our lives that He would supply us with this internal compass as we seek to do His will.

At the same time, the mature Christian will recognize that there is another way that God uses the fruit of peace to direct our steps. As we surrender to the lordship of Jesus Christ in our lives, He brings us to a place where we experience His blessed peace on an ongoing basis. Instead of anxiety, anger, or depression, the peace of God becomes the normal state of mind for the Christian. I have a friend named Daryl, and when I meet him in the hall at work, I ask him how he's doing. In a declaration of our biblical position in Christ, he always quotes the famous hymn, "It is well with my soul."

If I am in Christ, it truly is well with my soul. I am at peace with God, and I should be walking in peace in this world. That's not to say that each one of us won't have our share of problems — and sometimes we will have even more difficulties because of the spiritual warfare that swirls about us — but because we are God's children, and His Spirit comforts us and guides us, we can be at peace in spite of the circumstances.

So as maturing believers, when we are seeking after God's plan for our life, we must also be sensitive to a lack of peace in a particular direction. This absence of God's peace in the form of anxiety, stress, anger, or confusion, is also a strong indicator warning us that we are stepping out of the will of God. Just as the Lord will grant special peace to the believer when he or she discovers His plan, He will also remove His peace when a Christian strays away from His course for their lives.

Now I need to clarify that you don't leave your problems behind when you come to Christ. It might take years of working through the issues of your life until you come to the point where you are experiencing the peace of God on an ongoing basis — but it is God's desire for you. Even when you reach the maturity level where you are walking in God's peace, you will continually experience the testing of your faith.

I remember a song on Michael W. Smith's second album that illustrated our experience in Christ remarkably well. "On the day you were saved heaven and hell marked it down. Angels praised; devils raged; life became a battleground. So when hell starts to move and the enemy marches on you, stand strong, it's a fight. You've been marked by the army of night. You're a target."

But the song doesn't end with the battle. It continues, "When things get bad and you can't stand to look, it's time to read to the end of the book. Don't put it down 'till you get to the end, when Jesus comes and His kingdom begins...."[3]

For the kingdom of God is...righteousness and peace and joy in the Holy Spirit (Romans 14:17 KJV). The peace comes in knowing that the kingdom of God is here and now, *and* yet to come.

Have you ever had your peace upset by a proposition that was not from God? How did that feel? How did it affect your decision-making process?

_____

_____

Since the Bible says that the kingdom of God is righteousness, peace, and joy in the Holy Spirit — and you are a part of God's kingdom if you are born again — how should that make you view the circumstances that you confront and your attitude throughout each day?

_____

_____

_____

_____

_____

_____

_____

_____

Day Two: The Knowledge of God and the Will of God

A life lived in the Spirit is a life of peace because Jesus Christ is the Prince of Peace. When you invite the Prince of Peace to dwell on the inside of you, He brings His peace along with Him.

Read the prayer that the apostle Paul prayed for the saints in Colossae in Colossians 1:9–12. What did Paul pray that God would fill them with? (verse 9)

_____

_____

Through what would this come?

_____

_____

What would be the result of this "filling"?

_____

_____

In order to comprehend God's will, we must be filled with spiritual wisdom and understanding. We cannot comprehend the will of God unless our spiritual eyes are opened, and this spiritual vision comes when we are born again.

Read what Paul wrote to the church in Corinth in 1 Corinthians 2:12–14, 16. Why have we received the "Spirit who is from God"? (verse 12)

_____

What happens to a person without the Spirit?

_____

_____

What is the purpose of our being given the "mind of Christ"?

_____

_____

The natural man does not comprehend the things of God for they are spiritual in nature. The Greek word used here for "natural man" is *psuchikos,* which refers to a person's soul. The soul includes our mind, will, and emotions. Jesus said that those who worship God, or have a relationship with Him, must do so *in spirit and truth* (John 4:23). This can only happen when one's spirit is regenerated through salvation. If we will come to know God first, then we will grow to know His will. Out of His nature we will begin to sense His will. A person cannot truly discover the will of God for their lives unless they are in tune with the Spirit of God — and that only comes by being born again. But even if you have accepted Jesus Christ as your personal Lord and Savior, you have to desire to press into the deeper things of God — you have to want an ongoing personal relationship with Him, and you have to hunger for it above anything else.

That is why Paul prayed his prayer for the Colossians. They were already born again. He wanted them to be filled with the knowledge of God — to have an ongoing love relationship with their heavenly Father. From this they would grow to know the will of God.

Jesus taught us to pray, *Your will be done on earth as it is in heaven* (Luke 11:2). This must be our desire above all else. We must grow in the knowledge of God through daily communing with Him like Adam and Eve did in the Garden — through prayer, reading the Bible, listening to God's voice, obeying Him, learning from the trials and tests of life, trusting the goodness of God, and striving to be like Christ in every area of our lives.

As we grow in our love relationship with God, the peace of God becomes the normal emotion of our lives. We trust that our Father in heaven is taking care of us, and this brings great peace to our souls. We give our burdens to the Lord, and He gives us His peace. It is quite an exchange, and it's all about relationship.

How has your relationship with God brought peace to your life?

_____

_____

_____

_____

_____

_____

The General Versus the Specific Will of God

We receive the peace of God when we discover, develop, and then release ourselves to the plan of God for our lives. It is essential for believers to recognize that part of God's plan for our lives is His general will for all Christians, and another part is His specific will for our individual lives.

The general will of God, of course, is found in the Scriptures as He revealed His ultimate will to mankind in and through His Son, Jesus Christ.

Read the following scriptures and describe the aspect of God's general will given in each.

2 Peter 3:9

_____

_____

Matthew 5:48

_____

_____

Romans 12:2

_____

_____

1 Thessalonians 5:16–18

_____

_____

Hebrews 11:6

_____

_____

Isaiah 58:6–7

_____

_____

Isaiah 1:17

_____

_____

Luke 4:18–19

_____

_____

Psalm 34:13–14

_____

_____

As part of our role on earth in fulfilling the will of God, we are to be peacemakers. God wants us to live in peace, to seek after it, and to become brokers of peace in the midst of trouble.

God's general will is to bring blessing to His people. There is an often quoted verse that encapsulates God's desires for your life:

> *For I know the thoughts that I think toward you, says the LORD, thoughts of peace and not of evil, to give you a future and a hope. Then you will call upon Me and go and pray to Me, and I will listen to you. And you will seek Me and find Me, when you search for Me with all your heart.*
>
> —Jeremiah 29:11–13

What God has prepared for us is for our good and will bring joy and peace to our lives. His ultimate plan for our lives will be satisfying — it will delight us. The will of God for you is to bring forth that for which you have been created. God's plan for your life will be precisely what fits your talents and the joy of your heart. He has a general will that can be found in the Bible. And He has a specific will for each of our lives that will be discovered through walking in relationship with Him and paying attention to the seven keys of God's guidance.

If you will follow carefully the general principles of the Bible that are clearly stated, then God will reveal to you the specific details of His will for your daily life. He will teach you the hidden things of His kingdom. *Seek first the kingdom of God and His righteousness, and all these things shall be added unto you* (Matthew 6:33). As you do this, God will begin to speak to you about the specific areas of guidance in your life.

If you will embrace the general principles of the will of God found in the Bible, and will make them an intricate part of your life, then the Lord in His goodness will reveal to you the specific calling on your life.

I have visited Israel and have swum in the Dead Sea, the shoreline of which is the lowest dry land on earth. The countryside surrounding this amazing natural wonder is a barren, dry desert. They call it the Dead Sea because it is just that — dead. The water is so thick with salt and other minerals that no living creature can survive in it. Our tour guide warned us to only go into the water for ten minutes and then go and rinse off, then go in another ten minutes and rinse off again — and that was it. If we stayed in any longer than that, the minerals would burn our skin.

Someone has described the life of the believer as being either like the Dead Sea or the Sea of Galilee. The Galilee is a beautiful body of water, absolutely teeming with life. It is the sea from which Peter, Andrew, James, and John made their living. And there is something interesting about the Sea of Galilee that makes it different from the Dead Sea. Flowing down from the Galilean Mountains, streams of rainwater runoff flow into the headwaters of the Jordan River, which in turn flows into the Sea of Galilee, bringing a constant flow of fresh water. On the south side of the Galilee, the Jordan River continues to flow south until it reaches the Dead Sea. Like the Sea of Galilee, the Dead Sea constantly receives water from the Jordan River. But unlike the Sea of Galilee that receives refreshing and then passes it along downstream, the Dead Sea only receives, and that is where the flow of water ends.

God wants His children to be like the Sea of Galilee, and not like the Dead Sea. His general will for us is to receive His blessing and then to be a channel of that blessing to others, allowing the waters of God's Spirit to nourish us, and then passing that nourishment along in the stream of God's favor. When we receive and then give of God's life and blessings, then we ourselves have life, and we bring life to countless others that we touch in His name. If, however, we are like the Dead Sea, always looking to receive but never giving out the blessing that has been bestowed on us, we too will eventually lose the life that once flourished in us. We will become bitter, and people will only want to be around us for a short time — and after they leave our presence they may want to shower off, so to speak, so that the poison of our bitterness will not burn them.

May we yield to God's will for our lives to receive from Him, and then be an open spring of the water of His goodness, bringing life and refreshment to those with whom we come in contact in our lives. When we participate in this divine exchange of receiving and giving, we will grow in our knowledge of God, in our love for Him, and the fruit of peace will be ours to enjoy on an ongoing basis.

How can knowing and doing the general will of God bring peace to your life as a believer?

_____

_____

Is your life like the Sea of Galilee or the Dead Sea? Examine your heart to determine if there are ways that you've allowed selfishness to creep into your heart, creating a Dead Sea experience in your walk with God. Write down ways in which you can start giving to get the flow of God's blessings moving in your life again.

_____

_____

_____

_____

_____

_____

_____

_____

_____

_____

Day Three: Righteousness, Peace, and Joy

I want to share another e-mail that I received because it is helpful for us to see how other people struggle in trying to follow the leading of the Holy Spirit in their lives.

> I sometimes think that I hear the Lord's voice, but I become confused. I pray that the Lord will help me to discern the different voices. Many times when I am praying, verses of Scripture will just pop into my head. The other day, every time I prayed, the Lord put Mark 8 into my heart. I began to wonder if the voice was my own, or if it was from the Lord. I've also had verses come into my heart that do not exist...such as 1 Peter 6, for instance, since it only goes up to 5. So that confuses me.

> I have been disappointed in situations in which I thought I heard the Lord's voice, but it was actually my own thoughts or the enemy's voice. Pray for me that I would be able to discern God's voice. I take everything to God in prayer because I'm always afraid that my decision will not be a good one. I always want God to be part of everything that I do.

As Jesus said to the scribe who spoke to Him about the greatest commandment, *"You are not far from the kingdom of God"*(Mark 12:34). Or as my dad would often tell us jokingly, "You are on the right track." The person who sent this e-mail is doing many of the proper things necessary to hear God's voice and be led in His ways.

Read Hebrews 5:14. How are "those who are of full age" described?

_____

_____

_____

_____

The ability to clearly hear the voice of God — to discern between good, the voice of God, and evil, that which is not God's voice — comes with practice. And with practice comes maturity.

Listening to the voice of the Lord is in some ways like tuning into a radio station with the old-fashioned radio knobs. It may take some adjusting to get to the point where you are clearly hearing the signal from W-GOD (or K-GOD if you're from the western United States!) The thing to realize is that God is on the other end, transmitting His message with the most powerful station in the universe. Through persistent use, and by constantly adjusting the knob through the seven keys, you will mature to the point where you will be able to identify His signal and enjoy the sweet sound of His voice.

The peace of God, in harmony with the other keys of God's guidance, is like today's digital receivers that lock onto a signal, ensuring that you receive the message loud and clear:

• Through God's peace we can know if the Lord is using a particular Scripture to speak to us about guidance in our lives.

• Through the peace of God we can learn to differentiate between the voice of God, our own thoughts, the voice of the devil, and the voice of the world.

• The Lord will give you peace when a prophet of God is speaking on His behalf, and He will withhold peace when a false prophet is speaking to you, or when a godly person is merely speaking from his or her own mind and not from the Spirit of Christ.

• When seeking godly counsel, the Lord will provide peace when the advice being given is from Him, and He will often withhold His peace when that person is counseling outside of God's will — they may be giving you sound, even biblical, advice, but if it is not within God's will for you at that time in your life, you will not sense the peace of God.

• The Holy Spirit will provide you with God's peace when a particular circumstance is an indicator of God's guidance. And He will remove His peace if a circumstance is not a part of the collection of indicators that God is using to move you toward His will for your life.

Of all the seven keys to hearing God's voice, peace and the Scriptures are the two keys that must be evidenced in every decision. The lack of God's peace is a clear indicator of a red or yellow light in your path. When you experience God's peace, when you have considered the other keys, and when you are confident of God's timing, you will then have a green light to proceed in God's plan for your life.

What do you do if you think you heard from God, but later you find out it was actually not His voice — like the person who thought they heard "First Peter 6," but then realized that the book of First Peter only goes up to chapter 5?

_____

_____

_____

_____

How can the peace of God help us to differentiate between the voice of God, our own thoughts, the voice of the devil, and the voice of the world?

_____

_____

How can a lack of peace be a red or yellow light in your path?

_____

_____

Righteousness, Peace, and Joy in the Holy Spirit

In Ephesians 1, Paul used the phrase "in Christ" twelve different times. When we respond to the wooing of the Holy Spirit in our lives, and surrender ourselves to the lordship of Jesus Christ, we are made righteous in Christ. Paul declares that when we are "in Christ" through faith, we are made holy and blameless in His sight. And we are then given the promised Holy Spirit.

Read Ephesians 1:13–14. What is the "seal" that has been promised by God?

_____

_____

Jesus said that He would send the Holy Spirit, the Comforter. The word *comforter* means "with strength." The Holy Spirit guides us into all truth. He is the Advocate. He is the Revelator. As the Holy Spirit comes upon you, you become sensitive to the will of God for your life.

When we are *in Christ,* and the Holy Spirit dwells *in us,* there is peace and joy *in the Holy Spirit.* The peace of God comes with the presence of the Holy Spirit. The apostle Paul said:

> *And let the peace (soul harmony which comes) from Christ rule (act as umpire continually) in your hearts {deciding and settling with finality all questions that arise in our minds, in that peaceful state} to which as {members of Christ's} one body you were also called {to live}. And be thankful (appreciative), {giving praise to God always}.*
>
> —Colossians 3:15 AMP

Peace follows the indwelling of the Holy Spirit, and it helps to answer every question that arises in our hearts.

One of the classic Christian writings is from a little-known monk named Brother Lawrence entitled *Practicing the Presence of God.* This obscure cleric from the Middle Ages understood that his first duty on this earth was to practice the presence of God in all that he did. His assigned task in the monastery was menial: washing the pots and pans in the kitchen. But day in and day out, he did his job with joy and gladness, praising the Lord, meditating on the Scriptures, and practicing the presence of God right there in the kitchen.

Someone who has not renewed his or her mind to the things of the Spirit might think that this kind of existence would be a great waste of human potential. But in actuality, Brother Lawrence pleased God with his surrendered life. And the little booklet that he wrote has blessed millions of other believers around the world as they have yielded their lives to the Lord and practiced His presence in all things, great and small.

If you want God's peace, get into His presence. Be filled, and re-filled with the Holy Spirit. Praise the Lord, and watch your perspective change from anxiety to peace and joy in the Holy Spirit!

In what ways do you need to begin practicing the presence of God in your daily life?

_____

_____

How might that cause peace to multiply in your heart?

_____

_____

Day Four: Peace and God's Timing

Christian author Jennie Bishop shared this story with me of how a lack of God's peace allowed her to hear God's voice, which in turn prepared her for what could have been a devastating disappointment. It is an excellent example of how God will sometimes require us to step out in faith when we sense His direction through a lack of peace in our hearts.

The Christian Booksellers Association Convention in the summer of 2000 was sure to be exciting for us. I had written a book for children on purity called *The Princess and the Kiss* that would debut that year. The book had huge ministry potential, and we, and all my friends at the publishing house felt strongly about it.

Not only was I excited about the book's potential, but also about my opportunities as an author. I had an actual booth where I would be signing books, and this was a kind of "arriving" for me. I knew that the book was God's doing, but it was also a very great honor and "shot in the arm" for me to have the opportunity to sign my books for convention-goers.

But the night before the signing, I lay wide-awake in bed, aware that God had something to say to me. I could feel that heavy presence in the air that kept me from peacefully drifting off to sleep, and I opened my heart to Him. What He said shocked me.

Is it okay with you if you don't sign books tomorrow?

That immediately got my attention. I was all wound up to be signing books. I had come all the way to New Orleans to make a debut as a successful author. I had a booth reserved!

But I knew the Lord's voice. I couldn't mistake it. And how could I withhold anything from Him? Surely He had a good reason for asking me to make this sacrifice.

I gulped and sighed, *Okay, Lord. Whatever You want. It's okay with me.* Immediately I was at peace, and able to sleep.

The next day we received some difficult news. The books for the signing had not arrived. They were supposed to be flown in at the last minute, and they had not made it. There was no way we could do the signing. I was so excited! God had already prepared me for this setback, and I shared my story with the man in charge of marketing, a good friend of mine. He was amazed. My excitement encouraged the whole staff at a time when we could have been very discouraged.

We rescheduled the booth for Tuesday. The books still hadn't arrived on Tuesday morning, so we gave up the booth, and decided to make the best of it. Later that day, the books finally came in, so we decided to try for an impromptu signing at our booth on the floor the next afternoon. We swallowed hard and expected very few to show up — although we felt that somehow God must be up to something.

And He was. I signed more than 200 books that afternoon in the course of two hours ... at a completely unadvertised event. The line stretched all the way down the side of the CBA floor. I talked to bookstore owners from around the world, some of whom shed tears as they thanked me for writing the book. Mothers were especially touched. Reviewers stopped to say how special they thought the book was.

Later on, after the release, we heard stories of how moms were coming into the bookstores and crying as they read the book, then bringing back three more friends and saying, "You've got to get this book for your kids!" Crisis pregnancy centers all over the nation have ordered the book to use with their clients. Christian actors from New Jersey to Louisiana have called to ask permission to dramatize the story for use in abstinence presentations. A ministry called "The Princess Project" in Texas gives the book to girls at an overnight event that calls preteens to purity. An abstinence organization in Fort Wayne, Indiana, scheduled an event called "The Princess and the Tea" to be held in, of all places, an actual castle.

God made that CBA one of the most memorable conventions of my life, by asking me to step aside for a moment. And the success of the book in sales and ministry is no surprise to me. If it was important enough for God to schedule such an outstanding debut, then the story, which is obviously His, will continue to bear fruit and change lives for as long as He wills ... and as long as I keep my ears open to His voice.

Though we make our plans, and design our strategies, God is sovereign, and His plan is the best plan — even if it seems foolish to us at first.

Read 1 Corinthians 1:27–29.

The Lord will at times direct us in ways that may seem foolish in the world's eyes, but then He will provide us with His peace to assure us that it is actually His desire for our lives, just as it was for Jennie Bishop at the CBA. Remember, the Lord can lead us by supplying His peace when we are in turmoil, or by removing His peace when we begin to stray from His path. If we are seeking God and we don't sense His peace, we can be assured that we are either heading down the wrong path, or we are outside of His timing.

How does being flexible help you to maintain your peace in the midst of life's circumstances?

_____

_____

_____

_____

Here's another e-mail from a CBN.com viewer:

> I am having a lot of trouble hearing God's voice. I am in the process of making a life-changing decision that I have been planning for the last two years. I experienced all of the things listed in your article on CBN.com (peace, confirmation, prophetic word, godly counsel, etc.), but suddenly I am at a stand-still. I am not feeling any of those things anymore. I have been seeking God for two months now to find out why there is a blockage, but I haven't heard anything yet. Now I wonder, _Have I been experiencing a false peace all along? Have I fallen into a trap set by the enemy to get me out of God's will?_

When God gives us a word of direction from His throne, He will then knit that together with the other things that He has revealed, and as we continue to seek Him, He will begin to unfold His progressive will, including His timing.

I remember during one particularly important transition in my life, the Lord gave me a vision of an Apollo rocket ready to take off into space. You may have seen the impressive scene from the movie *Apollo 13* when the giant spacecraft is approaching liftoff. At the appointed time in the countdown, the man at launch control in Houston cries out, "Ignition!" At that moment the fuel is released from the mammoth tanks and thousands of sparks dance beneath the towering rocket. In an instant the gasses ignite, causing a tremendous plume of fire and smoke atop the launch pad. One by one the walkways and electrical cables connected to the giant ship are pulled away. Then, in a huge burst of energy, the spacecraft glides upward away from earth and toward its preordained destination.

The Lord gave me this analogy as I prayed about a pending major move for my family and myself. This was no small change of direction. I was going to quit my job, sell my house, and move my family hundreds of miles away, without any guarantee of a job waiting for me on the other end. Through many different avenues, the Lord made it clear that this was His will for me — now I was waiting for His timing. It was several months before the Lord gave clear and concrete direction on the timing of the move. This was a critical time in my life. I didn't want to lag behind the leading of the Lord, but neither did I want to move out ahead of Him. I asked Him to make His timing clear to me through confirmation and His peace. He was faithful to answer that prayer.

When He did confirm His will and timing, it was dramatic and unmistakable — and this gave me a tremendous sense of peace to move forward, giving notice at my job and putting my house up for sale. The Lord was faithful during that time, and my family has received innumerable blessings as a result of obeying God during that fateful transition in our lives.

Earlier I mentioned the concept of the harness of the Holy Spirit, when God reveals His will to us and then places us in a holding pattern to determine whether we will obey Him in walking it out in our lives. There are times when the promises of God and the desires that He places in our hearts are so exciting that the pursuit of them can take precedence *over* the pursuit of our relationship with God. The Lord is jealous of our relationship with Him, and He will, from time to time, test our love like He did with Abraham and Isaac.

There are some, however, who get to the point of testing or waiting, and they begin to doubt or complain. This attitude may put God's plan for their lives into a holding pattern until they repent for their lack of faith and their complaining. Sadly, there are many people who have heard God's word for their lives, they have determined His will, and they have begun looking for His way, but in the time of waiting and testing, they lost faith and began complaining. Like the children of Israel, they had to go around and around the wilderness mountain until they came to the place of confidence in God's goodness, and until they stopped complaining and began praising their heavenly Father.

Some people never learn this lesson. They complain about every trial in their life, and then they wonder why they're not moving ahead in their walk with God.

Read Philippians 4:4–7. Explain how the peace of God relates to the joy of the Holy Spirit.

_____

_____

_____

How can God's peace lead us in the timing of our decisions?

_____

_____

_____

Praise the Lord. Wait for His timing. Look for His peace — and He will guide you into His perfect will for your life.

Day Five: Peace and the Unfolding of God's Will

The will of God is not a blueprint that you receive at some point in your life that shows you exactly what God's plan will be for the remainder of your time on this planet. The will of God is revealed to you incrementally throughout life. Receiving direction from the Lord is in many ways dependent on your own desire and tenacity in going after it. Just as Jacob wrestled with God, unwilling to let Him go until he received the blessing, we must wrestle with God in a spiritual sense, not letting go until we receive the blessing of His direction in our lives. This divine struggle will occur again and again at key junctures of our walk with God.

God will not play religious games with you. His will for your life will not make you miserable. God will use you in a way in which you will excel, because He designed you for that purpose. This will bring peace to you. When that peace lifts, you know that you are out of the will of God. When you begin to have anxiety and agonizing doubts, or you even feel like someone has punched you in the stomach, you can say, "I have missed God."

The farther you get from God's best for you, the louder those alarm bells will ring. Be careful that you stay alert to these warning signs. A person can ignore the prodding of the Holy Spirit to get you back on track with the Lord. If this continues — if someone dismisses the lack of peace in their lives as merely the anxiety of daily living — they can desensitize themselves to the moving of the Holy Spirit in their lives. Over time, this can cause a rift in your relationship with the Lord, and it can lead you into deception in your life.

Be careful to guard your walk with the Lord. Spend time daily in prayer, Bible reading, and worship — talking to Him and listening for His voice. And if the peace of God is not dwelling on the inside of you — if someone has robbed you of your joy — find out why it's gone, and as King David did after he sinned with Bathsheba, ask the Lord to restore unto you the joy of your salvation (see Psalm 51:12).

How can you become desensitized to the prodding of the Holy Spirit in your heart?

_____

_____

_____

Has this ever happened in your life?

_____

_____

What should you do to get "back on track"?

_____

_____

_____

Be Careful of False Peace

Christians, especially new believers, need to be cautious of false peace that comes just because a decision has finally been made. There is also a deceptive peace that is only temporary, and is fleeting with time as we work through a decision. The peace that comes from God will withstand the test of time, of changing circumstances, and even our own changing ideas.

Another form of false peace can come as a result of feeding our flesh. The word *happiness* is associated with the word *happening*. People are *happy* because good things are *happening* for them. One can be happy, yet not have peace and joy. You see it every day. There are millions of happy people in the world who don't know Christ. They will try to fill the void of their empty hearts with all manner of things, from drugs, to sex, to relationships, to material possessions, and so on. False peace is like a pain reliever that dulls our spiritual senses, even though the cause of the unrest has not been dealt with.

There are countless Christians in the world today who allow false peace to influence their walk with Christ. They have allowed their senses to be dulled through entertainment, alcohol, parties, business pursuits, relationships with friends — the list could go on and on. These people have at one time made a commitment to the Lord, but they have walked away from an intimate walk with God and they are no longer hearing His voice. Some of them don't even want to hear His voice, because they know that if they stopped to listen to the voice of God, He would call them to repent and to come back to a walk of holiness in Him.

This is dangerous ground to be on! Be careful to keep short accounts with God. If you have sinned, repent quickly. Make things right with Him. If you have been wounded by someone, forgive them quickly. Don't hold on to bitterness and unforgiveness. Left unattended, bitterness will consume you. It will destroy you physically, and it can even destroy your spiritual life.

Don't be hasty in making decisions. The peace of God will be there in a month or in a year if the direction you are following is truly from the Lord. If it is not, you may find yourself going back and forth between peace and unrest. If this is the case, it is best to wait, if possible, until you have a sustained peace — especially in major decisions like your career, your marriage, or a geographical move. The peace that is from God is an everlasting peace.

Read 2 Corinthians 2:12–13. Why did Paul decide to leave for Macedonia?

_____

_____

The Lord had opened a door for ministry, but Paul had no peace because of the circumstances. We don't know why the Lord opened the door — perhaps it was to show Paul that this opportunity was there in Troas for a later time. Maybe Paul was going to send someone else to minister here. Perhaps the timing for ministry may not have been right. We see three of the seven keys at work here: the leading of the Spirit, circumstances, and a lack of peace. Paul did not have peace in his heart, and without that peace, he did not go through an obviously open door of ministry.

There are times when we won't have direction from God through all seven of the keys to hearing His voice. We may have two, three, or more, as was the case with Paul in Troas. But a key indicator is always the peace of God.

Write out Isaiah 55:12.

_____

_____

_____

Read 2 Corinthians 2:14.

This is the very next verse after Paul's description of his decision. How does this verse relate to our discerning of God's will?

_____

_____

This portion of Scripture reveals a liberating concept of God's guidance. As the apostle Paul exemplified, we are not bound to walk through a perceived open door — even if it is of the Lord. That door may be open, but it may be open for someone other than you. Our responsibility is to weigh that open door against the other keys of God's guidance. That includes considering how this opportunity may jeopardize the other responsibilities that God has already assigned to us — like looking after the Titus's in our life.

Something that I have learned in twenty-plus years of full-time ministry is that there are more open doors, more opportunities, more people who need to hear the Word of God than I have energy or resources to fill on my own. We can't do it all ourselves — we have to concentrate on doing what _God_ wants us to do, not what seems like a glaring need. Not every need constitutes a call. The peace of God can help us to differentiate between what is good and what is best; between what is a need and what is truly the call of God for us in every situation.

Why is an open door in itself not enough of a reason to make a decision?

_____

_____

What can we learn from the fact that the apostle Paul did not go through an open door of ministry because he lacked the peace of God?

_____

_____

_____

Are You at Peace in Your Life?

Who are you? Have you ever asked yourself that question? Who has God created you to be? If you haven't taken inventory of your life recently, perhaps it is time to do so now.

It may have been years since you have experienced peace in your life. I encourage you to examine your life to determine if a change in career or circumstances is necessary.

If you take a personality profile, and find that your makeup does not match your career choice, you may want to investigate making a change. Don't do anything hastily, but seek the Lord for wisdom, and then step out in faith as He directs your path.

You may have a lack of peace in your life for other reasons. In my years of ministry I have known many people who have been victims of abuse. Some have been abused physically, some emotionally, some verbally, and some sexually. These are dear people who love God and truly want to hear His voice and follow His direction. But the pain from past hurts often clouds their ability to sense God's peace in their hearts and makes it difficult to discern His leading in their lives.

If you are hurting and lacking peace in your life, take heart. The Prince of Peace is well able to bring His peace to your soul. It will take some effort on your part as years of abuse can leave deep-seated wounds. But there are some wonderful ministries that work with victims of abuse, and they can help you work through your wounds and come to a place of forgiveness and peace in Christ. Talk to your pastor about a Christian counselor in your area, or log onto CBN.com to receive a referral to some wonderful counseling ministries nationwide.

The bottom line is that God wants you to walk in peace — and He has given the fruit of peace to His children to act as a compass in their decision-making process. If you ask, the Holy Spirit will guide your steps and will lead you out in His peace.

In the prophetic utterance over his son, the high priest Zacharias declared these words over John the Baptist:

> *And you, child, will be called the prophet of the Highest; For you will go before the face of the Lord to prepare His ways, to give knowledge of salvation to His people by the remission of their sins, through the tender mercy of our God, with which the Dayspring from on high has visited us; to give light to those who sit in darkness and the shadow of death, to guide our feet into the way of peace.*
>
> —Luke 1:76–79

Jesus is the "Dayspring from on high," and He has sent His Spirit "to guide our feet into the way of peace." The peace of God is a vital component in the seven keys to God's guidance. It is a precious gift and keepsake of the Holy Spirit given to all who will believe on the Lord Jesus Christ.

Do you know who you are? Have you taken a personality profile or a spiritual gifts inventory? If so, write down the results here. If not, I encourage you to find a way to take either the D.I.S.C. or Meyers-Briggs tests to help you determine your personality type. This will help you to know if you are in the right career, serving your church or community in the proper way. It will also help you to understand how to relate with others, especially those closest to you.

_____

_____

_____

_____

_____

_____

_____

_____

_____

Are you at peace in your life? If not, what might you need to do to make a change in your circumstances or career to bring peace to your soul? Ask the Lord to show you some specific things that need to be changed, and make the determination to follow His leading.

_____

_____

_____

_____

_____

_____

_____

_____

_____

Personal Prophecy — Hearing God's Specific Voice to You

I was not having a good day.

I had put in a request to have a videotape duplicated at the Christian television ministry where I was working. I needed it by 5 o'clock to meet a deadline. Somehow the order form had gotten lost, and the job was not done. The tape would not be ready until the next morning.

So much for the deadline. I had to admit that I was having difficulty maintaining my joy. Suddenly one of my friends walked into the duplicating room and called out my name. "Craig, here she is," she said with a smile. The "she" whom my friend was talking about was one of the hosts of the national Christian talk show that this ministry produced.

Earlier that day, my friend had called and said that she had a friend who was going through a difficult time and needed prayer. She asked if I would be willing to pray over her — but she didn't tell me who it was. I said, "Sure, I'd be happy to pray for her. Call me later and tell me when and where to meet you."

Several hours went by, and I did not hear from her. And then the crisis emerged over the deadline and the missing videotape. Suddenly, in walked my friend with her friend, a nationally known Christian "celebrity"! I was certainly not in the mood to pray over anyone at that moment, especially not someone of her stature.

I smiled and greeted them anyway. "Do you have time right now to pray for my friend?" she asked.

"Sure," I responded, deciding to trust that when we are weak, He is strong. "Just let me finish what I'm doing here, and I'll be right with you." After I completed a new request form, I rushed out to meet them. In my heart I quickly repented for my frustration and silently prayed what I always do before I minister: *Let the words of my mouth, and the meditation of my heart be acceptable in Your sight, O Lord, my Strength and my Redeemer.*

We went into what is called the "green room," the place where guests sit and wait until they are led onto the set of the talk show. I shook my head at the thought of what was happening. Here I was in the green room of a national Christian talk show, getting ready to pray for this highly respected host. For a kid from Erie, Pennsylvania, it was spiritually heady stuff. *Lord, let what I say be from Your heart,* I silently prayed.

Almost as soon as we sat down, I received a very detailed prophetic vision from the Lord. I saw this young lady holding a baby in her arms, trying to protect it from a huge demon that was attacking them with a sword. The demon continually swung the sword at them, but an invisible force field was protecting them from the blows.

I had been trained in the prophetic ministry under Dr. Bill Hamon. One caution he always gave us is to be very careful with prophecies about major geographical moves, marriages, and babies. These are such highly-charged emotional issues that the minister must never put his own interpretation onto what God may be saying.

Because the vision I had involved a baby, I decided to put it on the shelf, concerned that it was just my imagination. My friend prayed over the young lady first, and then it was my turn.

I laid my hand on the young lady's forehead and started to pray. Tears ran down her cheeks as the Spirit of the Lord ministered to her heart. It was obvious that what God was saying through my prayer was reaching to the depths of her being. When I finished, my friend prayed for her again, and as she did, the same vision once again flashed in front of my eyes, exactly as it had the first time — with the same details and intensity.

This time I could not hold back from sharing what I saw. "There are certain things of which you need to be cautious when you minister prophetically," I began tentatively. "I have been taught to be careful about giving prophecies concerning marriage, babies, and geographical moves. The Bible says to test all things and hold on to what is good. So I want to encourage you to carefully weigh what I am about to share with you." The young lady nodded her head soberly as she wiped her eyes with a tissue.

I paused and then began to describe the vision. "I saw you holding a baby in your arms…" I hadn't even finished the phrase when she burst into uncontrollable sobbing. I waited while her friend rubbed her shoulders, comforting the young woman.

After a moment she grew quiet and I continued. "There was a large demon with a sword that was trying to attack you and the baby. The demon continually swung the sword at you, but you were surrounded by an invisible force field of some sort and the blows bounced right off. The demon was enraged that he could not harm you or your child, and he kept hacking away to no avail. The whole time you were crying out, 'Why won't my husband come and defend us from this attack?' But your husband was nowhere to be found."

I shared with her that I sensed the Lord wanted to give her and her husband a child, but the enemy was trying to thwart God's plan. I also sensed that the husband was not completely in agreement with God's plan, and wasn't even walking in right relationship with the Lord. That was why he was not defending her against the demonic attack. I prayed for God's perfect will to be done in their lives and in this situation.

When I finished praying, the young lady wiped the tears from her eyes and told us that the prophetic words were very accurate and timely. She had wanted to have a baby for some time, but her husband had been opposed to the idea. In the last year he had fallen away from the Lord and was seeking worldly pursuits. In the past few weeks he had come around and was now open to the idea of having children. In fact, she thought she might have been pregnant, but she had just started her period and was concerned that she may have lost the baby.

When she finished speaking, I asked if we could pray for her again. We prayed for her marriage, for her husband, and that the Lord would knit the two of them together in love for each other and for the Lord. Then we prayed that God would bless them with a child in His perfect timing.

Several weeks went by and I heard that this young lady had some news. I saw her after chapel, and she gave me a giant hug. "I just found out that I'm pregnant!" she exclaimed.

"Praise the Lord!" I responded.

"And not only that," she added with a big smile. "The doctor said that I have been pregnant for more than three months. That means that I was pregnant when you prophesied over me! Maybe the fact that I thought I was having my period was a sign of the attack that Satan was waging against the baby and me?"

"How did your husband take the news?" I asked.

"He was actually excited," she answered. "The Lord has really done a work in our marriage since you prayed for us."

I saw this young lady in the hall a few weeks later and asked her again how things were going. "God is 'the bomb'!" she replied as she whisked passed me on the way to a meeting.

I couldn't agree with her more.

Christians are faced every day with the difficult task of making decisions. Those who have asked Jesus to be Lord over their lives desire to know that they are walking in the will of God. The Bible gives us principles and general instructions about how to live our lives. But when it comes to making specific decisions about critical areas of our lives, Scripture is not always able to speak precisely to our circumstances.

Today, God can communicate with any believer through the Bible, and directly to his or her heart through the Holy Spirit. As he did with Adam and Eve in the cool of the day, God desires to have a daily personal relationship with each of His children. But sadly, not all Christians understand how to recognize the voice of the Lord. They are like Samuel, the boy prophet who thought he was hearing the voice of his master, Eli, when it was really God speaking to his heart.

Even Christians who know how to hear God's voice at times may not respond to the Lord in a biblical manner. Sometimes the circumstances of life can be so stressful and confusing that a believer needs outside confirmation to know for certain what God is saying to them. Personal prophecy is one of the keys of God's guidance that can bring that confirmation.

WEEK SEVEN
Day One: Prophecy in the Bible

Personal prophecy, along with the other keys to hearing God's voice, can help believers make important decisions in life. It is important to understand that God created us with a need for other people in our lives. He knows that human beings are sinners and prone to selfishness. No Christian is self-sufficient — we are a part of the body of Christ. The only way we can live a fruitful and productive Christian life is to be an active member of a thriving community of believers in a local church. Sometimes the Lord will purposely withhold information from a Christian to force him or her to seek godly counsel and confirmation of His leading. Through prophets and other believers in the local church who flow in the gift of prophecy, the Lord can speak to us and direct our steps.

Some would ask, "Is it scriptural to seek God's guidance through personal prophecy? Is it proper for a Christian to go to a prophet and expect to receive a specific prophetic word of direction, instruction, or confirmation?" The answer is yes — but like all the keys of God's guidance, that word must be judged against the Scripture and confirmed through peace, and in the mouth of two or three witnesses before it is acted upon.

Throughout the Bible we see God speaking to His saints through the prophets. In fact, through the prophet Amos the Lord declares: *Surely the Lord GOD does nothing, unless He reveals His secret to His servants the prophets. A lion has roared! Who will not fear? The Lord GOD has spoken! Who can but prophesy?* (Amos 3:7–8).

In the Old Testament, the Holy Spirit was not given to each person (see Numbers 11:25). Old Testament prophets were specially appointed and anointed mouthpieces for God, speaking on His behalf before paupers and kings. True prophets of God were consistently accurate, and as a result of their ministries, people were led to worship the Lord of heaven and Him alone. Though they were human and sometimes sinned, these prophets consistently bore good fruit in their lives and through their prophetic ministry.

It was vital that the Old Testament prophet speak an *accurate* word of the Lord, because this was the primary way that God communicated with His people at the time. Prophets like Moses, Daniel, Isaiah, and Ezekiel, and prophetesses like Deborah and Anna received the word of the Lord and then delivered it to God's people. If they didn't fulfill their calling, the people didn't hear from God.

That is why such a stern warning was given in the Mosaic law for prophets to speak only the words that were given to them by God.

Read Deuteronomy 18:20–22. What was the test to determine if the prophet was "of the Lord"?

_____

_____

What was the punishment for a "presumptuous" prophet?

_____

_____

Why do you suppose God required such a harsh punishment for false prophets?

_____

_____

Only one sin cast Adam and Eve out of the Garden of Eden. Only one mistake kept Moses out of Canaan. And under a strict interpretation of the law, only one unfulfilled word could cause someone to be judged a false prophet.

Why was the standard so stringent? Under the Mosaic Law, priests represented man to God through sacrifices in the tabernacle and later the temple. But the prophets represented God to humankind, and they had God's anointing to pronounce divine judgments and decrees in the name of the Lord. For that reason, and because the Holy Spirit only came upon a limited number of individuals for a specified time, prophets were required to speak the very word of the Lord every time they opened their mouths.

Read Ezekiel 3:18–19. How are prophets responsible for the words from God they receive?

_____

_____

_____

Many of the prophecies of the Old Testament had a particular application to an immediate situation as well as a long-term fulfillment centuries later, and they were captured in words that meant entirely different things in each setting.

One example is David's prayer in Psalm 22 that included graphic descriptions of the crucifixion (a method of execution that was unknown in David's time), but had other implications to David when he wrote it. Under the inspiration of the Holy Spirit, David prophetically wrote a song about his own oppressed state and unknowingly provided Jesus with the words He would later cry from the cross: *"My God, My God, why have You forsaken Me?"* (Psalm 22:1 and Matthew 27:46).

There are dozens of prophets in the Bible:
• Moses was a mighty prophet, who was also given the awesome responsibility of leading three million of God's people to the Promised Land.

• Miriam was a prophetess who helped to save the life of Moses as a baby. Later she would sing a prophetic song of the Lord when God delivered Israel through the Red Sea.

• Deborah was a dynamic prophetess who wisely judged Israel, bringing deliverance from their enemies.

• Samuel was a prophet who anointed two kings and served God valiantly throughout his life.

• Elijah was the great prophet who prophesied to King Ahab, *"There shall not be dew nor rain these years, except at my word"* (1 Kings 17:1). For three years the Lord held back the rain. Then Elijah prayed again, after putting to death the prophets of Baal, and the rain poured down from heaven.

• Elisha asked for, and received, a double portion of Elijah's anointing. After prophesying a son for a certain woman, the boy later died, but Elisha prayed and the boy returned back to life.

• Jeremiah and Ezekiel were great prophets who foretold the fall of Israel and also suffered severe persecution for their ministries.

• Isaiah was one of the Old Testament's leading prophets, who mightily foretold the coming of the Messiah.

• Jonah was a prophet whose warning turned the people of Nineveh from their sin, despite his ungodly attitude toward them.

• Daniel was an amazing prophet who ministered to kings and received a vision of the end of all things.

• Anna was a prophetess who witnessed to the lordship of Jesus as a baby and spoke of Him to all those who looked for redemption in Israel.

• John the Baptist was the last Old Testament prophet, having died before Jesus' death and resurrection — and before the Holy Spirit was poured out on the Day of Pentecost.

• Jesus Himself was the great Prophet, sent from heaven to embody the love of the Father to the world.

• Agabus was a New Testament prophet who foretold a famine and prophesied that Paul would be delivered into the hands of the Gentiles.

• Barnabas was a compassionate prophet who first brought Saul to the apostles. Later Barnabas and Saul were set apart as a prophet/apostle team by the Holy Spirit to take the gospel to the Gentiles.

The apostle John wrote in the book of Revelation that in the last days God will raise up two mighty prophets who will do signs and wonders in the name of the Lord.

Read Revelation 11:3, 6.

If the ministry of the prophet is no longer needed by the church because the Bible has replaced them (as some would teach), then why do we find them functioning in the end times, long after the canon was completed?

The Old Testament prophet Malachi foretold that God would send Elijah the prophet before the coming of the great and dreadful day of the Lord (see Malachi 4:5). When the angel appeared to Zacharias in the temple, he quoted Malachi when he announced the birth of John the Baptist:

> *"He will also go before Him in the spirit and power of Elijah, 'to turn the hearts of the fathers to the children,' and the disobedient to the wisdom of the just, to make ready a people prepared for the Lord."*
>
> —Luke 1:17

The Jews believed that Elijah himself would return to announce the coming of the Messiah, but Jesus explained that John the Baptist fulfilled Malachi's prophecy.

> *"But what did you go out to see? A prophet? Yes, I say to you, and more than a prophet. For this is he of whom it is written: Behold, I send My messenger before Your face, who will prepare Your way before You. And if you are willing to receive it, he is Elijah who is to come."*
>
> —Matthew 11:9–10, 14

The canonization of the Scriptures into the sixty-six books of the Bible did not eliminate the need for prophets in the church. And unlike Old Testament times, today millions of people across the globe have the Holy Spirit residing on the inside of them. God can speak to and through any believer who is willing to be used as His vessel.

Why is it sometimes difficult to get specific direction from the Bible?

_____

_____

How can personal prophecy, along with the other keys to God's guidance, help a person to make decisions about God's will in their life?

_____

_____

Why did the Holy Spirit only fall on certain persons in the Old Testament?

_____

_____

_____

Read Ephesians 4:7–8, 11–12.

To help bring Christians into a place of maturity, God has set within the body of Christ the ministry of the New Testament prophet with special anointing and authority. Through the manifestation of the Holy Spirit, He has also established the gift of prophecy to communicate in the local church. And as He inhabits the praises and prayer times of His people, He releases the spirit of prophecy to give testimony to the lordship of Jesus Christ in the earth today!

Dr. Bill Hamon defines prophecy as:

> …simply God communicating His thoughts and intents to mankind. When a true prophecy is given, the Holy Spirit inspires someone to communicate God's pure and exact words to the individual or group for whom they are intended. It is delivered without any additions or subtractions by the one prophesying, including any applications or interpretations suggested by the one speaking. To be most effective, it must also be delivered in God's timing and with the proper spirit or attitude.[1]

The Bible makes it clear that prophecy is a most powerful gift, and it is encouraged throughout the Scriptures.

Read 1 Corinthians 14:1, 39. What are we to "desire earnestly"?

_____

_____

As I have said before, God is love, and love communicates! God *wants* to reveal Himself to mankind, and He has given us a powerful gift for expressing His thoughts and desires to the world. The term "desire earnestly" is the Greek word *zeloo,* which means to have great desire, to be jealous over, and to be zealously affected. It implies fervency of mind, even the type of emotional jealousy a husband would have toward his wife, an intense hunger to hear from God.

God commands us to desire earnestly and covet the prophetic ministry. In fact, it is the only ministry that the Bible tells us we are to covet.

We receive spiritual gifts and manifestations of the Holy Spirit for our own benefit and enjoyment, but also to be a contributing member of the body of Christ.

Read 1 Corinthians 12:7–11. Why do you think God wants us to covet to prophesy?

_____

_____

When you realize that God desires to manifest His Spirit through you supernaturally, how does that impact your faith to move in the gifts of the Spirit?

_____

_____

_____

Edification, Exhortation, and Comfort

Prophecy in the New Testament is used by God to speak edification, exhortation, and comfort to individual believers, small groups of Christians, local churches, the church in a particular geographical area, and sometimes to the entire body of Christ (see 1 Corinthians 14:3).

Another word for edification is "up-building," which is the Greek word *oikodome,* meaning "to build a house." Paul was saying that prophecy is to be used to build up the household of believers by communicating the heart and thoughts of God. Personal prophecy can build up an individual in their walk with the Lord or encourage a congregation to move forward in the plan of God for them in their neighborhood, city, or region.

Jesus uses the term *paraclete* in the gospel of John to refer to the Holy Spirit. The apostle Paul uses the same root word for *encouragement* in 1 Corinthians 14:3, *paraclesis.* Through prophecy, the Holy Spirit encourages us in our Christian walk. He also exhorts us to fulfill all of God's will for our lives by His power and grace. "To encourage" is to speak words that drive away fear and build faith or "courage" in our hearts. That is what the Holy Spirit does through personal prophecy.

Paul uses the Greek word *paramuthia* for "comfort" in this passage, which means to exercise a gentle influence of consolation. The Holy Spirit will calm our fears and bring peace to our hearts through a prophetic word spoken in a gracious manner. Be careful to guard yourself against a prophetic word given in a harsh, judgmental, condescending, or critical manner. The New Covenant prophet gives words under the grace of Jesus Christ, through edification, exhortation, and comfort.

The ministry of the Holy Spirit and the writing of the Bible did not eliminate the need for prophets in the body of Christ. Prophets are used to vocalize the revelation of God as well as provide specific instruction for individual lives. Prophecy is God speaking to man, through man. New Testament prophecy is only one of the seven keys of God's guidance — but it is an important key that should not be overlooked.

In his book, *Prophets and Personal Prophecy,* Dr. Bill Hamon writes:

> God still wants the revelation of His will to be vocalized. So He has established the prophetic ministry as a voice of revelation and illumination which will reveal the mind of Christ to the human race. He also uses this ministry to give specific instructions to individuals concerning His personal will for their lives.
>
> The ministry of the prophet is not, of course, to bring about additions or subtractions to the Bible. Any new additions accepted as infallibly inspired would be counterfeits, false documents which would contain delusions that lead to damnation. Instead, the prophet brings illumination and further specifics about that which has already been written. And the Holy Spirit's gift of prophecy through the saints is to bring edification, exhortation, and comfort to the Church (1 Corinthians 14:3).[2]

The Lord wants to communicate directly to the heart of the individual believer. But whatever a person receives from God through the keys to hearing His voice must be confirmed in the mouth of two or three witnesses (see Deuteronomy 19:15; 1 Corinthians 13:1). This vital function can be fulfilled through personal prophecy.

The prophet and personal prophecy are never to take the place of the inner voice of the Holy Spirit within the heart of every believer. Prophets are an extension of the ministry of the Holy Spirit in communicating the mind of Christ to the church.

God approves of personal prophecy as long as we don't allow it to become a substitute for hearing the voice of God for ourselves in our own times of prayer, searching the Scriptures, fasting, and seeking His face. We must seek the Lord through the other keys to God's guidance, but from time to time when we need the Lord to speak to a specific area of our lives, and we have been diligent in seeking His will in our personal times of prayer, we can seek personal prophecy as another means of discovering His plan for our lives.

If you encounter a person who is giving a prophecy in a critical or judgmental tone, what should that tell you about that prophetic word?

_____

_____

_____

_____

Paul exhorts the Corinthian church to not be ignorant concerning spiritual gifts. How can a person's ignorance of spiritual gifts be a hindrance to their walk with the Lord?

_____

_____

_____

_____

_____

_____

_____

_____

Day Two: The Nature of Personal Prophecy

God did not design us with the ability to know or consider too much about our future. If we did, we would probably be fixated on it, neglecting to focus on the issues of the day.

Read Matthew 6:34. How did Jesus tell us we should view the future?

_____

_____

While the Lord does at times speak to our future through personal prophecy, typically He will reveal only those things that we need to know in order to help us properly prepare for what He has in store.

Now it must be stated emphatically that although personal prophecy is a manifestation of the Holy Spirit through the born-again believer, New Testament prophecy does not rise to the level of infallibility like Scripture. Because of the improper ways that people have abused personal prophecy and other forms of divine guidance in the past, whole churches and denominations have taken the position that the supernatural gifts of the Spirit are no longer valid.

But the Bible never states that the manifestation of the Holy Spirit in the world will cease — that is, until perfection has come. As I see it, only Jesus is perfect, and He hasn't come yet. Until He does return, we who are imperfect need His divine intervention, power, guidance, and love in order to be and do all that He desires in this highly imperfect world.

For the most part, God will providentially guide us without our being aware of it. But there are times when the Lord needs to get our attention to move forward in His plan for us. Someone once said that God's guidance could be compared to taking a long flight on an airplane. For the majority of the journey we are in that one vehicle, and the pilot is guiding us from one location to another as we enjoy the ride. But often when we fly long distances, we are required to transfer to another aircraft. When God wants us to make a major shift in our lives, or when we are just not getting the message, He will ordain a transfer in our journey from one plane to another. He often does this through supernatural, or special guidance — through a dream, vision, miracle, angelic visitation, heavenly voice, or personal prophecy.

There some pastors who accept that God will speak through prophets and personal prophecy, but they are so afraid of "wild fire" that they don't encourage prophecy in their congregations — and in effect, they are "quenching" the Holy Spirit. Speaking of the gift of prophecy and the manifestation of the Holy Spirit in the church, the apostle Paul wrote, *Let all things be done, decently and in order* (1 Corinthians 14:40). There are some charismatics who cry out, "Let all things be done!" while other evangelical or mainline Christians declare, "Decently and in order!" The Lord wants to bring the church into balance regarding the gifts of the Spirit to "let all things be done — decently and in order."

God is a Creator. Satan is an imitator. For every true, genuine gift of God there will be a counterfeit. In a way, knowing there is a demonic forgery of the gift of prophecy should encourage our faith to believe God for the real. If the devil can promote psychics, witches, astrologers, and the like, then we know that God has prophets speaking on His behalf in the world today!

Paul gave the Thessalonian church a guide for judging personal prophecy.

Write out 1 Thessalonians 5:19–21.

_____

_____

_____

_____

_____

There is a dual implication in verse 21. First of all, if we can hold fast to what is good, then Paul is telling us that personal prophecy is a good thing. The second implication is that if we are to test all things and hold fast to what is good, then not everything we might hear in a personal prophecy is good. In these cases we should eat the meat and spit out the bones.

The word *despise* in this passage is a form of the Greek word *exoudenoo,* which means "to make utterly nothing of." The apostle Paul is exhorting believers that they should not "make utterly nothing of" the gift of prophecy in their lives.

The Lord intends for believers to receive personal prophecy in their life, but to do so in a biblically balanced manner, with proper spiritual oversight. When we do this, we unlock the door to tremendous blessing both for us, our families, our churches — and through us, the world.

How can a person quench the Spirit or despise prophecies?

_____

_____

_____

How can you avoid quenching the Spirit or despising prophecies?

_____

_____

_____

Personal Prophecy Is Partial, Progressive, and Conditional

In order to properly incorporate personal prophecy into our lives, we must understand that it will always be partial, progressive, and conditional. Paul declared that _"we know in part and we prophesy in part"_ (1 Corinthians 13:9). Personal prophecy is only a small insight into God's overall will for our lives. We can only do what the Lord reveals for us to do.

Read Deuteronomy 29:29. To what might the "secret things" in this verse refer? To whom do they belong?

_____

_____

_____

Personal prophecy is _partial_ in that God only reveals what we need to know in order to do His will in a particular area of our lives. A prophecy may only speak to a certain "chapter" of our life story. Knowing that prophecy is partial helps us to understand that just because the Lord doesn't speak about a certain area of our lives, that doesn't mean that He doesn't want us to move forward in that area if we have been led through the other keys of God's guidance.

Besides being partial, personal prophecy is also *progressive*. The Lord will unfold and reveal His will through prophecy gradually over a lifetime, with each prophetic word adding new information and revelation. For this reason, time is often the greatest trial of faith for believing the promises of the Lord given to us through personal prophecy.

Abraham and Sarah had to wait twenty-five years for the fulfillment of God's prophecy about Isaac — and they were already elderly when the promise first came to them. The apostle Paul had to wait years before the prophecy of his ministry to the Gentiles would be fulfilled. King David waited for nearly twenty years between the time he was anointed as king by Samuel and the time he actually ascended to the throne. Joseph received his prophetic dream when he was a teenager, but it wasn't until twenty-two years had passed before he saw a fulfillment of God's revelation in his life.

In considering how the Lord leads us through personal prophecy, we also need to understand the fundamental difference between conditional and unconditional guidance. The majority of God's guidance is unconditional — the Lord directs our steps, often without our even realizing it. God will sovereignly act regardless of whether we are obeying Him fully or not. God's unconditional guidance works in our lives because we are His people, and because He honors His Word — not because we deserve it, but because we are His children, having been redeemed by the blood of Jesus.

Personal prophecy, however, is often *conditional*; it can be cancelled, altered, reversed, or diminished based on the response of the person receiving the word. For prophecy of this kind to come to pass requires the proper faith and action on the part of the person receiving the word.

Although we have God's assurance that He will guide us, there are other occasions when the Lord will give us a promise and preface it with a condition. From biblical examples, we discover that personal prophecy is not always fulfilled. Prophecies that are conditional have part of their fulfillment based on human behavior. In the life of Abraham, the promises spoken by God to him over the years were partial and progressive, expanding and unfolding over a lifetime. We see in God's words to Abraham that it was as a result of his obedience to the tests that he became the father of many nations, as God had promised.

And He said, "Do not lay your hand on the lad, or do anything to him; for now I know that you fear God, since you have not withheld your son, your only son, from Me. "By Myself I have sworn," says the LORD, because you have done this thing, and have not withheld your son, your only son — blessing I will bless you, and multiplying I will multiply your descendants as the stars of the heaven and as the sand which is on the seashore.... In your seed all the nations of the earth shall be blessed, because you have obeyed My voice."

—Genesis 22:12, 16–18, emphasis mine

The life of King Saul provides a tragic example of a personal prophecy being revoked because of disobedience. Though Samuel had anointed him king, Saul failed to completely obey God's directions to him. The heart-rending rebuke through Samuel makes it clear that Saul's attitude of rebellion and disobedience caused the promise to be withdrawn.

And Samuel said to Saul, "You have done foolishly. You have not kept the commandment of the LORD your God [personal prophecy], which He commanded you. For now the LORD would have established your kingdom over Israel forever. But now your kingdom shall not continue. The LORD has sought for Himself a man after His own heart, and the LORD has commanded him to be commander over His people, because you have not kept what the LORD commanded you."

—1 Samuel 13:13–14, comment mine

How is personal prophecy partial in the life of a believer? Why doesn't God give us a fuller picture through the prophetic gifts?

_____

_____

_____

_____

How is personal prophecy progressive in the life of a believer?

_____

_____

_____

In your own words, explain the difference between conditional and unconditional prophecy.

_____

_____

_____

Only for Confirmation?

Some people teach that personal prophecy is meant only to confirm, and not to give direction. It's true that prophecy will often be used to confirm the Lord's will in your life, but the Bible never says that it cannot be used for direction. In fact, the Scripture shows numerous examples of prophets speaking directional words. Some teach that the New Testament does not give any examples of such a word, and neither does it speak to the issue, but this too is not factual.

One basic rule of biblical interpretation is that if the New Testament does not do away with certain practices or ministries available in the Old, then they are still available in the church age. No scriptures in the New Testament state that a prophet in the church does not have all the ministry rights of the prophets of old. All the Law and Prophets were fulfilled in Christ, but then, as we have already seen, when Jesus ascended into heaven, He gave the prophets to the church, along with the other ministry offices.

The late Demos Shakarian shares an amazing example of a directional prophecy. His family lived in the village of Kara Kala in Armenia, at the foot of Mount Ararat. All of them were Christians, having received the gospel through the witness of Russian Orthodox believers at the end of the nineteenth century. In his village there lived an eleven-year-old illiterate boy whose name was Efim. One day this lad heard the Lord calling him to a time of prayer and fasting. After seven days and nights, the Lord gave him a vision:

> Efim could neither read nor write. Yet, as he sat in the little stone cottage
> in Kara Kala, he saw before him a vision of charts and a message in a
> beautiful handwriting. Efim asked for pen and paper. And for seven days,
> sitting at the rough plank table where the family ate, he laboriously copied

down the form and shape of letters and diagrams that passed before his eyes. When he had finished, the manuscript was taken to people in the village who could read. It turned out that this illiterate child had written out in Russian characters a series of instructions and warnings. At some unspecified time in the future, the boy wrote, every Christian in Kara Kala would be in terrible danger. He foretold a time of unspeakable tragedy for the entire area, when hundreds of thousands of men, women, and children would be brutally murdered. The time would come, he warned, when everyone in the region must flee. They must go to a land across the sea. Although he had never seen a geography book, the boy prophet drew a map showing exactly where the fleeing Christians were to go. To the amazement of the adults, the body of water depicted so accurately in the drawing was not the nearby Black Sea, or the Caspian Sea, or even the farther off Mediterranean Sea, but the distant and unimaginable Atlantic Ocean! There was no doubt about it, nor about the identity of the land on the other side; the map plainly indicated the east coast of the United States of America.

But the refugees were not to settle down there, the prophecy continued. They were to continue traveling until they reached the west coast of the new land. There, the boy wrote, God would bless them and prosper them, and cause their seed to be a blessing to the nations.

More than fifty years passed and Efim, then an aging man, announced to the village that the time had come to obey the prophecy. The Shakarians, along with several other families, sold their goods and moved to America. But many of the villagers did not heed the prophecy. Not long after this, in 1914, the Turks began a genocide that killed more than one million Armenians, including every single person in the village of Kara Kala.

The Shakarian family obeyed the word of the Lord and settled in California, where they started what would become a hugely successful dairy farm. As the prophecy foretold, the family prospered in this new land. Later, at the leading of the Holy Spirit, Demos Shakarian founded The Full Gospel Businessmen's Fellowship, a ministry that eventually touched the lives of millions of people in America and around the world — fulfilling the prophecy that their seed would be a blessing to the nations.[3]

The Bible tells us, *Believe in the LORD your God, and you shall be established; believe His prophets, and you shall prosper* (2 Chronicles 20:20).

What benefits does believing God's prophets bring to a Christian's life?

_____

_____

_____

_____

How should you respond if you receive a directional personal prophecy?

_____

_____

_____

_____

_____

Day Three: Receiving Personal Prophecy

The apostle Paul spoke of the proper biblical response to personal prophecy in his letter to the Corinthians.

Write out 1 Corinthians 14:39–40.

_____

_____

_____

The Bible provides us with general guidelines to help us properly respond to personal prophecy.

1. Does the word line up with Scripture?

Someone may say to you, "I've had a vision about your life," or "The Lord has given me this great word for you." God does lead supernaturally, there is no doubt about it. But whenever you are considering any form of special guidance, you need to judge it against the light of God's Word to see if it is true. The apostle Paul gave the litmus test for prophets in his letter to the Corinthians.

Describe the test that Paul set forth in 1 Corinthians 14:37.

_____

_____

_____

In other words, you should ask, does the prophecy line up with the Bible? The Holy Spirit will never act in contradiction to the written Word of God. He is the One who inspired the Bible in the first place.

Christians should know the Bible and memorize key portions of it. It is the Word of God that will protect us against false doctrine, deception, and spiritual manipulation. Always check a prophetic word against the other seven keys, beginning with the Bible. If the prophecy contradicts the Scriptures, you can obviously ignore it.

2. Is the prophecy given in love and grace, or in anger and judgment?

Prophecy in the New Testament flows from the Spirit of Christ, which is a spirit of grace and love. As we have already considered, the majority of personal prophecy should be given as edification, exhortation, and comfort (1 Corinthians 14:3).

Read 1 Corinthians 13:2. How should love and the giving of personal prophecy relate?

_____

_____

_____

It is interesting that the portion of Scripture that has become known as the "love chapter," 1 Corinthians 13, is sandwiched between the two chapters that deal with the manifestation of the Holy Spirit. Through these gifts God shows His love to the world, and He expects His ministers to do the same.

3. What is the character and fruit of the person giving the word?

The personal character of a prophetic minister, or any minister for that matter, is the foundation of his or her ministry. Character is a primary guide for determining whether someone is a true or false prophet.

Dr. Hamon has given a list of what he calls the "10 M's" for maturing and maintaining ministry. These key character attributes are a good guide for determining the fruit of the person giving a prophetic word:

• Manhood – Are they the man or woman that God intends for them to be in Him?

• Ministry – Do they exhibit the mature fruit of a loving, grace-filled ministry?

• Message – Do they speak the truth in love, in a balanced, scriptural manner?

• Maturity – Do they display a right attitude and heavenly wisdom in every relationship?

• Marriage – Is their life biblically in order, with the right priorities (God first, wife and family second, and then ministry)?

• Methods – Are they righteous, ethical, honest, and full of integrity, or are they manipulative or deceptive?

• Manners – Are they unselfish, polite, kind, and discreet? Are they a gentleman or a lady?

• Money – Do they have a love of money, or the proper perspective of stewardship in their finances?

- Morality – Are they virtuous and sexually pure? Do they display the right attitudes, thoughts, and actions in all situations?
- Motive – Is their motive to be seen or to serve?[4]

4. Is there some sort of religious bias in the attitude of the person giving the word?

Sometimes a person will bring what could be termed a doctrinal "hobby horse" into a prophetic situation that can twist a true prophecy and give it an unbalanced presentation. Be careful to judge the word against the Bible, and not against the positions of a certain denomination.

5. Do I sense a witness from the Holy Spirit?

When a guitarist tunes his guitar, he will play one note and then match the next string on the guitar to the note on the first string. A true musician can hear the dissonance when their instrument is out of tune, and they will tinker with the tuning key until there is resonance between the two strings.

Bruce Yocum writes of this principle regarding our spirit and the Holy Spirit's witness in our heart:

> Objects have certain characteristic frequencies at which they vibrate. If you cause one object (for instance a bell) to vibrate near another object with the same characteristic frequency (another bell of the same size and weight and shape), the second object will begin to vibrate by itself. That is something like what happens when we hear the voice of the Lord — we resonate.[5]

When the Lord is speaking to us, no matter what method He chooses, our born-again spirits recognize the voice of the Good Shepherd. Jesus made it clear in John 10 that His sheep know His voice, and the voice of a stranger they will not follow. If a personal prophecy is not of God, the born-again Christian will get what is known as a "check" in their spirit — an uncomfortable feeling in the pit of the stomach telling them that something is not right.

6. Don't reject a directional word, but test it against the other keys.

If the word is something new that you have never heard before, it may be a directional word from the Lord, but don't act on it right away. Test it like you would any other guidance from the Lord.

What sensations do you experience when you know someone is not in tune with the Holy Spirit? Do you have unrest in your emotions? Do you experience physical discomfort, like a tension in your neck? Think back on a time when you knew someone was speaking something to you that did not line up with the Spirit of God. Write down how you felt or what you experienced.

_____

_____

_____

Earlier we examined the concept that many personal prophecies are conditional. How does this fact affect your judgment of whether a person is a true or false prophet?

_____

_____

_____

How might a prophet's character cause their prophecies to be false?

_____

_____

How might a person's religious bias affect a prophetic word that they give to another person?

_____

_____

What should you do with a prophecy that you sense is correct overall, but that perhaps the person giving it has added some of their own interpretation or religious viewpoints?

_____

_____

_____

Personal Prophecy Versus Psychics and False Prophets

A viewer of *The 700 Club* sent in an e-mail stating that he believed the words of knowledge received during the show are psychic abilities in operation. He said, "When you are spiritual and intend to help others, then psychic results happen."

In his book, *Bring It On,* Pat Robertson responds:

> It helps to understand three words in the New Testament Greek: *pneuma,* which means "spirit, wind, or breath;" *psuche,* which means "soul." This is the word from which we get the word *psychic.* And *soma,* which is "body." Human beings are tripartite creatures, comprised of body, soul, and spirit.
>
> The Bible says that the *psuchikos* man, the soulish man, receives not the things of the Spirit of God, for they are foolishness unto him. Neither can he know them (1 Corinthians 2:14). So if a person is operating on the soulish, psychic level, he is not dealing with the Spirit of God. The information received may be merely human, or it may come from a spirit, but it is not directed by the *Holy* Spirit. When you delve into psychic things, you inevitably discover that it is soulish and demonic as opposed to God's Spirit.
>
> In 1 Corinthians 12 and 14, the enablements of the Holy Spirit are described. These *charismata,* or manifestations of the Holy Spirit, come about through the operation of the Holy Spirit in a human being. For instance, when we receive a word of knowledge, it is the Holy Spirit speaking to our spirit the things God wants to reveal. That is not psychic. The psychic attempts to imitate many of the things the Spirit of God does through His people.
>
> Certainly, most of us have powers in our minds that we may or may not exercise. Our minds send out both FM and AM radio waves. We can do amazing things in the psychic part of ourselves. The full potential of the human mind and soul has never been realized. But the Bible never tells us to stir up our psychic part or our soulish powers, because the psychic part of unredeemed humanity will ultimately lead to worship of the devil and rebellion against God. Scripture does instruct us to stir up our spirit. It says, "For the one who sows to his own flesh shall from the flesh reap corruption, but the one who sows to the Spirit shall from the Spirit reap eternal life" (see Galatians 6:8).
>
> We should stay far away from any psychic phenomena that is not under the control of the Holy Spirit, including psychics on television, tarot card readers, fortune tellers, and other occult practices the devil uses in an attempt to seduce us from God into falsehood.[6]

The Lord will protect you from receiving anything through a psychic or satanic source. In fact, a false prophet or psychic might use all the right biblical words, they might speak "christianese," but you still won't feel the peace of God because they are speaking out of the *psuche*, and not from the Spirit of God.

The Bible clearly condemns the practice of divination.

Read Deuteronomy 18:9–14 and Leviticus 19:31. Why do you think God's judgment of psychic practices is so severe?

_____

_____

_____

_____

A person who practices divination peers into the future, not with a renewed spirit, but through the soul or *psuche*. All of the practices listed in Deuteronomy 18 are Satan's copy of God's prophetic giftings, including personal prophecy, word of knowledge, word of wisdom, and discerning of spirits. Remember, Satan and his demons still have a certain amount of power in the spirit realm here on earth. They can do any number of impressive tricks to try to deceive and get you to take your eyes off of Jesus Christ. Someone may be able to tell you details of your life, like your birthday or the address of the home you grew up in, but if they are exhibiting a spirit of pride or judgmentalism, or if they are not giving glory to Jesus Christ, you may be dealing with someone caught up in divination. Do not receive such a word — reject it, and pray for the eyes of that person to be opened to the truth of the gospel.

Another kind of false prophet that can be more difficult to detect is someone who claims to speak in the name of God, but the fruit of their life does not line up with the Christian life. Jesus warned of these kinds of false prophets.

Read Matthew 7:15–20. How does Jesus say we will recognize true or false prophets?

_____

In his book, *Prophetic Gatherings in the Church,* David Blomgren says:

False prophets may be detected by their character and conduct. A false prophet will live a sinful life, while a true prophet will exemplify conduct and character which are consistent with God's character. A false prophet will bring forth evil fruit, and a true prophet will display good fruit.[7]

False prophets have no qualms about taking Scripture out of context to fit their own interpretation of what they think the Bible means. They will use manipulation to try to control or influence the lives of people around them. They may even use prophetic utterances as a means of making money. The true prophet of God is not motivated by money, and is very cautious of being manipulated by money or influence. The true prophet of God is not a respecter of persons — he or she will be obedient to speak the word of the Lord to whomever God commands, in whatever way God leads them to speak it.

Read 1 Timothy 4:1–2.

As the time for Jesus' return grows closer and closer, we must have special discernment to distinguish between God's prophets and Satan's counterfeits. I am convinced that both will grow in power and prominence in these last days. We must study to show ourselves approved in these critical times — we must know the Word of God! (See 2 Timothy 2:15.) When we allow the Spirit of God to shine the light of the Bible, the darkness is immediately overcome.

How does knowing that psychics pull from the *psuche* affect your view of their powers?

_____

_____

_____

Why do you think God allows Satan and his followers to have a certain amount of supernatural power on the earth? How can you avoid being deceived by these abilities?

_____

_____

_____

Day Four: Responding to Personal Prophecy

The apostle Paul wrote in 1 Timothy 4:14–15 NRSV: *Do not neglect the gift that is in you, which was given to you through prophecy with the laying on of hands by the council of elders. Put these things into practice, devote yourself to them, so that all may see your progress.* The following are some practical ways that a believer can respond to a personal word.

1. If possible, record the personal prophecy.

Recording a personal prophecy is beneficial for several reasons. First, the person receiving the word can listen to it several times, thus retaining more of what is said. Most people forget a large amount of what they hear, even soon after a word is given. It is always amazing how much the Lord speaks to me each time I listen to a tape recording of a prophetic word.

The other advantage of recording a word is that you have new and different perspective on what the Lord is saying as time goes by. As the Lord reveals more to you, and as you experience more of life, your prophetic words take on new meaning and often greater significance as the things that God speaks of are fulfilled in your life.

Recording a personal prophecy also provides accountability, both for the person giving it and the one receiving it. It helps the person who received the message to recall precisely what the prophet says. It also prevents the prophet from being misquoted or part of the prophecy being taken out of context.

2. Transcribe, read, and meditate upon the word.

It is wise to transcribe audio recordings of prophecy to keep for future reference. These words can then be reviewed with one's pastor, mentor, or spiritual covering as a means of counseling and as a way to track your own spiritual growth. Share the word with someone you respect who understands how to test personal prophecy. As you review your word, ask the Holy Spirit to enlighten any areas of the word on which you need to focus. Are there any conditions to the prophetic word's being fulfilled?

When reviewing a prophecy, it should be noted that not every element of the word will be applicable to your present experience. As I have already pointed out, the Bible warns us to prove and judge prophecy, not the prophet, if some elements may not seem to relate at the present time. Be careful not to interpret the word based on your own desires. Our approach to prophecy, and the other keys of God's guidance, should always be, "Not my will, but Your will be done."

3. Seek the Lord for the timing of any prophetic word.

The writer of Hebrews spoke of the importance of waiting on the Lord to fulfill His desires in our lives.

Write out Hebrews 6:12.

_____

_____

What do we have need of? Why?

_____

_____

Seeking the way of God is vitally important, and yet it is probably the one area of God's guidance that most Christians fail to consider when seeking His will for their lives. God's way requires a process of trusting God to give us the specific timing for obeying His Word and His will. The Bible tells us that God showed *His acts* to Israel, but He made known *His ways* to Moses. Let us pray that we would be like Moses, not only knowing about God's acts, but also knowing His Word, will, and way.

Make sure you wait on the Lord to know not only what He wants you to do, but when He wants you to do it.

4. Be sure to fulfill the conditions of the prophetic word.

As we have said, in some cases prophecy is unconditional — God has promised and He will do what He says. But in many instances the Lord will require a certain response of faith and corresponding action from you.

Some people will tell you that you have to put every personal prophecy on the shelf, and just allow God to fulfill them when He chooses. This idea sounds very religious, but it is not biblical, nor does it make practical sense. The process of receiving a fulfillment to a prophetic promise from God is similar to the process of receiving salvation in many ways. In our salvation experience, God sends forth His Word by the Holy Spirit, we respond in faith and declare the lordship of Jesus with our mouth, and then God's grace comes on the scene and we are born again. In personal prophecy, God sends forth His word by the Holy Spirit, we respond in faith, and then we act on that word, doing what we can do in the natural to obey the conditions that the Lord sets forth. Then in God's perfect timing, grace comes on the scene, God moves on our behalf to fulfill His promises, and we receive the fulfillment of the prophetic word.

One minister tells the story of how his baby grandson received a prophetic word that said, "This child is a worshiper." Not long after that the child was severely injured in an automobile accident. As he lay in the intensive care unit, the doctors did not give much hope for his survival. But this man of God remembered the promise that God had given through the prophet, and as he stood next to the child's bedside he cried out to God, reminding Him that He said, "This child is a worshiper." Through the night he interceded for the wounded lad, standing on the promises of Scripture. But he kept coming back to the prophetic word, and in faith he reminded God of His promise. Miraculously the child survived the night, and then he slowly recovered from his injuries.

The first Sunday after the grandson was released from the hospital, the family brought him to church, where a different prophet just happened to be ministering. He called the family forward, not knowing what they had been through. Laying his hands on the little boy he declared, "This child is a worshiper"!

5. Don't do anything differently unless you are definitely directed by God.

Do nothing major in life based only on a prophetic word. When a prophetic word refers to transitions in life such as romance, geographical moves, changing churches, and so forth, it is important that a person never make hasty moves until prayer, godly counsel, and much reflection has been done. Through careful prayer, counsel with spiritual leadership, and cautious small steps of faith, God's purposes can be established.

The Bible gives many examples of caution in the face of a prophetic word. David tended sheep for many years after being told he would be king (see 1 Samuel 16:13). Jehu received very specific instructions when he was anointed as king (see 2 Kings 9). King Jehoshaphat was told to follow all divine directives in detail (see 2 Chronicles 20). It is imperative that we not only hear God's word, but also listen for the way and the timing on how that word is to be fulfilled.

6. Remove all hindrances to receiving the promise.

When dealing with spiritual realities like prophecy, a Christian must be willing to judge themselves to make certain they are able to hear from God. Attitudes that can hinder our hearing from the Lord include a negative mindset, inflated or low self-image, pride, self-justification, blame-shifting, self-preservation, a people-pleasing attitude, carnal reasoning, and procrastination.

7. Wait patiently upon the Lord.

Extend your faith to believe that God will fulfill the prophecy in His own time and way. Do what you can do in prayer and in natural preparation to receive the promises of God in the prophetic word, and then trust God for the rest.

Read Isaiah 40:31.

The principle of waiting on the Lord is found throughout Scripture. The biblical meaning of "waiting" is active, expectant faith.

8. Allow God to form your character in the process.

God's primary intent in the life of the believer is to call leaders and to test every area of their lives in preparation for ministry. Prophecies given to us about future ministry should be received with joy, and with respect for the process God will use to prepare us for that leadership. Men in the Bible like David, Joseph, Abraham, and Moses were tested before they were given dynamic ministries. Women like Deborah, Esther, and Priscilla were women of character. God developed these people through testing, trying, and time.

9. Don't be a prophetic "groupie."

I traveled with a Christian rock band for five years. During that time we had several people that I would describe as "groupies" — people who identified with what we were doing and followed us around as we ministered to young people through music. Many of these folks volunteered to help us set up our equipment, watch our tape and T-shirt table, and load the trucks at the end of the day, but they weren't a part of the ministry.

I have noticed in some circles that there can be prophetic "groupies" — people who go from one prophetic meeting to another seeking "a word." It's great when you receive a word of prophecy, but you must be careful that you don't become complacent in hearing the Lord's voice for yourself, or acting on the words that God has already given you. It's great if you receive another prophetic word tomorrow, but what good will another word do for you if you have not acted in faith on the things that God spoke to you about three years ago?

This life that we're living is all about learning to be obedient to our heavenly Father. God's purpose for every Christian is that we grow and mature to the place where we are a reflection of His Son, Jesus Christ. Only Jesus is God, so we will never reach that perfection here in this life, but we can strive to be imitators of Him — to be true disciples. Jesus said, *"If you abide in My word, you are My disciples indeed. And you shall know the truth, and the truth shall make you free"* (John 8:31–32). The key is "abiding" in His Word — being obedient to the principles of Scripture and to the direction that He gives in your life.

Don't despise prophecy, but don't make it an idol either. Don't just accept a word just because it comes from a famous prophet, or even your own pastor. Test all things, and hold on to only that which is good.

Why is it wise to record a personal prophecy?

_____

How can transcribing and meditating on a personal prophecy help you to better understand what God may be speaking to you?

_____

Why is it important to wait on God's timing, even when you know what He wants you to do and how He wants you to do it?

_____

_____

How can you act in faith to receive a personal prophecy and do your part to see it fulfilled?

_____

_____

Day Five: Personal Prophecy and the Seven Keys

The Scriptures show us that many people of God have missed God's best for them by not receiving His word in faith. Hebrews 4:2 says, *For indeed the gospel was preached to us as well as to them; but the word which they heard did not profit them, not being mixed with faith in those who heard it.* While the accomplishment of any prophetic directive is largely up to God, our role in the process is to put aside doubt, and to give God freedom to make whatever changes in us that are necessary to bring about His plan.

In addition, it is best to judge a prophetic word in the same way you judge the other keys of God's guidance — by weighing the word against what you are perceiving through the other keys.

• Does the personal prophecy line up with the Scripture? If you're not sure, read through your Bible to find assurance that what was said lines up with the Word of God. You may want to get further advice from other mature Christians, asking them what they think of the prophetic word.

• Does the personal prophecy line up with what you believe the Lord has spoken to your heart? At this point you should be careful, especially if you are a younger Christian, because it takes time to learn how to discern the word of the Lord. Remember that there are four voices we can hear in our heads: the voice of the Lord, the voice of the devil, the voice of our own fleshly desires, or messages we have picked up from the world. Weigh any personal prophecy against the impression of your heart, and against the other seven keys to see if the Lord confirms it.

• Does the personal prophecy line up with any other prophetic insight that you have received? Remember, personal prophecy is progressive, so a word may very well give further clarity and insight to other prophecies you have received.

• Have you received godly counsel in the matter? Take the word to your spouse, your parents, your pastor, or a trusted Christian counselor to receive their input on what the Lord is saying through this word. God may use another mature Christian to help you to discern what God may be saying through a prophetic word.

• Has the Lord confirmed the prophetic word in the mouth of two or three witnesses? Perhaps the personal prophecy, word of knowledge, or word of wisdom is one of the confirming words to let you know whether the overall direction you are sensing is of God. Again, don't be afraid to speak with several mature believers about your decision. The more important the decision, the more vital it is that you seek a multitude of godly counsel.

• Do you have peace about the prophetic word? When it comes to personal prophecy it is vitally important to check your peace level concerning both the word and the person giving it. If you don't have peace on one or both, you may want to put that word on the shelf. If you sense a controlling spirit, fear, or confusion surrounding the word, you may be well advised to reject it outright. The fruit of a word from the Lord will bring joy, peace, and clarity of mind.

Be careful, however, that you don't confuse your own inexperience with the prophetic with a negative feeling about the prophetic word or the minister who is giving it. You may be uncomfortable at first in receiving personal prophecy because it is new to you, or because someone told you that it is not for today, or even that it is of the devil. If you are just dipping your toe into the prophetic waters, you would be wise to find a mature Christian friend or leader to help you to interpret what the Lord may be saying to you through the prophetic word.

You may have peace about one aspect of the word, but not all of it. Or, you may not have a peace about it at all. Grasp hold of the portion of the word that means something to you, and leave the rest for a later time. It may be that part of the prophetic word is speaking to where you are now, part of the word is speaking to where you will be in a year, and part of it is speaking to where you will be twenty years from now. The Lord will give you peace to grasp the portion of the word that is meaningful to you when the time is right.

Wait until you have peace about your decision before moving forward based on a prophetic word. Let the peace of God rule in your heart.

• Does the prophetic word line up with the circumstances of your life? It may be a really exciting word. The Lord may be declaring victory and breakthrough for your life. The word may line up with the Scriptures, with what God is saying to your heart, with other prophetic words that you have received, with what other godly leaders have said to you, and with the peace in your heart — but if the circumstances are not lining up, it may be that the timing to move forward on this word has not yet come. Again, God gave us a mind to help us responsibly think through the leading that we are receiving and to determine what is the correct decision to make. Part of the process of seeking God's will for your life is asking yourself, "Does this make sense?" God won't have you do something that is foolish.

Personal prophecy is a wonderful gift from God. But it must be given and received in a balanced, biblical manner, with proper spiritual oversight and safety mechanisms. One should not reject personal prophecy, but neither should one put too much weight onto a prophetic word — no matter what the source.

Remember, personal prophecy is only one of the seven keys of God's guidance, and it alone should not be leaned on in making major decisions in our life. However, it is an important way that God guides the New Testament believer, and it should not be overlooked in seeking God's direction for our lives.

The bottom line is that personal prophecy is a gift that Christ has given to the church, but it should never replace our need to have an ongoing, personal relationship with God in which we hear His voice for ourselves.

Why is it important to weigh a personal prophecy against the other keys to hearing God's voice?

_____

_____

_____

What have you learned from this chapter that may have changed your perception of the gift of prophecy or the office of the prophet?

_____

_____

_____

_____

_____

WEEK EIGHT

Confirmation — Hearing God Again... and Again...and Again

DAY ONE   How Does God Confirm His Guidance?

DAY TWO   Humility and Surrender

DAY THREE   Guided by the Desires of Our Hearts

DAY FOUR   Hindrances to Confirmation

DAY FIVE   The Law of Use — And Disuse

It is one of my most common prayers: *Lord, please confirm somehow what I am sensing You are saying to me...*

The apostle Paul declared in 2 Corinthians 13:1: *By the mouth of two or three witnesses every word shall be established.* This principle originated in the Old Testament, was confirmed by Christ, and then was repeated in several places in the New Testament.

Moses established this principle in the book of Deuteronomy:

> *One witness shall not rise against a man concerning any iniquity or any sin that he commits; by the mouth of two or three witnesses the matter shall be established.*
> —Deuteronomy 19:15

Jesus spoke of it in the gospels: *"It is also written in your law that the testimony of two men is true"* (John 8:17). *"But if he will not hear, take with you one or two more, that 'by the mouth of two or three witnesses every word may be established'"* (Matthew 18:16). Paul also referred to the practice in 1 Timothy 5:19: *Do not receive an accusation against an elder except from two or three witnesses.*

Our Father in heaven is well able to confirm His direction in our lives. Not only that, but I believe He *desires* to confirm it for His glory, and so that you will know with certainty that you are hearing His voice.

Day One: How Does God Confirm His Guidance?

I have often said this about God's direction: "If God appoints, He anoints. If God calls, He equips. And what God orders, He pays for." We can trust that if God calls us to do something difficult on behalf of His kingdom, our loving Father will supply us with all we need to accomplish His will in our lives — if we are humbly following Him.

David Wilkerson has said that the will of God is that thing that just won't leave you alone. If God wants you to do something, He keeps putting it in front of you. It just will not go away. It may be an idea that just keeps coming back to your mind. It may be a strategy, or an invention, or a pathway. If it is God's will for your life, and if you are surrendered to His lordship, He will make that thing so obvious to you that you will have a hard time ignoring it. In fact, if you do ignore it, it will only be because you are rebelling against the Lord's plan for your life.

Write down something that is a desire of your heart that just won't go away. Maybe there is a list of unfulfilled desires in your heart. Pray right now that the Lord would confirm whether those desires are of Him, and if you should begin taking practical steps to pursue those dreams.

_____

_____

_____

Why might your own desire be an important factor to consider when seeking God's guidance?

_____

_____

_____

This e-mail question came to me at CBN.com:

> What practical steps can I take to make sure that I am listening to the voice of the Good Shepherd, and not following after another voice?

That is a good question. There is a cacophony of voices vying for our ear in this world. Many people claim to speak on behalf of God. How can we know which voice is truly the Good Shepherd, and which is not?

In the Bible we can see many examples of God speaking to His people. Look up each of the following verses and describe the method God used to communicate His will to His people.

Luke 1:19

_____

_____

Genesis 15:1

_____

_____

1 Kings 3:5

_____

_____

Exodus 28:30

_____

_____

1 Kings 19:11–13

_____

_____

Exodus 8:20–25

_____

_____

Amos 3:7–8

_____

_____

How has God ultimately revealed Himself in the New Testament?

_____

_____

God spoke to His people in the Bible, and there is no indication in the Bible that He has stopped speaking to His people today. On the Day of Pentecost the Holy Spirit was poured out on the disciples, and the promise of Joel 2 was fulfilled.

Read Acts 2:17–18.

There is nowhere in Scripture or in the history of the church to indicate that the Lord has rescinded the gift of the Holy Spirit. He is available to the believer today, not only to dwell inside of us, but also to empower us for service.

God is a God of order, and He will reveal truths from His Word to us to help us to grow up in Christ. Having said that, however, it is important to understand that God is God, and He can reveal His will to us in any way that He chooses to do so. Because He loves us, and because He does things in an orderly fashion, God will most often confine Himself to the ways that He has dealt with mankind through the ages as revealed in the Bible. We must be careful, however, not to put God into a box. He alone is God, and all that we know of Him is what He has chosen to reveal through His Word. I can tell you about the hundred and one ways that God has led His people in the Scriptures, and He can come up with a thousand and one different ways that He will lead you into His will for your life — being God, He has that right.

If God in His sovereign will decides to do something differently, He's not limited by the principles in this book. But rest assured, typically He leads us through the seven keys that we are considering in this study.

I should also add that God will move supernaturally in the lives of His people, especially if they are crying out to Him for direction and extending their faith to believe that He will reveal Himself.

As my pastor, Mark Stafford, always says, "If you ask for Jesus to lead you, He will lead you. If you ask for the Holy Spirit, you're going to get the Holy Spirit." Always remember that Satan is merely a fallen angel, and we serve the Creator of the Universe. Our heavenly

Father is not going to allow the devil to play some kind of trick on you. When you sincerely ask God to direct your path, and you are doing all you can to walk in obedience to Him, He will be faithful to answer your prayer. You can take that to the bank!

Write down a list of all the different ways that God directed His people in the Bible.

_____

_____

_____

_____

Now write down all the ways you have been led by the Spirit of God in your lifetime.

_____

_____

_____

_____

From what you've learned so far in this Bible study, what are some of the ways that God leads that you have not yet experienced, but that you may extend your faith to believe for in the future?

_____

_____

_____

How does the promise, "When you ask for the Holy Spirit, you're going to get the Holy Spirit," bring peace to you as you seek God's direction for your life?

_____

_____

_____

_____

WEEK EIGHT
Day Two: Humility and Surrender

The Bible says, *God resists the proud, but gives grace to the humble* (James 4:6). What attitude should we have when approaching God about His will? Above all else, we must be humble.

Pride was the original sin of Lucifer. It was part of the downfall of Adam and Eve. In many ways it is the worst sin we could commit, because it is the root of so many other sins. Pride says, "I'm going to do it *my* way. I can do a better job of running my life than God can! I want my own will rather than God's will." The proud man is self-sufficient, but if you want to hear God's voice and discover His will for your life, you must humble yourself, acknowledge your need for His direction, and surrender to what He tells you to do.

Read Matthew 5:3. How would a person who is "poor in spirit" be in a better position to hear God's voice than someone who is not?

_____

_____

Another way of describing the poor, or humble, in spirit is as spiritual beggars, those who are crying out to God, pleading with Him to guide their steps. These people don't seek their own way, but they recognize that God's way is always best. They don't just seek God for what He can do for them; they seek Him for who He is.

Read Proverbs 16:18 and Daniel 5:19–20. What happens to a person whose "spirit is hardened" with pride? What happened to King Nebuchadnezzar?

_____

_____

Pride also leads to self-deception:

> *Your fierceness has deceived you, the pride of your heart, O you who dwell in the clefts of the rock, who hold the height of the hill! Though you make your nest as high as the eagle, I will bring you down from there, says the Lord.*
>
> —Jeremiah 49:16

Pride will make a person foolish: *Do you see a man wise in his own eyes? There is more hope for a fool than for him* (Proverbs 26:12).

Pride will hinder a person from coming to God: *The wicked in his proud countenance does not seek God; God is in none of his thoughts* (Psalm 10:4).

A proud person will not be open to the seven keys to hearing God's voice. A proud person will reject the notion that the Bible is the inspired Word of God. A proud person will not take the time and energy to pray and listen for the still small voice of the Savior speaking to their heart. A proud person will reject the notion that God will speak through modern-day prophets, or through another believer who has the gift of prophecy. A proud person will not seek the counsel of others, and will reject the notion that God will set them under the spiritual authority of another. A proud person will reject the nudging of the Holy Spirit through confirmation, peace, or circumstances because they believe that they know best, and any outside suggestion is inferior to their own wisdom.

Read Proverbs 22:4. What comes as a result of humility and a fear of the Lord?

_____

_____

From humility comes the fear of God, from the fear of God comes wisdom, and from wisdom we can discern the will of God.

Part of humility is recognizing that not every need we see around us equals a calling on our lives to fulfill. There are times when you may see a need, and it may be a kingdom calling for someone in the body of Christ to fulfill, but it may not be *your* calling. We need to be very careful that we don't allow the compassion that Christ has put into our hearts to overwhelm the discernment He has also placed there.

When someone is not yet mature in the Lord, they may jump at every opportunity that they perceive to be from God. Wise believers allow time when seeking a potential direction. They pray about it over the course of days, weeks, months, and sometimes even years. They think it through, checking that bit of direction against the other seven keys. They don't try to make it happen immediately, but they wait for the Lord to unfold His desire, His strategy, and His timing. If a particular direction is of the Lord, it will be confirmed.

The apostle Paul makes it clear that the only behavior in this life that makes sense is to surrender completely to the lordship of Jesus Christ.

I beseech you therefore, brethren, by the mercies of God, that you present your bodies a living sacrifice, holy, acceptable to God, which is your reasonable service. And do not be conformed to this world, but be transformed by the renewing of your mind, that you may prove what is that good and acceptable and perfect will of God.

—Romans 12:1–2

By humbly giving every area of our lives to God, we will receive the mind of Christ, and will be able to prove what is God's good, acceptable, and perfect will for our lives.

How can humility help us to better hear God's voice?

_____

_____

How can you determine if an identified need is actually a calling from God?

_____

_____

Revelation Follows Surrender

I was blessed to attend Christian school from first through tenth grades. One of the first scriptures I was required to memorize was the familiar passage of Proverbs 3:5–10. The reason these verses are so popular is that there is so much fundamental truth in them.

Trust in the LORD with all your heart, and lean not on your own understanding; In all your ways acknowledge Him, and He shall direct your paths. Do not be wise in your own eyes; Fear the LORD and depart from evil. It will be health to your flesh, and strength to your bones. Honor the LORD with your possessions, and with the firstfruits of all your increase; So your barns will be filled with plenty, and your vats will overflow with new wine.

God wants His children to trust Him. He is a loving Father, who cares very deeply for those who belong to Him. It blesses Him when we put our faith in Him.

Part of trust is believing that God's way is the best way for our lives. It may sound simplistic, but it is the starting point of our relationship with Him. We must come to the point where we recognize Christ's lordship in our lives, and our need, not only for salvation to get into heaven, but for salvation in every area of our lives.

We need to be careful that we don't allow our own understanding of a situation to thwart the will of God for our lives. When it comes to being led by the Spirit, we must be like little children. One of the most dangerous things we can say is, *Lord, yes, I want Your will, but...* The word *but* is always an indication that you are leaning on your own understanding, as if you believe you have more wisdom than God in a certain matter. *Yes, I sense You are telling me to start such and such a business venture, but don't You know about thus and so...?* Of course, God knows about it! He is the Author of all wisdom. Any knowledge or understanding that you have today is because God has given it to you.

Lean not to your own understanding — Father truly knows best!

Now I must say as a balance that in seeking direction from God, we are not to forsake wisdom. In fact, the writer of Proverbs tells us to diligently seek wisdom.

Read Proverbs 2:2.

God has given each of us a mind, an intellect, and analytical ability. He wouldn't have equipped us with these things if He didn't expect us to use them. We must guard ourselves from becoming overly "spiritual" when it comes to seeking direction from God. Analytical thought and logical reasoning with which God has endowed human beings must be engaged in the decision-making process — especially when it involves a potentially life-changing decision.

Sadly, many business people, politicians, and other leaders have gotten into trouble because they entered into some agreement or venture based on some sort of inner revelation, prophecy, or spiritual experience that they believed to be the will of God — in most cases ignoring the other keys of God's guidance. We should seek after, and lean upon the will of God, but we must also employ our understanding in making every decision.

But while we seek wisdom and understanding, and we rely on our human reasoning skills to make wise decisions, the starting and ending point of our deliberations must be our relationship with God. *The fear of the LORD is the beginning of wisdom, and the knowledge of the Holy One is understanding* (Proverbs 9:10).

In all our ways we must acknowledge Him and He will make our paths straight. To acknowledge Him means to consider the will of God in every area of our lives. In other words, it is to truly make Jesus the Lord in every aspect of our lives — in our relationships, in our homes, with our children, in our business, in our finances, with our friends — everywhere to put God first. When we fulfill our responsibility in this relationship with God — putting Him first — then He will fulfill His promise — directing our paths.

How can you balance the portion of Scripture that says *lean not to your own understanding* with the practical need to make wise decisions based on the best information you can gather?

_____

_____

_____

_____

_____

_____

_____

Name some practical ways that you can "acknowledge God" in your own life.

_____

_____

_____

_____

_____

Day Three: Guided by the Desires of Our Hearts

The psalmist wrote, *May He grant you according to your heart's desire, and fulfill all your purpose* (Psalm 20:4).

The Lord gives us some wonderful promises in His Word concerning the desire of our hearts. One of the most striking is found in Psalm 37:

> *Trust in the LORD, and do good; Dwell in the land, and feed on His faithfulness.*
> *Delight yourself also in the LORD, and He shall give you the desires of your heart.*
> *Commit your way to the LORD, trust also in Him, and He shall bring it to pass.*
>
> —Verses 3–5

Just like an earthly father who delights in providing his children with the things that they write on their Christmas list, our heavenly Father delights in giving us the things we desire — but not all of them.

There are times when we desire something that seems good to us, but from God's point of view it would not result in our ultimate good.

Our Father in heaven truly knows what is best for our lives. There are times when we want certain things that He knows would be a hindrance to us. My dad often tells the story of an interview he once watched with a world-class pianist. The reporter remarked that he would love to be able to play the piano as well as this man did. With a slight smirk, the musician replied, "No you wouldn't."

The reporter was shocked. "What do you mean?" he asked.

"To be as good as me you would have had to have begun studying piano not long after you learned to walk. When your friends were out playing games, you would be inside playing your scales. You would have to play for eight hours every day, and then perform nearly every night. You would have to travel around the world, moving from one hotel to another. You would be constantly lonely, not being able to maintain long-term relationships. No, you wouldn't want to be as good as I am."

There is such a thing as a divine rejection. There are times when we cry out to God, *Lord, this is the desire of my heart! Please give it to me,* but the Father knows that the thing that we want so badly is actually bait on a sharp hook. If we were to swallow that bait, it would take us to places we did not want to go. In His great love for us, God may withhold certain things to protect us.

Have you ever experienced this "divine rejection"? If so, what were the circumstances? What was the end result?

_____

_____

_____

_____

In other cases, there are things we desire that may not be at all harmful, but the Lord will keep them from us because He has something even better in mind for us. How many of us have prayed to be in a certain job, or marry a certain person, or receive a certain material blessing, only to realize later that that job, or person, or thing was not all that we thought it was! Many times, when the Lord has withheld something from me, I have later come to realize that it was for my protection and my long-term good. It is always best to pray that God's will would be done!

Describe a time in your life when you asked God for something, and He did not give it to you at that time, but later He gave you something even better. What did you learn from this experience?

_____

_____

_____

_____

_____

It is also important to realize that sometimes the Lord will plant His desires in our heart and then cause those desires to grow so that we will seek Him. And at some point in the process, He may require that we surrender those dreams back to Him. This is called "dying to the vision," and it is a test that the Lord will often put His children through to determine their love for Him.

God may promise something to us and place a desire for it in our heart, and then require the very thing from us that He had promised. With Abraham, God promised him an heir in his old age. The birth of this baby brought so much joy to Abraham and Sarah that they named him Isaac, which actually means *laughter*. But when Isaac was a teenager, the Lord tested Abraham's faith by asking him to offer Isaac as a sacrifice to God. In obedience Abraham built an altar, placed the wood in position, bound the hands of his son, and laid him on it. Just as he raised the knife to slay his son, the angel of the Lord stopped him. God provided a ram, caught in the thicket, for Abraham to sacrifice to the Lord instead of his son (see Genesis 22).

If we will die to the vision that is in our heart, and allow the Lord to have everything in our lives, He will not only give us that thing that He promised, but it will be better than we could have ever imagined in our own minds.

Have you ever had to die to a vision? What was the end result of surrendering it to the Lord?

_____

_____

_____

The great holocaust survivor Corrie Ten Boom often spoke these words of wisdom, "Hold loosely to the things of this life, so that if God requires them of you, it will be easy to let them go."

God will give us the desires of our heart, but the first desire of our heart should be to serve Christ Himself. When we have Christ as our chief desire, all of the other desires of our heart will be submitted to His lordship, and we can willingly pray, _Not my will, but Thine be done._ When that happens, God will give us our hearts' desire, which will also be His desire for us!

Often God will use different circumstances to lead you in life. Sometimes He won't reveal certain things to you until you need to know them — for many different reasons. At other times, the Lord will conceal His direction because He knows that if He revealed it to you, and you knew what was to come, you wouldn't go down that path — but that is exactly the direction that He intends for your life.

When things don't seem to be working out, or you're having a hard time, is it not always because you're out of the will of God. It may be that you are directly in the will of God, and He is controlling the circumstances of your life to bring about His purpose for you. In these times you must remain prayerful, and consider the combination of ways that He is guiding you through your personal relationship with Him, and through the other seven keys to hearing God's voice.

There are thousands of Christians who are wasting their lives, waiting for God to make clear to them their calling. God has given them the Scripture, which reveals God's general will for all believers. In that alone, they can see that the Lord does not want them to bury their talents but to use them to His glory. When Moses was questioning God in front of the burning bush, he said, *"Suppose they will not believe me or listen to my voice?"* (Exodus 4:1). The Lord replied to him, *"What is that in your hand?"* (verse 2). Of course, we know that what was in Moses' hand was the rod that the Lord used as an instrument to demonstrate His power.

The Lord is asking you today, "What is that in your hand?" You may have read in the Bible that the Lord has a unique calling for your life. You may have heard some specific direction from the Lord concerning that calling, but you still are waiting for it to happen in your life. I ask you today, "What is that in your hand?" Do what is in your hand to do. Move forward in faith in the things that you have heard from the Lord, and God will meet you where you are. Like Peter in the boat on that stormy night, you may have heard the voice of the Lord saying, "Come out on the water." You have to make a decision to lift your foot over the edge of that boat and step out, trusting that you have heard His voice, and keeping your eyes on Him in the midst of the storm.

God will provide you with the grace and strength that you need to get it done, but you must take that first step in obeying His will for your life.

Search your heart right now. Are you waiting on God for some spectacular revelation before you obey what He has already placed in your heart to do? If so, write down what you believe God has called you to do, based on your heart's desire and other factors of God's guidance that you have read in this study.

_____

_____

_____

_____

_____

Now pray and ask the Lord to confirm that what you are sensing is from God, and then start taking tangible steps toward seeing that thing fulfilled in your life. Write out your prayer to the Lord in the lines below.

_____

_____

_____

_____

_____

_____

Day Four: Hindrances to Confirmation

I recently read a book by a major Christian leader who had fallen into moral failure and lost his ministry and his family as a result. As he sat in prison, paying for his sins, he began to take Bible college courses. After several months of study, he came to the conclusion that one of the leading reasons for his downfall was that he had followed after popular teaching without properly searching the Scripture to see if it was actually God's truth. By floating along on the "winds of doctrine," he floated right into a series of ungodly relationships, which led to ungodly decisions, which in turn led to ungodly behavior. All of this led to the ultimate collapse of this man's life.

This dangerous practice is called *proof texting,* to look for a particular phrase or passage of Scripture that seems to line up with your own particular "belief," and then pull it out of context and use it to justify that idea. This is an extremely unhealthy approach to biblical interpretation, and it can get any of us into serious trouble. In the case of this man, it led him into a series of disastrous circumstances that nearly destroyed his life.

Thankfully this man learned from his mistakes and is now out of prison, remarried, and serving the Lord once again in ministry. Thank God for His faithfulness — even if we stumble, we won't be utterly cast down!

What examples of proof texting have you seen in your experience?

_____

_____

_____

How can the practice of proof texting keep you from doing God's will?

_____

_____

_____

Another major hindrance to properly confirming the direction of the Lord is trying to hear what we want to hear, rather than truly being open to the lordship of Jesus Christ in our decisions. George Muller was the leader of a large orphanage in England. He was a great man of prayer, and during his prayer times he received specific guidance from the Lord. Someone once asked him what the secret was of receiving such clear direction from heaven, and he replied, "Have no mind of your own in the matter."

When you want to know the will of God for your life, it is best that you come to the Lord with no agenda of your own. You should have no preconceived notions, no position to advocate before God. If you want to truly be led by the Lord, you shouldn't come into your time of prayer with a to-do list for which you want God's help. Instead, you should ask the Lord what He wants you to do, listen for His voice, and then obey His leading.

Have you ever come to God with your own agenda and attempted to seek His blessing? What was the result?

_____

_____

How might this have been a hindrance in discovering God's true will for your life?

_____

_____

As Paul declared, *Bad company corrupts good character* (1 Corinthians 15:33 NIV). It is important that we surround ourselves with people of godly character. We can be just as unequally yoked in our friendships as we can be in a marriage. One of the ways that we can be hindered in seeking confirmation is to seek the advice of unscrupulous or worldly people. This is one way in which many of us neglect to "acknowledge God in all our ways."

For example, you may own or be in charge of a particular business or organization. Since you want your business to gain prominence in your community, you may invite some well-known, influential people to sit on your board of directors. In the course of time, you may discover that one of them is a womanizer, or a drunkard, or has participated in some immoral, unethical, or even illegal activity. To keep that person on your board because they have connections, or because they could be helpful to you business-wise, is not honoring to God, and it may lead you into trouble. You could yourself become entangled in their wrongdoing. Your reputation could be ruined if people began to assume that you are guilty by association. Or you could take their unscrupulous, or unbiblical advice, and find yourself in a terrible mess. Be careful of whom you bring into your inner circle, and from whom you receive counsel.

In some ways it is equally dangerous to surround yourself with so-called "yes" men and women — people who will only tell you what they think you want to hear. This perilous situation has confronted many great Christian leaders in ministry, business, politics, education, and other positions of power. But even individual Christians can make the mistake of surrounding themselves with people who will not tell them the truth. I have seen numerous instances of "mutual-deception" societies in which co-dependent people latch onto one another to maintain a state of denial about areas of weakness in their lives. Sadly, there have been numerous believers who have come to ruin because they would not allow the people close to them to "speak the truth in love" and help them clearly see areas of weakness, and even sin, in their lives. (See Ephesians 4:15.)

On the other hand, if God has spoken to you, and you know it is His voice beyond a shadow of a doubt, even if you receive contrary counsel from everybody else, you should do what God says. Be sure to consider all the keys of God's guidance, and ask the Lord to confirm His word to you with two or more witnesses. If you have done all these things, and are confident in God's direction, then move forward.

There are times when God may blind the eyes of those around you as to His will in your life to test you and see if you are really following Him or have become too dependent on your mentors, family, and friends. That's not an easy place to be. When I left the evangelistic music ministry, there were many around me who counseled me not to do it. But I knew beyond a shadow of a doubt that it was God's will for me, and obeying Him was more important to me than pleasing my family and friends. God has blessed that decision, though for a time it caused a strain in some of those relationships. If they are truly godly friends and counselors, they will come back in fellowship with you in time, even if you don't follow their advice. Conversely, the person who breaks off their relationship with you because you don't follow their advice was never truly a friend to begin with.

How can you tell the difference between a true and a false friend when it comes to seeking counsel?

_____

_____

Why do you think God would allow the eyes of those around you to be blinded when you are seeking godly counsel? Have you ever experienced this situation? If so, describe what happened and the end result.

_____

_____

_____

_____

Signs and Fleeces

There are times when God may confirm His direction to us through a specific sign. Often He will do this when He wants us to see something or do something specific for Him. He will make His will very clear, as He will require very specific obedience from us. But it is important to point out that Jesus rebuked the scribes and the Pharisees, and even Thomas, when they sought a sign for confirmation. It is much better to have faith in God's ability to confirm His word to us in the way that He wants, rather than asking for some specific sort of sign.

One reason that signs can be so dangerous is that they can be manufactured by the devil and used to take us off course. The devil can come disguised as an angel of light, and false signs may be sent by Satan to confuse us in our major decisions. As an example, Moses and Aaron performed signs in front of Pharaoh to confirm that they were sent from God. Immediately, Pharaoh ordered his diviners to duplicate these signs with false miracles, and they did so.

Describe how God tested His people in Deuteronomy 13:1–3. Why might someone be able to perform a "false sign or a wonder"?

_____

_____

_____

_____

_____

_____

Jesus Himself warned of false prophets with false signs:

> *Then if anyone says to you, "Look, here is the Christ!" or "There!" do not believe it. For false christs and false prophets will rise and show great signs and wonders to deceive, if possible, even the elect. See, I have told you beforehand. Therefore if they say to you, "Look, He is in the desert!" do not go out; or "Look, He is in the inner rooms!" do not believe it.*
>
> —Matthew 24:23–26

Read 2 Thessalonians 2:9. What does this verse have to say about Satan's ability to work miraculous signs and wonders?

_____

_____

_____

Jesus warned that many will be deceived by the devil's lies because they will not have known the truth of God's Word. False miracles and false prophecies can lead us away from God's will. The seven keys we are studying in this book can help you to discern between the voice of God and the voice of the devil.

Another issue that should be examined at this point is the difference between confirmation and the practice known as "setting out a fleece." The practice of setting out fleeces stems from Gideon's need for a "sign" that God was truly speaking to him. It was an indication, not of faith, but of doubt. (See Judges 6:36–40.) God honored Gideon's request in that day, but that does not mean it is a practice that we ourselves should follow.

In our day and age, someone might seek confirmation of a certain direction by setting out a "fleece" before God, by saying to God something like, *If there is a rainbow in front of my house tomorrow, then I will know that You want me to do such and such a thing.* The danger in this approach to seeking confirmation is that it places too much emphasis on *you. You* are telling God how He should or shouldn't confirm His will in your life. It is much safer to allow God to determine how He will show us His direction.

The other potential danger with setting out fleeces before the Lord lies in the realm of coincidence. What if you happened to say to God, *I want to see a rainbow in front of my house as a sign that I should marry this person,* but because of the atmospheric conditions in your city the next day, there just happened to be a rainbow that appeared — not because God was showing you His will, but because a coincidence took place! It might have been going to rain that day regardless of your prayer — the weather patterns were such that rainfall naturally occurred, and then the sun shone through the humid atmosphere and a rainbow appeared, just like every other time these events take place in the natural world.

Fleecing is *not* a God-inspired method of seeking guidance. In the story of Gideon, God accommodated his unbelief by answering his prayer for guidance through the fleece — but that also took place in Old Testament times. Today, we have the Holy Spirit available on the inside of us to show us which direction to go — a luxury that Gideon did not have.

It is dangerous to make any decision based solely on some sort of a sign. We could so easily misinterpret something as being a "sign" when it is nothing more than a coincidence. I'm not saying that God does not give us signs to help guide us on our way — He absolutely does. But *any* "sign" should be weighed against the other keys of God's guidance, and it is best to allow *God* to choose what way He is going to confirm His direction in your life, rather than making that determination for Him.

What do you see as the primary dangers in setting out a fleece?

_____

_____

_____

When you realize that God was merely accommodating Gideon's lack of faith, how does it make you think about using a fleece for guidance?

_____

_____

_____

_____

_____

_____

Day Five: The Law of Use — And Disuse

In the parable of the talents, Jesus described the reaction of the ruler to his servant who took the five talents he was given and gained five more talents through his obedience and industry:

> *His lord said to him, "Well done, good and faithful servant; you were faithful over a few things, I will make you ruler over many things. Enter into the joy of your lord."*
>
> —Matthew 25:21

Jesus contrasted this with the reaction of the ruler to the servant who took the one talent that he was given and buried it in the ground out of fear of the master:

> *But his lord answered and said to him, "You wicked and lazy servant, you knew that I reap where I have not sown, and gather where I have not scattered seed. So you ought to have deposited my money with the bankers, and at my coming I would have received back my own with interest. Therefore take the talent from him, and give it to him who has ten talents. For to everyone who has, more will be given, and he will have abundance; but from him who does not have, even what he has will be taken away. And cast that unprofitable servant into the outer darkness."*
>
> —Matthew 25:26–30

The principle that Jesus was conveying is what Pat Robertson calls the "Law of Use." The person who will diligently use what God has given him will see that talent multiplied in their life. God will bring forth much fruit from the life of the person who plants and tends the heavenly seed of talent and ability that God has given to them.

However, I cannot emphasize strongly enough that the other extreme of this principle is equally true. The person who will not use what God has placed in his life will not only lack fruit, even the things that they have will be taken from them.

In his book, *The Secret Kingdom,* Dr. Robertson speaks of the principles of the kingdom of God. When he deals with the "Law of Use," he uses the example of the body builder who lifts weights to increase his muscles' mass and tone. He explains that a weight lifter will start out small, lifting only a few pounds. It may be difficult at first, but the more he disciplines himself to go to the gym and lift the weights, the easier the process becomes. In time his muscles will develop to the point that the amount of weight he is lifting will seem too light. He will add more weight to the bar, and the process begins all over again. As he continues this regimen, the size and tone of his muscles will increase, and it will become obvious to everyone else that he has been lifting weights.

In contrast, if you took that same person and taped his arm tightly to his side so that he was unable to move it, and you left him in that condition for several weeks or even months, when you removed the tape that person would not even be able to lift his arm. From lack of movement, the muscles would have deteriorated to the point that they would be useless. Because the muscles of his arm were not exercised, even the muscle mass that had been there in the beginning would be lost.[1]

It is the same in our walk with the Lord. God will give you talents and abilities, and then He will instruct you on how and where to use them for His glory. If you are obedient, He will say, "Well done, good and faithful servant," and He will bless you with even more talents and responsibility so that you can be a tool in His hands to reach the world with His love. But if you ignore God's direction in your life and fail to use the talents and abilities that He gives you, in time those abilities will begin to diminish, and you will not be blessed with anything further from the Lord — that is, until you follow through with what He has already given.

You're better off to know nothing than to know the will of God and not do it. To whom much is given, much is required. You are accountable before God for the talents He has given you and the truths He has entrusted to you. Open disobedience to God will bring condemnation to your life. Once you know God's will, you are accountable to obey it. When you obey God's plan, you will be blessed, and God will open even more of His riches to you. But if you reject God's direction, you will reap the consequences of open rebellion to God. Knowingly disobeying God's revealed will is very dangerous, both to you spiritually, and in every area of your life.

Are you using the talents and abilities that God has given you for His glory? How could you be hiding your talent in the ground, not willing to use it for Him? Or, how might you be using your talents to promote the kingdom of God?

_____

_____

_____

_____

In addition, sin and rebellion against God will bring darkness in a person's life. There is no way to get around it; sin will blind you to God's will for you.

You may be crying out to the Lord, asking Him to give you direction in your life, but you may be frustrated because you feel like you're not hearing anything from God. If that is the case, it may be time to take inventory of your life. Are you habitually committing some sort of sin? It could be a sin of commission — some action, attitude, or pattern of speech that is contrary to the principles and promises of the Bible. Or it could be that you are committing a sin of omission — you are neglecting to do something that you know God has instructed you to do. God may not be answering your prayers because you have failed to forgive someone who has wronged you. You may be harboring bitterness toward someone — or even toward God — for something that happened in your life that wounded you in some way.

As it is often said, "Keep short accounts with God." Repent for that sin in your life. Don't just say you're sorry, but renounce it, turn away from it, get it out of your life. Flee youthful lusts. Forgive the person who harmed you. If you believe that in some way God has harmed you or withheld something good from you that you think He should have given to you, then bring it before Him — yes, you can even forgive God. Don't let the sun go down on your anger. Seek peace and pursue it.

Read 1 John 1:7–9. Describe how you can begin to "walk in the light as He is in the light."

_____

_____

_____

_____

If you will do works of righteousness and walk in love and holiness, in time you will begin to experience the flow of the Spirit in your life and once again hear His voice.

How can sin and unforgiveness keep you from hearing God's voice?

_____

_____

_____

Right now take an inventory of your heart. Is there some hidden sin? Are you harboring bitterness or unforgiveness toward someone? Take a moment to forgive that person, or to ask God to forgive you.

_____

_____

_____

_____

_____

Learning Through Our Mistakes — And the Mistakes of Others

I have learned much from my father and am deeply in his debt for the wisdom he has shared with me over the years. One simple thing he told me when I was still an adolescent was, "Learn from the mistakes of others. You don't have time in life to make them all yourself!"

We can learn from the lives and mistakes of others. And we must also ask the Lord to help us learn from our own mistakes as well. God can teach us through negative circumstances in life as much as He can through the positive things that happen to us. But we must step out of our comfort zone and be willing to make some mistakes in order to grow in our ability to hear God's voice.

But of course, the best situation would be if you could learn from someone else's mistakes without having to repeat them yourself! Try to reap as much wisdom as you can, from as many individuals as you can. There is no one with a monopoly on wisdom. There are people who go through things in their life that we ourselves will never experience. We can gain the wisdom of their experience if we are willing to humble ourselves, listen, and learn from them.

God Wants to Confirm His Direction in Your Life!

You absolutely can be led by the Lord and know His will! Don't be afraid to ask God to confirm His will to you. He will not be offended by that request. It is almost always better to wait until you are at peace with the leading of the Lord than to rush out ahead of God and possibly miss His timing.

God wants to lead us. He wants to reveal His will to us through many different means — through the Bible; the voice of the Lord speaking to our hearts; personal prophecy; godly counsel; peace; circumstances; visions; dreams; angelic visitations; various signs — all of these things can be used by God to confirm His will for your life.

God can speak to you in one of a million ways, and more. He is God, and He can reveal Himself to you any way He wants to — but the greatest thing is that He does want to!

What are some of the mistakes you have made in the past that God has used to teach you valuable lessons?

_____

_____

_____

_____

Have you ever learned from the mistakes you have seen other people make? What were some of those lessons?

_____

_____

_____

_____

Write down as many ways as you can think of that God might confirm His plan for your life to you.

_____

_____

_____

_____

Circumstances — Hearing God in Everyday Life

One of the strongest man-made structures in the world is the suspension bridge. This modern engineering marvel can carry an amazing amount of weight and strain because of its unique design. On every suspension bridge there are two anchors at each end of the structure that bear the load of the bridge. Then giant copper cables are strung back and forth from one anchor to the other. The actual roadway is suspended in midair from these enormous cables. If there were a failure in one or the other anchor the entire structure would collapse. That is why the towers or mountains that support a suspension bridge need to be massive and incredibly strong.

But not only is it a practical part of our modern transportation system, the suspension bridge is also a thing of awe and beauty. When you think of some of the great man-made structures, suspension bridges like the Golden Gate and the Brooklyn Bridges come to mind.

A proper biblical worldview sometimes demands that we approach God's truth in a balanced fashion, weighing the Scriptures and opinions on both ends of an issue, and then coming to a balanced position in the middle — like the roadway on a suspension bridge. I call this philosophy "truths in tension," and you see numerous occasions where it is demonstrated throughout the Bible. For example, there are many scriptures that admonish the community of believers to take care of the poor. But the Bible also says if you don't work, you don't eat. The truth of how to respond to the poor among us is somewhere balanced between the two truths.

When considering how God uses circumstances to guide us, we should consider the balance of two truths: First, God can and does use circumstances to guide us into His will; and second, circumstances are not always an indication of God's plan for our lives.

It is probably easier to be swayed by circumstances than by any of the other keys to God's guidance. Circumstances are so real to us in the physical world. Anything that touches our person in this world is circumstance — joy, sorrow, hunger, pain, happiness, cold, heat, birth, death. When it comes to being led through circumstances, it seems that many Christians are clinging to one or the other end of the suspension bridge. Some Christians are convinced that the manifestation of the Holy Spirit, and God's willingness to speak to His children, ended with the death of the last apostle. These folks are hanging onto the anchor that God only leads through the Bible and circumstances. Then there are those who are on the other end of the bridge, believing that God leads only through supernatural signs and guidance, and not at all through circumstances.

The truth lies in a balance between both extremes. As we have already seen in our study, God does lead His children in many different ways: through Scripture, by speaking directly to their spirit, through godly counsel, and through other supernatural guidance like personal prophecy, signs, dreams, visions, and so forth. But He will also use the circumstances of our lives to direct us into His will. Many "super-spiritual" believers have walked right out of God's will because they did not want to be bothered by the circumstances. The ramifications of this spiritual arrogance can lead to a major catastrophe in life. Other "grounded evangelicals" have ignored the voice of the Lord speaking to their heart and have focused only on the circumstances that they perceive with their natural senses. These folks are often either extremely limited in their impact for the kingdom of God, or they are completely blind to spiritual matters, like the perilous men described as *having a form of godliness but denying its power* whom Paul warned against in 2 Timothy 3:5.

The truth is that you are a spirit, you have a soul, and you live in a body. God can and will communicate with all aspects of who you are. He will use every means necessary to reach you with His message of love and grace.

God is love — and love communicates.

Day One: Open and Closed Doors

Abraham Lincoln is an amazing example of a person who, despite hindering circumstances, pushed forward in life until he achieved his divine destiny. He was born into poverty, and in 1816 his family was forced out of their home. As a youngster, Lincoln had to work to help support the family. In 1818 his mother died. In 1835 he was engaged to be married, but his sweetheart died unexpectedly, leaving him with a broken heart. The next year he suffered a nervous breakdown and was bedridden for six months. And over the course of his career, Lincoln lost eight elections and went bankrupt twice.

After losing one of two elections for the United States Senate, he proclaimed his optimistic outlook: "The path was worn and slippery. My foot slipped from under me, knocking the other out of the way, but I recovered and said to myself, 'It is a slip and not a fall.'"

Lincoln is a member of a distinguished group of winners who refused to believe it when people said they were losers:

• After Fred Astaire's first screen test, the memo from the testing director of MGM, dated 1933, said, "Can't act! Slightly bald! Can dance a little!" Astaire kept that memo over the fireplace in his Beverly Hills home.

• An "expert" said of Vince Lombardi: "He possesses minimal football knowledge. Lacks motivation."

• Beethoven handled the violin awkwardly and preferred playing his own compositions instead of improving his technique. His teacher called him hopeless as a composer.

• Walt Disney was fired by a newspaper editor for lack of ideas. He also went bankrupt several times before he built Disneyland.

• Albert Einstein did not speak until he was four years old and didn't read until he was seven. His teacher described him as "mentally slow, unsociable and adrift forever in his foolish dreams." He was expelled and was refused admittance to the Zurich Polytechnic School.

• Louis Pasteur was only a mediocre pupil in undergraduate studies and ranked fifteenth out of twenty-two classmates in chemistry.

• Leo Tolstoy, author of *War and Peace,* flunked out of college. He was described as "both unable and unwilling to learn."

• Babe Ruth, considered by sports historians to be the greatest athlete of all time and famous for setting the home-run record, also holds the record for strikeouts.

• Winston Churchill failed sixth grade. He did not become prime minister of England until he was 62, and then only after a lifetime of defeats and setbacks. His greatest contributions came when he was a "senior citizen."

God will often use the so-called "closed doors" in our life to mold our character and prepare us for the time when we will fulfill His destiny for our lives.

In *My Utmost for His Highest,* Oswald Chambers explained that not everything that happens to us as Christians makes human sense. "To turn head faith into a personal possession is a fight always, not sometimes. God brings us into circumstances in order to exercise our faith."[1]

Maturity comes to believers when they allow the Holy Spirit to break them of their vulnerability to circumstances in life. One of my favorite teachers, Larry Tomczak, said, "You're not under the circumstances; you're above the circumstances. You're not contending with the devil for a place of victory; you overcome the devil from your position of victory." Circumstances, taken apart from consideration of the Scriptures and the peace of God, can lead us astray.

We can learn to discern God's hand in both positive and negative circumstances. But neither favorable nor unfavorable circumstances can be taken alone as a sign that we are in or out of the will of God.

What do you think Oswald Chambers meant when he said, "God brings us into circumstances in order to exercise our faith?"

_____

_____

Why do you think that some people are guided by circumstances alone, while others almost completely ignore circumstances when seeking God for direction? Where is the balance for you?

_____

_____

_____

There are two types of circumstances that God will use to lead us — closed doors and open doors.

Closed doors restrain us from moving forward in our pursuits. This can be frustrating at times, and when it happens, it should force us to seek the Lord as to why the door appears to be closed, especially if we think we already have had clear guidance to move in that direction. Some Christians will automatically think that a closed door is Satan's attempt to prevent God's plan from happening in their lives. Others will believe the closed door is a sign that God is saying no to that pursuit. Both of these extremes can be dangerous, because they may be right, or they may be wrong. We need spiritual discernment to discover God's purpose in the closed doors of life — and that can be found in using all seven keys to hearing God's voice.

We often interpret the negative circumstances of life in one of four ways. We may say:
1. "God is putting me through a test;"
2. "I'm reaping the wages of my sin;"
3. "I'm being attacked by the devil;" or
4. "I'm being persecuted for righteousness' sake."

Any of these statements could be the true diagnosis of the situation. But it takes more than an analysis of circumstances to know:
• If the unfolding situation is a test from the Lord that you need to endure;
• If you are reaping something that you sowed and you should repent;
• If this is an attack by the enemy that should be resisted; or
• If it is merely persecution that should be endured with God's grace.

Which of these viewpoints do you tend to take?

_____

_____

Why might your view be correct or incorrect?

_____

_____

_____

_____

Just because a door is closed doesn't mean it will be closed forever. Sometimes the Lord puts us in a holding pattern while He works on our character, or while He is setting the stage for our later success. Always keep in mind the tremendous promise of Psalm 37:23: *The steps of a good man are ordered by the LORD, and He delights in his way.* The Bible and history show us innumerable instances of people persevering through difficulties and delays along the path to their destiny.

God can also lead us through the seemingly open doors that circumstances present. These potential open doors can be exciting, and can seem like a clear indication of God's will for our lives. But one must beware. Not every open door is from God. Blaine Smith classifies open doors into two categories — suggestive or confirming: "Suggestive circumstances imply possibilities. Receiving a scholarship would suggest the possibility of attending a particular college. But this circumstance should align with the other guidance factors of desire, ability, and counsel. Confirming circumstances merely confirm the choice, which we believe to be God's will. If you have already determined that you are to marry a particular person, then circumstances may simply confirm your decision."[2]

When things don't seem to be working out, or you're having a hard time with the circumstances in your life, it is not always because you're out of the plan of God. Often you are directly in His will! Sometimes circumstances can help you determine the will of God, but they should never be an ultimate indication of it. It is important to take everything you are hearing from God into account — and use all seven keys to evaluate the message.

The Bible makes it clear that our days are numbered and planned by God. King David wrote in Psalm 139:16: *Your eyes saw my substance, being yet unformed. And in Your book they all were written, the days fashioned for me, when as yet there were none of them.* We can rejoice, knowing that the sovereign God has things well in hand, no matter what the circumstances may seem to say.

How can you rightly discern if an open or closed door is from the Lord?

_____

_____

_____

Describe a "closed-door" situation that has occurred in your life? How did you react to it? What was the end result?

_____

_____

_____

_____

Now describe an "open-door" situation you have experienced. How were you able to tell the open door was of God? What was the result?

_____

_____

_____

_____

_____

_____

_____

Day Two: The Fire of Delayed Answers

Waiting for God's timing is a critical element of being led by the Spirit. Circumstances can help us to gauge the timing of the Lord, which is often like a traffic light. There is the red light of stop, the yellow light of caution, or "slow down," and the green light of go. We may have God's direction on a matter, but the circumstances don't line up — the light of God's timing is red. Other times we may know God's will, and it seems like things are coming together, but we still wait for certain key issues to fall into place — the light of God's timing is yellow. But when we know God's will, all the circumstances have fallen into place, and we have peace in our heart, the light is green — it is time to move forward.

What does Revelation 3:7 have to say about open and closed doors?

In his book, *When God Winks*, Squire Rushnell talks about how God will lead us through life's circumstances:

> A God Wink is…a message of reassurance coming when you most need it: when you're at a crossroads in your life, and when instability is all around. It might be said, in fact, that coincidences are the best way for God to establish a perpetual presence in your life. Think about it. If you were God and wanted to communicate with human beings without using a human voice, how would you do it? You'd perform little miracles, wouldn't you? You'd create little miracles. Like coincidences, that cause people to say, "What are the odds of this ever happening?" Those are God Winks.[3]

Isn't that a wonderful way of describing how God is constantly at work, leading us into His perfect will for our lives? It should give us great peace to know that our heavenly Father takes such care in guiding our steps.

Have you ever experienced a "God Wink" in your life? What happened? How did you know it was from God?

_____

_____

Circumstances can be a factor in the leading of God in our lives, but we don't necessarily want to be controlled by circumstances. In the power of God, circumstances can change.

Circumstances should be considered, but they are not to be a controlling factor in our lives. We have to be careful that we don't invest meaning into ordinary circumstances that really have no significance whatsoever.

Blaine Smith writes:

> Often we attach too much importance to circumstances, viewing them as an infallible indication of God's will. In fact, circumstances should play a very limited role in making major decisions.… We can safely assume that the normal obligations of our commitment are part of God's will. He then will use circumstances as the primary means of guiding us in making everyday minor decisions. Furthermore, circumstances stress the importance of yielding to the Lord's will.[4]

How can circumstances help us balance the practical and spiritual considerations when making a decision?

Sometimes the answer to our difficult circumstances seems to be delayed — but this is one way that God may use to direct our steps.

There may be times when the Lord allows you to go through things that don't make sense. It may seem that He is not answering your prayers. It may seem that the devil has been given a "free pass" to harass you. It may appear that your whole world is crumbling around you — and that may even be true! The Lord may be allowing you to be tested for a season to show you your own heart and to help you to grow in godly character.

James writes of this phenomenon in the Christian experience:

> *My brethren, count it all joy when you fall into various trials, knowing that the testing of your faith produces patience. But let patience have its perfect work, that you may be perfect and complete, lacking nothing.*
>
> —James 1:2–4

God will deliver us from affliction, but sometimes He will delay the answer for the purpose of refining us by fire. In this life we are in the process of growing into maturity in Christ. The Lord wants to produce His character in us so that we can be an example of His love and grace to a lost and dying world, and so He allows us to go through various trials and tests.

What do the following passages have to say about "refining circumstances"?

Psalm 66:10

_____

_____

Isaiah 48:10

_____

_____

Zechariah 13:9

_____

_____

Malachi 3:2–3

_____

_____

Bob Sorge is a pastor and a worship leader, a person who uses his voice both to minister the gospel and earn a living. Over a period of time, Bob began noticing that he was losing the ability to speak and sing. Finally, it came to the point where he was only able to talk in a whisper. As he sought the Lord for healing, and for an explanation to this major blow to his career, he began to see that God was allowing a refining fire to come into his life.

In his book, *The Fire of Delayed Answers,* he writes:

> When the fires of persecution have given way to a pseudo-toleration of Christianity, what should God do? Should He just allow the church to mutate and to degenerate into a lukewarm, milquetoast, insipid, self-centered, powerless form of religion? No, He's too jealous for that to happen.
>
> So what does God do? (To understand this, we must be convinced that His ways are higher than ours.) In His mercy, He allows other things first to put the heat on our lives: financial distress; physical distress (sickness, infirmity); family distress. Without the heat, so often our love grows cold. You say, "Those things can't be from God because He has given us specific promises in His Word that He would deliver us from those things." He does deliver us, but He uses the delay period (while we're waiting for the deliverance) as a purifying fire in our lives.[5]

Some of us have been in the kind of fire that Bob Sorge experienced, suffering from confusion and even deep depression. Unless you've been through it, it is hard to understand the depth of pain and sorrow that this type of Job-like test can produce. But when the Lord brings His peace and grace to the situation, our love for Him grows even deeper.

God wants His first commandment — to love the Lord our God — to be the first priority in our lives, and the second commandment — to love others — to be second. He uses the fiery circumstances of life's tests and trials to bring us to a deeper love for Himself, and from that love flows our desire to minister to others.

If you have done all that you need to do to receive God's direction, and the answer has not yet come, then stand firm in faith, and trust that the Lord will bring it about in His good time. God is good, all the time! He delights in blessing His children — but He also delights in seeing His children mature and become the men and women that He desires for them to be. If you are "in the fire" today because of a delayed answer, rejoice! Remember that the journey is the destination. Ask the Lord to do His full work in you during this time. Take this opportunity to grow closer to Him, and allow Him to show Himself faithful to you. Your testimony on the other end will be that much more glorious if you hold on until the time of deliverance.

How does God use the fire of delayed answers to draw us closer to Him?

_____

_____

_____

_____

Are you waiting on something from God today? Write down your request, and ask the Lord to give you the grace to wait on His timing for that answer.

_____

_____

_____

_____

_____

_____

_____

_____

Day Three: The Harness of the Holy Spirit

Horses are one of the most beautiful and powerful of God's creatures. Left to run wild, a horse is a ferocious and potentially dangerous creature. But once it is trained — and under the bit and bridle of its master — a horse can perform amazing feats of strength and skill and is one of the gentlest creatures on earth.

You and I are a lot like that, aren't we? We need God to temper us and to lead us. As the Twenty-third Psalm says, *He leads me beside the still waters* (verse 2). Without His leading, how lost we would be?

It's especially important to have God's leading when we go through difficult times. In the dark days, we must strive to be "tuned in" to the voice of the Lord. And when we hear His voice, we must then submit to His leading.

The Lord showed me an illustration of this principle during a difficult transition in my life. For nearly five years I had traveled with a Christian rock band called Insight. The Lord had blessed us as thousands of young people committed their lives to Christ through our ministry. But in my prayer time, the Lord began to tell me that I had completed the work He wanted me to do with the band — and He had other plans for my life. I felt like Abraham when the Lord called him out of Ur of the Chaldees. The Lord had promised to lead me, but He didn't tell me where I was going!

It was difficult for many people in my life to understand why the Lord would take me out of such a fruit-bearing field and put me into the wilderness. But as I read the Bible, I discovered that this is often His pattern for training leaders. Jesus was tempted in the desert. Paul, Moses, John the Baptist, King David, and others spent years in the wilderness learning to hear and trust God. If I were to be a servant of Jesus Christ, I would have my desert experience as well.

I spent a grueling year seeking the Lord's direction for my life. During this time, I worked a construction job. While I enjoyed working with my hands, doing manual labor as a full-time job was not what I wanted in life.

One day as I worked in the hot, dirty attic of a 100-year-old house, I cried out to the Lord: *God, have You brought me out to the desert to kill me? I am engaged to be married, and I don't even have a real job! I left college after three years to manage the ministry. Now You tell me to leave the band but You don't tell me where to go.*

But then the Lord suddenly reminded me of the days when I would go horseback riding with my friends in college. We would ride over the grassy hills of the Allegheny Mountains, feeling the exhilaration of such a mighty creature moving at our command. God designed horses to run. A horse would run all the time if it could. What a wonderful thing it was to experience a part of the joy that this majestic animal felt as he galloped over the rolling hills.

I remembered the times when we used to take the horses into the woods. "Be careful," my experienced friend would caution. "Hold very tightly to the reins as we pass through the trees. There are fallen logs and moss-covered rocks that the horse could slip on if you don't take it slow." If a horse is injured in the woods, it is almost impossible to save it.

I remembered how my arms would become strained pulling back on the reins, trying to keep that beautiful beast from going any faster than a slow walk. The struggle became even more intense as we approached the edge of the thicket. The horses sensed that the clearing was near, and it became increasingly difficult to keep them from running. It took all of my might to hold those reins tight. When we finally emerged into the meadow, without any prodding at all, the horses took off in a full-speed gallop.

So many times, we are like those horses — straining to run, even when God is guiding us through the woods. We were designed to run, but at times, our Master asks us to wait for His command. He is holding tight to our reins so that we won't slip on a moss-covered rock or trip over a fallen log. And soon enough, we will emerge into the spiritual meadow in which we will run free in the calling that He has for our lives.

The psalmist wrote, *The LORD confides in those who fear him; he makes his covenant known to them* (Psalm 25:14 NIV). He is always speaking to us, always leading our steps. Once we learn to hear His voice, we must cooperate with His plan and His timing.

How may you have been like a horse, straining at the reins when God was trying to slow you down?

_____

_____

_____

When have you experienced the "harness of the Holy Spirit"?

_____

_____

_____

At times the "harness of the Holy Spirit" may include what we call "divine rejections," God's withholding of something good, or maybe not so good, to make way for His best for us.

My father's favorite scripture is Romans 8:28: *And we know that all things work together for good to those who love God, to those who are the called according to His purpose.* You'll notice that this promise, like so many others in the Bible, is conditional. Some people say that "all things will work together for good," and leave it at that, but that is not a true statement! This verse makes it clear that the promise is only for "those who are called according to His purpose" — in other words, committed Christians.

In our walk with the Lord, we need to realize that it is absolutely no problem at all for God to meet our every need. He is the Creator of the universe; taking care of one person is no sweat! So why is it that there are times when we are doing all the things a Christian should — spending quality time with the Lord every day in prayer, reading our Bible, loving our spouse and our children, faithfully attending a Bible-believing church, sharing the gospel with non-believers, tithing, being obedient in every area of our life — but with regard to one particular prayer, it seems as if the heavens are brass and the answer will never come?

My dad's motto is connected to Romans 8:28: "Every blessing becomes a burden, and every burden has its blessings." Many times God will use divine rejections — the times that He says no to our requests — to move us from what is *good* to what is *best* for us. Or He may use a divine rejection to protect us from something that looks good, but in reality is harmful. Only God in His sovereignty knows the end from the beginning, and only He knows the purposes of men's hearts. To us, the rejection may look on the surface like God is withholding something from us. But in reality, by keeping us from taking that job, marrying that person, buying that property, or whatever else it might be, God could be protecting us from some unseen danger that is lurking down the road.

How good God is that He leads us through all the seasons of life with a firm but gentle hand! *He leads me in the paths of righteousness for His name's sake* (Psalm 23:3). He knows when to let us run free and when to hold us back. As we listen for His voice and seek to do the will of the Lord, let us always remember that our Father in heaven knows what is best for us — even when we can't see it.

How has God used divine rejections to mold your life? Have you seen God's hand in that circumstance in the long run?

_____

_____

_____

_____

Have you ever been angry with God for a divine rejection? Write out how you felt or may still be feeling about that time in your life. You may need to forgive God for that divine rejection, or you may need to ask God to forgive you for any bitterness that you still harbor.

_____

_____

_____

_____

_____

_____

_____

_____

Day Four: Staying the Course

There may be times in your walk with the Lord when you receive a word from God, beyond the shadow of a doubt, and the other keys of God's guidance will confirm it. You move forward with great anticipation of the Lord's blessing and grace and proceed in faith, when suddenly you find yourself facing all sorts of opposition to the very thing that God called you to do. You may wonder why God is not protecting you from the attacks of the enemy. After all, you are doing what He told you to do!

If this is occurring in your life, don't be dismayed — this scenario is very common in the Christian life. Jesus promised persecution to those who would follow Him — but He also promised His grace to help us through those times. When guidance is clearly given by the Lord, confirmed by witnesses, and established in your heart, you can bet that the devil will do what he can to get you off track — and that may include bringing adverse circumstances into your path. At those times, you must set your face like flint to do what God has clearly revealed, no matter what is happening around you to take you off course.

Read Mark 4:35–40. What was Jesus' command to the disciples?

_____

What adverse circumstances seemed to stand in their way?

_____

_____

Why should the disciples not have had fear in the situation?

_____

_____

How did Jesus demonstrate that He had control of the circumstances all along?

_____

_____

Jesus had made His will known to the disciples: *"Let us cross over to the other side"* (Mark 4:35). When you have the clear word of the Lord, with no ambiguity, there is no reason to fear when the circumstances turn sour. In fact, you can almost expect it to happen!

Read Mark 4:14–15, 20. What does Satan do "immediately" after the Word of God is sown?

_____

_____

What is the "good ground" in this parable?

_____

_____

How does our heart attitude affect the ability of the seed to bear fruit?

_____

_____

The destiny of the seed in this parable was connected to the condition of the soil. Besides the heart on the wayside, Jesus also speaks of a stony heart, a heart that is concerned with the cares of this world, the deceitfulness of riches, and the desires for other things. In all of these instances, the circumstances arise to choke or destroy the seed of God's word as a result of the condition of the heart.

We must be careful to guard the soil of our heart, keeping it tilled, resisting the deceitfulness of worldly pleasures. Then when the sower sows the word into our lives — when we clearly hear God's direction — the seed will take root and will grow, producing good fruit. When our hearts are soft and pliable before the Lord, we will receive His Word, and no amount of adverse circumstances will sway us from allowing it to take root. We are constantly navigating a labyrinth of contrasting circumstances in life. Mature Christians will not merely react to what they see or sense in the natural world, but they will consistently seek the Lord for discernment on how to interpret the circumstances that they are facing.

Have you ever known beyond a shadow of a doubt that God had directed you to do something, but negative circumstances were holding you back from moving forward in that plan? What did you do to overcome those circumstances? If you have never faced this scenario, what do you think you should do if it ever does happen to you?

_____

_____

_____

_____

_____

_____

Learning from Our Mistakes

The Lord can redeem the tragedies and mistakes of our past, even when they are completely our fault! In fact, this is one of the ways that God makes Himself real to other people in our lives. When our family, friends, and acquaintances see how God has moved dramatically to change our character and circumstances, they have to ask how it happened. The wonderful transformation in our lives gives us the opportunity to tell them about a relationship with God through Jesus Christ!

How could overcoming the negative circumstances of life — "staying the course" — be a witnessing tool for you?

_____

_____

_____

_____

_____

_____

_____

Day Five: The Shepherd of Our Circumstances

Big decisions in life are often stressful — who to marry, what job to take, what house to buy, where to go to college, whether or not to start a business — the pressures of life can sometimes bring great anxiety. When faced with such life-changing decisions, it is often difficult to hear the Lord's voice. Our emotions are often very loud. In these times, it is vitally important to prayerfully consider all the seven keys of God's guidance.

The Lord is very familiar with the frailty of men, and in His mercy He will often use circumstances as signposts to point us toward His will when we are at an important crossroad.

For example, you may desire a certain house, but it is at the top of your price range. It is everything you have ever wanted in a home, and it's in the neighborhood of your dreams. Because the price is high you have a slight check in your spirit, but you're not sure if it is a lack of peace or just anxiety about the situation. This neighborhood is so hot that houses are selling fast, so you don't have time to pray and fast for forty days — you've got to make a decision quickly.

You consider the seven keys in your prayer time with the Lord. The Bible tells us that the Lord will provide our every need, including the need for a home. But the Scriptures also warn that the debtor is slave to the lender, so you know you shouldn't become mortgaged to the hilt. You have prayed about this neighborhood for some time, and you believe that this is the general location to which the Lord has led you by His Spirit. You may have a prophetic word that speaks of God's plan to bless you with the home that you desire. You've talked to your pastor about the decision, and to other wise godly friends and mentors. They have given you their counsel, and you have weighed their different opinions against the other keys. You have considered the circumstances of the price of the house against what you can afford — although it may be tight, you believe you can afford it, especially if that expected raise comes through. And although it is a stressful situation, you sense the peace of God in your heart that this could be the right place for you to live.

After careful consideration of all the keys of God's guidance, you believe you have enough confirmation to make a bid. You have now done all that you can do, and the rest is in God's hands. You can rest in knowing that He will line the circumstances up according to His will for your life. This may not be the right house for you. The Lord may have a better house, one that is ten-thousand dollars cheaper in the same neighborhood! In His love for you, He may allow someone else to purchase the property. When the timing is right, He will lead you to the place that He has ordained for you and your family. Or, this may be the place that He wants for you, and He is wanting you to stretch your faith to believe for His best. He may give you tremendous favor with the sellers, the realtor, the bank, and the lawyers, making the sale as smooth as silk for you as a blessing. For good measure, He may have your raise come through even more quickly than expected, allowing you to move in with no worries whatsoever.

In either case, we should trust the sovereignty of God in every circumstance, whether positive or negative, and praise Him that our steps are ordered of the Lord. As we mature in the Lord, He gives us the grace to find peace in all things.

Read Philippians 4:4–13. How does Paul respond to whatever circumstances in which he finds himself?

_____

_____

What attitude should we have to our circumstances?

_____

_____

When we have this attitude, what will "guard our hearts and minds" in the decision-making process?

_____

_____

If you believe God is speaking to you through circumstances, pray that He will confirm His direction through one or more of the other keys to hearing God's voice. Remember, the direction that you take must line up with the Word of God, and if it truly is of the Lord, it will be accompanied by God's peace.

God has the power to ordain the circumstances in your life to direct you toward His will. He can bring negative circumstances to show that you are veering away from His plan for your life. Be aware when little annoyances start building around you — a flat tire, personality conflicts at work or home when it is normally peaceful, a series of things breaking in your car or your house — if your peace is upset for an extended period of time, it may be that God is trying to get your attention.

One of my pastors would always talk about the "umbrella of God's protection." When you are walking in right relationship with God, listening for His voice and then obeying His commands, the Lord provides an umbrella that shields you from the storm. Now there are times when the Lord allows things to get through this shield of faith to test our character. There are other times when the devil will bring an attack. But for the most part, the Lord protects His sheep from the wolves on the outside and from their own foolishness inside the pen.

Read Psalm 23. According to verse 4, what does the Lord's rod and staff do for us?

_____

_____

_____

If you've ever watched a shepherd with sheep before, you know that the shepherd will, from time to time, nudge the sheep with his staff to get them to move forward or to keep them away from danger. Thank God that He uses the rod of circumstances to nudge us into His will or away from things that would harm us!

God must be sovereign in our lives. If we are truly surrendered to Him, praying for His will to be done, He will bring His good pleasure to pass. If God wants you to have that house, He will give you the means to buy it, the right price to offer, and sellers who are favorable to you and your family. If God wants you to marry that person, He will put the desire in both of your hearts, and He will confirm it to both of you. If God wants you to move across the country to take that job, He will give you the peace that the move is of Him, and He will give you favor with your potential employer. If none of these things happen, rest assured that God is still God, and He has a wonderful plan for your life! As His very own child, your steps _are_ ordered of the Lord — and He delights in your way!

It is imperative that Christians seek with all their hearts to be in the center of God's will. Remember, hearing God's voice is all about having a relationship with the Father. God is pleased when His children desire to do what He wants us to do. It is a sign of our love for Him that we are willing to humble ourselves and say, "I want Your plan more than I want my plan."

Bob Mumford tells the story of an evangelist who was driving across Florida with his family. When his wife said, "Let's stop in this town and get some orange juice for the children," he agreed and they just happened to turn off at a certain exit, drove down a block or two, and happened to pull up in front of a certain fruit stand. Before he even had time to get out of the car, a lady came running across the street.

"Are you a minister?" she asked breathlessly.

"Yes," he replied.

"Praise the Lord!" she exclaimed. "This morning I prayed that God would send a minister who would lay hands on me and pray for my healing. God said you'd be driving a station wagon and pulling a trailer." She looked at the evangelist's brown station wagon and trailer and asked, "What took you so long?"

Bob Mumford explains that this evangelist and his wife didn't know anything about God's plan for them that afternoon. They hadn't heard a voice say, "Turn off at this exit and drive two blocks to the fruit stand where there is a lady I want you to pray for." But they had committed their day to God and prayed before leaving that His will and plan for that day would come to pass. And so the circumstances of the children's thirst and need for vitamin C caused them to move into the sovereign plan of God for them and for the woman who needed prayer.

When we completely yield ourselves to God's plan, sincerely praying, *Not my will, but Thy will be done,* it is amazing how the Lord will orchestrate circumstances to move us toward His desire for our lives. We will often find ourselves in just the right places at the right time for God's providence to work in our behalf.

You can take comfort in knowing that no matter what the circumstances are at the moment, God has a plan for your life, and He will guide you into that plan as you seek

Him with all your heart. He has given us His promise: *Being confident of this, that he who began a good work in you will carry it on to completion until the day of Christ Jesus"* (Philippians 1:6 NIV).

When you are facing a stressful decision, how can your circumstances be a guidepost of God's direction?

_____

_____

_____

_____

At the same time, how might circumstances lead us away from God's plan? How can we tell the difference?

_____

_____

_____

_____

How does the Good Shepherd use the rod of circumstances to nudge us into His will or away from danger?

_____

_____

_____

_____

Truly Hearing God — Seeking the Maker of the Stars

In a recent Barna Research study, 68 percent of all adults surveyed, including 58 percent of non-Christians, and 83 percent of born-again Christians, said that they are facing a decision for which they "would like to get direction from God."[1] It is interesting that so many people — Christian and non-Christian alike — admit to wanting direction from the Lord. After all, that is the way God wired us. The more we allow the Lord to work in our hearts and lives, the more He will strip any self-sufficiency from us, and the more dependent we will be on Him in every area.

Guidance is a step-by-step walk with the Lord. Hearing God's voice and being led by His Spirit comes down to recognizing that we are totally dependent on the Lord, and without Him we are a ship adrift at sea. Jesus clearly painted the picture of our condition in this world when He told His disciples, *I am the vine, you are the branches. He who abides in Me, and I in him, bears much fruit; for without Me you can do nothing* (John 15:5).

In our final week of study, we will put all of the pieces together and see how using all seven keys will help us to discern God's will in our lives. But let's never forget the most important key of all: to "abide in the vine," to keep our relationship with our Creator, the Maker of the stars, the most important priority in our life.

Day One: Intimate Moments with the Savior

It was an issue of blood — but not blood only. You see, the diabetes that wracked my friend Dick's body had also damaged his liver and destroyed his kidneys. But it was the issue of blood — the lack of circulation — that made Dick's trial most evident to the rest of us. This was especially true in the past year when he underwent surgery to amputate his leg.

The diabetes that he had fought so valiantly against these many years finally claimed Dick's life on a beautiful day in May.

Working together at CBN, Dick and I had experienced the presence of God during times of prayer or worship. But when I heard that Dick had gone to be with the Lord, I was reminded of one particularly sweet moment that we shared — it was an intimate moment with the Savior.

I was asked to lead chapel in our department during a telethon a little more than a year before Dick's death. As I prayed about what I was to share, I felt like the Lord wanted me to read from a very special devotional by Ken Gire called *Intimate Moments With The Savior.*[2]

Before the meeting began, I was told that Dick was facing yet another surgery. He had already had some of his toes removed, and it appeared that the doctors were going to have to amputate even more from his foot. The diabetes was cutting off circulation, and if they didn't act, gangrene would set it.

My heart was heavy as I opened our time of prayer, and I could see the weight that Dick was carrying on his shoulders. I opened the devotional to where we had left off the day before. Providentially, we read about the woman with the issue of blood from Mark 5:24–34.

Read Mark 5:24–34. Describe the circumstances in this woman's life.

_____

_____

_____

_____

After the Scripture passage, Gire writes his interpretation of the events:

> God only knows how much she's suffered. She has lived with a bleeding
> uterus for twelve humiliating years. She has been labeled unclean by the
> rabbis and subjected to the levitical prohibitions. "Orphaned by society."
> And orphaned also by God, or so she thinks. She has prayed. She has
> pleaded. But for twelve agonizing years God has been silent.
>
> She is destitute now. And being out of money, the doctors finally admit
> there is nothing they can do for her. Her life is ebbing away. The steady
> loss of blood over the years has taken its toll. She is anemic, pale, and
> tired. So very, very tired.

**How might the woman have heard — or not been able to hear — the voice of God
in her situation?**

_____

_____

A wave of emotion washed over me. I looked across the table and saw that Dick was
stooped over, like an old man carrying a pack that he could barely lift. His eyes were
tightly shut, and he was drinking in the details of this sad story. I continued to read:

> She no longer dreams of marriage and a family — of being taken care of
> in her old age by loved ones — of golden memories she can treasure. Her
> suffering has whisked those dreams into little broken piles.
>
> But stories of another physician reach down to pick up the pieces of
> those dreams. A physician who charges no fee. A physician who asks
> nothing in return. Who has no hidden agenda beyond making a sick world
> well again.
>
> She has heard of this physician, this Jesus who comes not to the healthy
> but to the sick. Who comes not to the strong but to the downtrodden. Who
> comes not to those with well-ordered lives but to those whose lives are
> filled with physical and moral chaos.
>
> She has heard of Jesus' success among incurables — _Certainly,_ she
> thinks, _if I can find this Jesus and but touch the fringe of his garment, I too will be
> cleansed and made whole._

As I conveyed the story, a strange mixture of emotions swept through me. It was as if I could see into the future to experience the struggles that would confront my friend. I was overcome with sadness and I began to weep.

But the words that I read aloud about the love and compassion shown by Jesus to this woman mixed into my sadness a comforting feeling of hope and peace. As I continued, I was suddenly confident that the same loving care that Jesus showed to this woman two thousand years ago would be shown to my friend by a loving God.

> This desperate woman pushes her empty hand through a broken seam in the crowd and, for a fleeting moment, clutches the corner of his garment. Jesus is pulled back. Not by the grasp of her hands so much as by the grasp of her faith. Power leaves him to surge through the hemorrhaging woman, and immediately she feels the rush of her youthful health returning — How ready Jesus is to respond to the hand of outstretched faith.

I was overcome with the revelation of God's grace and His kindness — again the tears flowed down my cheeks, and I had to stop reading. I glanced through my clouded eyes at Dick. He, too, had tears, but they were just small pools collected in the corners of his eyes. Dick and his family had cried many tears as they faced the same indignities and humiliations as the woman in the story — he may not have had any more tears to cry.

But if his ongoing ordeal had made him bitter, he never let us know.

As a matter of fact, Dick was one of the most joyful Christians I knew. He always smiled when we greeted each other in the hall. He was an encourager, giving other employees a word of praise for a job well done. And he was always there when it was time to pray; he knew that the intimate moments with the Savior were what sustained him.

The presence of the Lord was so strong in our little gathering on that day, and I knew God was doing something special. When I finished reading, I asked the others to join me in praying for Dick. We gathered around and laid our hands on this dear man. You could sense him drawing strength from the words of faith that were being lifted up to heaven on his behalf. When we finished, many were wiping tears from their eyes.

As we rose to leave, Dick asked to borrow my devotional. "I have a feeling I'm going to need to experience more of these intimate moments with the Savior," he declared.

He told me later that he read through the small book several times. He needed to know God's presence — in the weeks and months that followed, the doctors amputated most of Dick's foot, and then his leg below the knee.

Dick returned to work in a wheelchair. As the year progressed, his body slowly succumbed to the disease. His kidneys failed, and he was placed on the donor list for a liver transplant.

But through it all, Dick continued to find strength in the Savior. He made it to work as often as he could; and his work for the Lord at CBN was stellar.

He had recently been reassigned to a new project within CBN. On his final day of work, he finished all of his tasks from his previous project, cleared his desk, and handed the books to his supervisor. His coworkers gathered around to pray for him and send him off to his new role with a blessing.

Little did they know.

On the final day of his life, Dick took his family to church. After the service, his wife and kids treated him to his favorite restaurant for lunch. Later that evening, as Dick worked at his dining room table, he was given his new assignment — and his new home.
It was an issue of blood.

Dick had surrendered his life to God. The shed blood of Jesus that purchased Dick's redemption was the life force that sustained him when his own circulation began to fail. God only knows how much Dick suffered over the years, just like the woman with the issue of blood. Ken Gire finishes the story:

> The crowd blurs in the watery edges of her eyes. For an intimate moment she sees only Jesus. And he sees only her. Face to face, physician and patient. And with the tender word "Daughter," he gives this orphan a new home within the family of God. He gives her healing. And he gives her back her dreams.

For my friend Dick, in an intimate moment, God gave him back his dreams — and a new, glorified body.

Dick's walk with God through the years of pain was an issue of faith. His joy in the midst of the trial was an issue of praise. And his new assignment in the presence of his Lord and Savior was an issue of blood.

I share this story of my dear friend to encourage you as you seek to hear the voice of God in your relationship with him. This life is filled with the struggles that we all face — some are physical, like what my friend Dick faced. Some of us deal with challenges in our marriages and families. You may be facing financial hardships. Others battle with emotional difficulties, like depression or anxiety. Then there are those who face the more subtle obstacles in life. Things seem to be going great, like you can do no wrong. You may struggle with pride, anger, lust, or a controlling spirit.

Whatever our challenges in life, we all have issues that can potentially hinder us in our relationship with God. In my public speaking course, I identify this problem for my students as "noise." In the communication process there is a speaker and a receiver, and they communicate across a channel. If we were set up like a computer network — God as the super-computer and all of us wired into Him — there would be no problem. We could just download whatever we needed from Him whenever we needed it. But our relationship with the Lord is much more complex than that.

The Lord wants to communicate with us, and he is constantly sending His messages, and as much as we desire to be a receiver, there is the constant distraction of noise. In this modern world the noise is both internal and external. It can be psychological, emotional, spiritual, and even physical. There will always be something that will potentially distract us from hearing God.

What distractions, or "noise," have you faced as you have struggled to hear God's voice?

_____

_____

_____

_____

_____

We live in a loud world. There are people I know who can't go a minute of their day — including their sleeping hours — without some sort of sound. If it's not the television, it's the radio, CD player, or Internet — anything to keep them from being quiet. Some of these people are hurting so much they don't want to face the world inside — and they definitely don't want to hear God's voice.

Then there are the people who live loud — they are on the move, in charge, the alpha-male types, with the cell phone in their hand night and day. They go from the power breakfast with the other partners in the company, to the power lunch with the key client, to the elegant dinner with the beautiful woman. They don't see their need to hear the voice of God.

And then there is the person like my friend Dick, who truly loved the Lord, wanted to follow His plan for his life, and do the best job for God and his family as possible. But like Dick came to realize, the challenges of living in this fallen world can constantly distract from the walk with God that you desire.

I suspect that this description fits you as you are reading this right now. You wouldn't have gotten this far in this Bible study if you didn't truly want to learn to hear God's voice and follow His direction for your life. I want to encourage you — you are on the right track!

Read Psalm 1:1–3. What will be the end result in the life of someone whose "delight is in the law of the Lord"?

_____

_____

_____

That's how Dick lived his life. It didn't matter what challenges he faced in his physical body, or in his emotional reaction to the obstacles that came against him, he continued to press forward in God. In observing the Passover meal, the children of Israel ate the bitter herbs, but they also enjoyed the sweet meat of the lamb. It is the same in our walk with the Lord today. Like Dick, we all experience the bitterness of life's difficulties. But as Dick so gracefully displayed in his life of joyful, diligent service to the Lord, we can also enjoy the sweet meat that comes from a daily relationship with the Lamb of God.

Dick understood that hearing God's voice and walking in His blessings is all about relationship.

No matter what you face in life, or how loud the noise gets, find a place where you can go to be alone with God and listen for His voice — because it is all about relationship.

Describe your own relationship with God.

_____

_____

_____

_____

_____

How does your relationship with Him affect your ability to hear His voice?

_____

_____

_____

_____

What might you be able to do this week to shut out the "noise" of the world and focus on hearing God's voice?

_____

_____

_____

_____

_____

_____

_____

_____

Day Two: Finally Making a Decision

After all of the seven keys have been considered in the decision-making process, the time has finally come to make the actual decision — but even then, it is still imperative to hear God's voice and receive His guidance.

The prophet Jeremiah prayed a prayer in the Old Testament asking God for guidance, and it is still a good prayer for us to pray today.

Write out Jeremiah 10:23–24 as your own prayer to the Lord.

_____

_____

_____

_____

We can't make it on our own! We must be totally dependent on the leading and the grace of almighty God. But that dependency doesn't mean that we have to constantly feel the presence of the Lord to know that He is present, to know that He is guiding us. The longer we walk with the Lord, the more we grow to understand that the Christian life is based on faith, not on feelings.

We are saved by faith through grace. We are baptized in the Holy Spirit by faith. We prophesy according to the measure of our faith. We receive healing and provision by faith. Without faith it is impossible to please God. Receiving guidance from the Lord begins with having childlike faith. Those who are truly mature are the believers who are the most dependent on the Lord — the most childlike. They are humble, and they are teachable, and they are willing to go wherever the Father desires for them to go, and do whatever the Father desires for them to do.

Explain what this phrase means to you: "Receiving guidance from the Lord begins with having a childlike faith."

_____

_____

_____

_____

The immature Christian goes where he or she wants to go. The mature Christian goes where the Father wants them to go. We must all adopt the attitude of John the Baptist who declared of Jesus, *"He must increase, and I must decrease"* (John 3:30).

When you are in the midst of making a major decision, you need to ask the Lord to give you grace to walk in holiness so that there will be nothing hindering you from hearing His voice. Unconfessed sin, including pride, unforgiveness, and anger can blind you. Also ask the Lord to help you live at peace with those around you. Be aware of the devil's schemes to stir up trouble with your family, friends, business associates, and others when you are trying to make a decision. The more critical the decision, the more likely you will find the nest stirred, either to distract you, or to make you yield to anger, jealousy, or unforgiveness. But if you stumble into sin during these critical times remember the promises of God: *There is therefore now no condemnation to those who are in Christ Jesus, who do not walk according to the flesh, but according to the Spirit (Romans 8:1). And: If we confess our sins, He is faithful and just to forgive us our sins and to cleanse us from all unrighteousness (1 John 1:9).*

When making a major decision, why is it important to have peace with God and with others?

_____

_____

Prayer is essential when you are facing a crossroads in your life — and big decisions require big prayer. Don't just pray here and there during the day, but have a special time each day set aside to commune with the Lord. But don't just speak prayers out loud, listen for the voice of the Lord as well. Keep a journal so that you can write down what the Lord speaks to you in these special times.

During times of important decision-making, you may also want to fast as the Lord leads you. Fasting combined with prayer is an essential Christian discipline that should be a part of every mature believer's life. It is important, however, to understand that we cannot manipulate God into performing the way we would like Him to in any given situation. Fasting doesn't impress God, but it helps you to overcome your flesh, and it purifies you so that your spiritual senses are more keen to hear God's voice. You can't manipulate God when you fast and pray, but participating in this spiritual discipline does please Him. The Lord will often honor your efforts to become closer to Him, to be obedient to Him, and to strive to walk in a holy manner. Bill Bright of Campus Crusade once said that fasting is the "atomic bomb of the spirit." Do you want things to happen in your life? Spend time in fasting and in prayer.

Explain why fasting and prayer is important when making a major decision.

_____

_____

While the Holy Spirit will be active in our lives, revealing His will to our hearts and then confirming that will through the other keys of God's guidance, He will also be communicating through the passive aspect of His presence and the peace of God in our lives. As we have said, the Holy Spirit will tell us whether we are "safe" or "out" in any guidance we are considering.

Be careful that you don't allow certain concerns to keep you from moving forward in a decision. Some Christians mistakenly believe that you must come to a place of "perfect peace" before you can move forward with a commitment or a decision. They think that if God is speaking to us, there will be no fears or doubts whatsoever. The Bible does promise the peace of Christ, but it never guarantees complete peaceful feelings. There are often concerns in a decision, but the Lord gives us an underlying assurance that He will be with us and guide us through.

How much "peace" do you usually require before moving ahead with a decision? How can you tell the difference between false peace and the peace of the Holy Spirit?

_____

_____

_____

_____

Blaine Smith wrote the following about the peace of the Spirit:

> His peace is the grace that transcends our fears, allowing us to move ahead in spite of doubt. Emotional peace will not be experienced until after we step out in faith. Furthermore, waiting for absolute peace before making every major decision would be paralyzing. Taking the first step is vital to experiencing peace — and God's blessings. Biblical faith is the resolve to forge ahead, despite the fear of change.[3]

Once we have submitted ourselves to God, and made things right in a spiritual sense, it is time to practically consider the decision we are making. We have examined the decision in light of the seven keys: the Scripture, what the Holy Spirit has revealed to our heart; godly counsel; the peace of God; personal prophecy; confirmation; and circumstances. Before making a final decision, carefully examine the entire situation using your God-given intellect. Ask yourself these questions:

• Is this new direction biblical?

• Is my spouse in agreement with this decision? (if you are married)

• Does it complement my spiritual gifts?

• Can I use my God-given talents and abilities in this new role?

• Does this new direction line up with the long-term desires of my heart?

• Do I have the personal resources to move forward in this direction? Will I have to wait on God's timing to bring those resources to me or to my organization?

• Do I have the experience necessary to excel in this new area of responsibility? Or is God asking me to go out and gain the experience needed to move into this new venture?

• Is it ethical? Is it legal?

• Do I have the peace of Christ — not necessarily a complete and total freedom from concern — but do I have an assurance from the Lord that He will guide me in this new path?

• Will my decision fulfill a desire that has been planted in my heart?

• What are the key people around me saying about this new direction — parents, pastors, professors, mentors, and friends — how has my decision been balanced on the scales of their opinions?

• Are the circumstantial doors open or are they closed?

• If the doors seem to be closed, does that mean I should back away, or do I have enough assurance through the other keys to wait in faith for God to bring the circumstances in line?

• If the doors seem to be open, do I have enough assurance through the other keys for me to move forward in this decision?

• Am I willing to die to my own desires if the Lord directs me in a way that I did not expect?

• Am I willing to allow God to give me the desires of my heart, even if it means new, possibly frightening challenges and a loss of my comfort zone?

Once you are confident that you know God's will, and you have His peace to move forward, take that step of faith and watch what God will do. Just like He did with Peter, when you lift your foot over the edge of the boat and step onto the water in obedience to His call, grace will come on the scene and God will do what it takes to see His will accomplished in your life.

As you make your decision, remember that second thoughts are normal. Everyone experiences doubts, fears, and uneasiness during a major transition in life. Trust the Lord every step of the way. Go back and remember how the Lord made His will known to you, and rejoice that you have the Word of the Lord to sustain you through the challenges in any transition.

It is also normal to mourn what you are leaving behind. Blaine Smith writes:

> No matter how strongly you want a change, you are still leaving behind something cherished. Even the person who is most eager for marriage is forsaking the benefits of single life. It is normal to feel genuine grief over lost benefits. Allow time to work through your feelings, but don't let them hold you back from moving on to God's best.[4]

Why is it necessary to make room for mourning the thing that you are leaving when you make a major decision?

_____

_____

Have you ever experienced mourning when you made an important life-changing decision? Explain the situation.

_____

_____

_____

_____

A person can bear almost any hardship if they know they are in God's will. When you know the will of God, you can truly be thankful in every circumstance — having a grateful heart in all things and for all things. God is sovereign in our lives. He rules the circumstances that we face. As we see in the story of Job, the devil can only do to you what God allows. So if this is the case, we can trust that our Father will only allow those things into our lives that will promote His ultimate purpose for us — and God is a good God!

Bob Mumford tells the story of a retired medical missionary who lived by herself in a little cottage right in the middle of a ghetto in a Florida town. In her neighborhood there had been looting, arson, and rioting — right outside of her door. Whenever there was unrest, her friends would ask, "Aren't you afraid of being alone at night? Maybe you ought to get a big watchdog!" The lady always smiled and shook her head. "There is no safer place in the whole world than in the center of God's will. He placed me here, and He is my mighty fortress."

In his salutations to the church in Colossae, the apostle Paul mentioned his co-laborer Epaphras, who joined with him in praying for the church:

> *Epaphras, who is one of you, a bondservant of Christ, greets you, always laboring fervently for you in prayers, that you may stand perfect and complete in all the will of God.*
>
> —Colossians 4:12

Paul and Epaphras seemed to think it was worthwhile to pray that the believers would be perfect and complete in the will of God. This verse assures us that we can walk in God's will, as we devote ourselves to hearing God's voice and obeying His commands.

In the list of questions to ask yourself when making a decision, which questions stand out to you, and why? If you are facing a major decision right now, which questions are critical to ask at this time?

_____

_____

_____

_____

_____

_____

Day Three: Our Choices and Our Character

Every person is known in two ways: by what they say and what they do. You and I are defined by the words we speak and the choices we make. We face decisions in life almost every moment of every day. Some of them are purely natural, such as what to eat for breakfast, what to wear, or which road to take to work. But there are also spiritual decisions that define us as well. They stem from ideas, desires, fantasies, and concepts that can come from either God or Satan.

We need to be aware of the fact that we are part of a larger spiritual dimension, and there is an ongoing struggle taking place between the Creator of the universe and Satan. Both God and Satan want to be expressed through what we say and what we do. In yielding to either of them, your will is involved in the choices that you make.

Explain how our choices reveal the nature of our will.

_____

_____

_____

Your will plays an important role in defining your character. Your character is defined by the nature of your actions and attitudes over time. Your will is also involved in the choices that result in your actions, attitudes, and words. Your soul is a very important part of your personality — which is comprised of your mind, will, and emotions. These are the three things that go into making a person who we know them to be. We are very familiar with the intellect and emotions, as a great deal of attention is usually given to them. But the one element of personality that is often ignored or misunderstood is the will.

Read James 1:5–8. What does this passage have to say about the importance of a person's will? How does it describe someone who has a weak will?

_____

_____

_____

In the process of making a decision on a direction, the mind moves the will to choose from the options that are presented to it — both good and evil. The end results of the will's actions become the physical, emotional, and intellectual expressions of who we are as people — and this is how our character is defined.

It is vitally important that we seek to hear God through the seven keys as we are making these decisions. We are known by what we say, and by what we do. Our character is defined by the choices we make.

A secular person has no reliable standard for judging which options are worthy of expression and which options should be denied. Culture and socialization are the major influences that define the character of the secular person. The Christian, on the other hand, has a standard that can be applied to the options presented to his or her mind or spirit. That standard is the Bible. And the Lord has also given us the seven keys through which we can judge every possible choice with which we are confronted.

Over time, the choices we make will reveal the spiritual direction our lives are taking. You will either be on the road that leads to life in Christ, or on the road that leads to death.

Read Matthew 6:24. How does this passage of Scripture relate to the choices we are confronted with every day?

_____

_____

_____

Maybe now is the time for you to take an objective look at the direction your life is taking. Paul says if we judge ourselves we will not be judged, but if we do not judge ourselves, we will be judged by the Lord so that we will not be condemned with the world (see 1 Corinthians 11:31–32).

As you are reading this book you may recognize that your life is headed in the wrong direction. The good news is that every day is a new beginning in God. Right now you have an opportunity to make a correction in the course of your future. Your ability to do this depends upon your obedience to God and His Word. If you are willing to see the corrections that need to be made, God will strengthen your will so that you can resist the evil options and choose the good.

When you look back over your life, how pleased are you with the person your choices have defined? God is giving you an opportunity to make a correction today. How strong is your determination to pursue your choices?

What is your response to these questions?

_____

_____

Of course, the most important choice you will ever make is to accept Jesus Christ as your personal Savior. If you haven't already done so, make Jesus Christ the Lord of your decision-making process. Perhaps you have known the Lord, but recently you have not sought Him in your decisions as you should. Take the time right now to ask for His forgiveness, and for His continued guidance in your life.

As you examine all options through the seven keys, God will give you a sense of destiny that will energize you to move forward in zeal and will comfort you in the difficult times of life. God has a destiny for each of His children, and we reach that destiny through our choices. We must choose to do His will. If we are prayerfully pursuing the will of God through the seven keys, He will enable us to follow His will.

How does the fact that you make decisions by using the Word of God help to define maturity in your life?

_____

_____

_____

Understanding that over time, the choices we make will reveal the spiritual direction our lives are taking, how do you feel about the place you are in life? Do you think there are some corrections that need to be made? Write out your thoughts.

_____

_____

_____

_____

_____

Day Four: Life in the Spirit

Every person is born with the ability to hear God's voice. As we have already seen, that ability is increased dramatically when you are born again. Every believer has the opportunity to live in the Spirit and experience God's power. It operates mightily in His kingdom, and when you are born again you become a part of that kingdom.

The ultimate source of power is God Himself. He is the Author of power. The sun, the moon, the stars, the galaxies, any light in our universe — all of this power flows from God. Since God is a Spirit, the ultimate source of life and energy is in the spiritual world. As you walk in the Spirit and submit yourself to God, you can tap into a source of unimaginable power. As you put into practice the principles that you have learned in this book, the power of the kingdom will begin to be demonstrated in your life. And then you can become a channel of God's blessings to this lost and dying world.

From God's Spirit, power flows to the human spirit, and then from the human spirit to man's mind. This is what life in the Spirit is all about, and it is available to all who will believe. God has given mankind dominion on the earth. Satan stole it away from Adam and Eve for a time. But that dominion has been restored by the death and resurrection of Jesus Christ. He holds the keys to death and hell, and He has received all authority on earth as the Son of man.

As we submit ourselves to His lordship, Christ gives us the authority to be His witnesses on the earth. After His resurrection, He told the disciples to go back and wait in the Upper Room until the Holy Spirit came, and then they would be endued with power to be His witnesses. As we also wait on God, and allow Him to fill us with His Holy Spirit, we too will be endued with power to be His witnesses on the earth — to be a channel of His love, peace, and blessings to a lost and dying world.

What does the phrase "life in the Spirit" mean to you?

_____

_____

_____

How can the Holy Spirit be a source of power for you in your Christian life and witness?

_____

_____

Through this life in the Spirit, you will begin to hear God's voice so that you can obey His leading in your life, both for today, and for the long term. His Word is a lamp unto your feet today, and a light unto your path tomorrow. But to hear God's voice, and to be filled with His Spirit, you must maintain a daily relationship with Him. Just like a baby who grows to know their parent's voice, a believer grows to know the voice of his heavenly Father. This happens through times of prayer.

Jesus is our example. The gospel writers showed that before any major decision or event in His life and ministry, He spent numerous hours in prayer. The spiritual discipline of prayer is an indispensable part of hearing God's voice.

Read James 5:16. How could this verse relate to a prayer for wisdom in a difficult decision?

_____

_____

Trusting in God's Sovereignty

In His sovereignty, God is leading your life for His kingdom purposes. In those purposes He is going to do good for you — but you are also part of a bigger picture. God has a grand design for our lives — and for the world. We can rest in knowing that the Lord truly does order the steps of the righteous person.

When we come to the place of trusting God in His sovereignty, we begin to realize that the trials and calamities in life can become a mirror that can show us our real selves. Challenges help to expose sin in our lives that needs to be dealt with — pride, fear, anger, rebellion, insecurity, false humility, negativity, and so on. Just like the pain from a hidden tumor or a ruptured appendix, the difficulties in life, coupled with our reaction to them, help us to diagnose sin that needs to be addressed. God exposes these things to us so that we will recognize they are there and allow Him to heal and deliver us from them. The

Lord will often use the difficulties in our lives to woo us back to Himself. When troubles come, we need to thank God and ask Him to do His complete work in the midst of them. Remember, Satan is God's devil. If God didn't have any use for him, He would have bound him and cast him into the pit after Jesus rose from the dead. But the Lord allows this fallen angel and his demons to still operate in the earth because he is the one who creates the needs that drive us to Jesus.

God alone rules over all creation. *"I am the LORD, and there is no other,"* He declared through the prophet Isaiah (Isaiah 45:5). Nothing takes Him by surprise. As my teenage son would say, "He rules!"

We are all human. We all make mistakes. God made us, and He is well aware of our weaknesses. If you have sinned, repent. If you have made a mistake, learn from it. The biggest mistake in life is wallowing in the sorrow of past mistakes. The only failure in life is when we fail to get up and start over after we have made the wrong choices.

As you have already learned, this doesn't mean that we don't have to diligently seek Him. God's sovereignty doesn't negate our responsibility in life. Someone who doesn't rightly balance the truths of God's sovereignty and man's free will might adopt an irresponsible attitude that says, "Whatever is going to happen is going to happen. God already has my life planned out — He'll make sure it all comes together." This is a dangerous position that, sadly, many Christians have adopted.

When God called Billy Graham to a ministry of evangelism at a young age, Billy had to respond to that call and "do" something about it. He had to go to Bible school. He had to formulate a plan for his ministry. He had to start a non-profit corporation and register that with the IRS. He had to print flyers and take out ads in the media. He had to organize thousands of volunteers. He had to prepare his sermons. He had to get on an airplane and travel to the sight of the rally. And finally, he had to preach the gospel message and give the invitation. And when he had done all of those things, God intervened and touched the hearts of the people who heard him, and they were saved.

The wonderful plans that God has for our life don't just happen — we have to cooperate with the guidance of the Lord by not just "hearing" His voice, but also "doing" His will.

But when we step out in faith and do what we believe God is leading us to do, God's grace arrives on the scene and amazing things happen — even beyond what we planned!

Why do you think God allowed Satan to remain active after Jesus rose from the grave? What is his purpose in the earth today? Does he have any authority? Does he have any power?

_____

_____

_____

_____

What is it that God has called you to do? Perhaps as you have worked through this Bible study, the Spirit of God has been speaking to your heart. Write down some of the things that you know God has called you to do.

_____

_____

_____

_____

Now, write down some ways that you can begin stepping out in faith to "do" what God has called you to.

_____

_____

_____

_____

_____

Day Five: It's All About Relationship!

In the quest to hear God's voice and obey His commands, Scripture tells us that *if you are willing and obedient, you shall eat the good of the land* (Isaiah 1:19). Seeking to hear God's voice shows your willingness. Following through in faith and action displays obedience. The Bible says that if you do these things, God will bless you with good things.

The key is that we seek *Him* and not just what *He can provide.* It is all about relationship.

Write out Matthew 6:33.

_____

_____

_____

In the midst of His sermon on life's priorities and God's care for us, Jesus dropped this anchor of truth for us to keep us balanced. We should not seek God for what we can get from Him. We should seek Him because we recognize who He is — the Creator of the universe, the Giver of life, the Sustainer of all things. He is our heavenly Father. When we realize His love for us, displayed in the sacrifice Jesus made for us at Calvary, we fall in love with Him; we want to know more of Him; and we want to serve Him, hear His voice, and do His will. The wonderful thing about God is that He rewards us when we do. He is truly an awesome God!

More than anything, God wants to have a relationship with us as individuals. He is concerned about our character. He wants to reproduce the attributes of Jesus Christ in our lives.

Listen to God's plan for us found in Psalm 37:3–5 (comments added by me):

> *Trust in the LORD* (have faith in God)*, and do good* (good things come from God, so do what He says to do); *Dwell in the land* (have dominion over everything the Lord brings into your sphere of influence), *and feed on His faithfulness* (enjoy the peace that comes in knowing that He is true to His Word). *Delight yourself also in the LORD* (fall in love with your heavenly Father, get to know Him, and do what He tells you to do), *And He shall give you the desires of your heart* (this is a bonus of seeking first the kingdom of God and His righteousness). *Commit your way to the LORD* (don't ask God to bless what you're doing, but ask to be doing what He is blessing), *Trust also in Him* (God is good and can be trusted to give you a future and

a hope), *And He shall bring it to pass* (every promise of God is conditional, but if we do our part, He will most assuredly do His!).

If we really want to hear His voice, and if we are truly striving to be obedient to His Word, He will plant His thoughts into our heart and our mind. Our desires will become His desires. When that happens it is "no sweat" to believe Him for the outcome.

It all comes back to our relationship with God. God truly does love you. He has an amazing plan for your life. And the way to discover that plan is by daily communicating with the Lord, to get back to the basics:

• Spend daily time in prayer.
• Read your Bible every day. Pray and meditate on what you read. Ask the Lord to reveal Himself through His Word.
• Build systematic Bible study into your weekly schedule. The Scripture will leap off the page as you use techniques like inductive Bible study to examine God's Word.
• Keep a journal of the things that God is speaking to you through the seven keys. Refer back to it from time to time to see how God is directing your steps.
• Find a church that believes in the Bible. Get to know your pastor and other mature Christians in your fellowship.
• Find a small group or Bible study that you can plug into. More growth happens in Bible studies than in any other church gathering.
• Build some close friendships with mature Christians in whom you can confide. Everyone needs an intimate circle of friends. Make sure you choose these close friends wisely. They will have a major influence on your life. Prayerfully seek the Lord on whom you allow into that inner circle.
• Become involved in the church. Find a way to use your God-given gifts. As you sow into the body of Christ, you will reap benefits that will boggle your mind. Give of your time, your money, your expertise, your friendship, and most importantly, your prayers. You cannot outgive God.
• When the time is right, find ways to start making disciples. As you prepare lessons for small group Bible study, one-on-one mentoring relationships, street evangelism, and so on, the Lord will open your eyes to His will for your life.
• Forgive those who hurt you. Never hold onto a grudge. Your lack of forgiveness doesn't hurt the person who offended you, but it will keep you in a prison that can negatively affect you spiritually, emotionally, mentally, and physically.
• To hear God's voice you must commit yourself to living a holy life, as much as you are able. If and when you fall into sin, confess it, repent, and move on.
• Look for opportunities to share your faith with other people. If you ask for opportunities, God will give you divine appointments. When those doors open, walk through

them with grace and love. God's heart beats for the lost — the Great Commission is the highest thing on His agenda. As you share your faith with sinners, God will lavish His blessings upon you — and that includes guiding your steps.

• Have faith in God, even when the way does not seem clear. Don't give up on Him. *Trust in the LORD with all your heart, and lean not on your own understanding; In all your ways acknowledge Him, and He shall direct your paths* (Proverbs 3:5–6).

• Ask the Lord to help you walk in the Spirit and not in the flesh (Romans 8).

Ultimately, being led by God comes back to the greatest commandment of all: *"'You shall love the LORD your God with all your heart, with all your soul, with all your strength, and with all your mind,' and 'your neighbor as yourself.'" And He* [Jesus] *said to him, "You have answered rightly; do this and you will live"* (Luke 10:27–28).

God has provided us with these seven keys so that we can have daily communication with Him. Our loving heavenly Father wants to walk with us in the cool of the day as He did with Adam and Eve in the Garden. He wants to bless us so that we can be a blessing to others. And we, too, can experience the sweet fellowship of knowing God, not only as Lord and Savior, but as a loving Father. It's all about relationship.

How have the truths you learned in this Bible study changed the way you make decisions?

_____

_____

What does the phrase, "It's all about relationship," mean to you?

_____

_____

How will your relationship with God begin to help you to hear His voice more clearly?

_____

_____

If you wish, write a prayer of dedication and commitment to the Lord to put into practice the things that you have learned — that you would be not just a "hearer" of His Word, but a "doer" also.

_____

_____

_____

Notes

Week One

[1]Corrie Ten Boom, "A Faith Not Hidden," interview by Pat Robertson, *The 700 Club,* Christian Broadcasting Network, 1974.

[2]*Fiddler on the Roof,* 1971, Metro-Goldwyn-Mayer Studios.

[3]Henry Blackaby and Claude King, *Experiencing God* (Nashville: Lifeway, 1993).

[4]Dr. Bill Bright, "The Four Spiritual Laws," (Campus Crusade for Christ: 1995).

Week Two

[1]Merrill F. Unger, *The New Unger's Bible Dictionary* (Chicago: Moody Bible Institute, 1988), "plumb line."

[2]Pat Robertson, *12 Principles of God's Guidance* (Virginia Beach, VA: CBN Publishing, 1979).

[3]Dr. Bill Hamon, *Prophets and Personal Prophecy* (Shippensburg, PA: Destiny Image, 1987), 32.

[4]Ibid., 87.

[5]C. S. Lewis, *Mere Christianity* (New York: Touchstone, 1943), 144.

[6]Pat Robertson, *Answers to 200 of Life's Most Probing Questions* (Nashville: Thomas Nelson, 1984), 49.

[7]Ibid.

[8]J. Rodman Williams, *Renewal Theology: God, the World, and Redemption* (Grand Rapids: Zondervan, 1988), 37.

[9]Robert H. Gundry, *A Survey of the New Testament* (Grand Rapids: Zondervan, 1994), 87.

[10]C.S. Lewis, *Mere Christianity,* 145.

[11]Bob Mumford, *Take Another Look at Guidance* (Plainfield, NJ: Logos, 1971), preface.

[12]Dr. Richard D. Dobbins, "Seeking God's Will," DayForward online, 2002.

Week Three

[1]Dr. Jimmy Williams, *Evidence, Answers, and Christian Faith* (Grand Rapids: Kregel, 2002), 95.

[2]Rene Pache, *The Inspiration and Authority of Scripture* (Chicago: Moody Bible Institute, 1969), 124.

[3]R. Laird Harris, *Can I Trust My Bible?* (Chicago: Moody Bible Institute, 1963), 124.

[4]Robert P. Lightner, *The Savior and the Scriptures* (Nutley, NJ: Presbyterian and Reformed Publishing, 1970), 28–29.

[5]Dr. Jimmy Williams, 84–85.

[6]Millar Burrows, *What Mean These Stones?* (New York: Meridian, 1956), 52.

[7]Gordon D. Fee and Douglas Stuart, *How to Read the Bible for All Its Worth* (Grand Rapids: Zondervan, 1981), 11.

[8]Ibid.

[9]John Wesley, *Preface to Explanatory Notes upon the Old Testament* (Edinburgh, April 25, 1765).

Week Four

[1]Charles G. Finney, *Revival Lectures,* "Lecture V: The Prayer of Faith."

[2]See http://www.comp.mq.edu.au/~len/christian/cho.html.

[3]Jack Hayford in Cindy Jacobs, *The Voice of God* (Ventura, CA: Regal, 1996), 11–12.

[4]Pat Robertson with Bob Slosser, *The Secret Kingdom* (Nashville: Thomas Nelson, 1982), 52–54.

[5]John and Paula Sandford, *The Elijah Task* (Tulsa: Victory House, 1977), 170.

[6]Jacobs, *The Voice of God,* 217.

[7]Dr. James Dobson, *Complete Marriage and Family Home Reference Guide* (Carol Stream, IL: Tyndale, 2000).

Week Five

[1]Pastor Larry Albanese, First Assembly of God, Erie, PA.

[2]Blaine Smith, *Guidance by the Book* (Virginia Beach, VA: CBN Publishing, 1992).

[3]Mike Fehlauer, *Exposing Spiritual Abuse* (Lake Mary, FL: Charisma House, 2001).

[4]Ibid.

Week Six

[1]Thomas Paine, *The American Crisis,* December 23, 1776.

[2]Larry Tomczak, *Biblical Confessions to Increase Your Faith,* audio cassette, 1998.

[3]Michael W. Smith and Mike Hudson, "End of the Book," on *Michael W. Smith 2,* Reunion Records, 1984.

Week Seven

[1]Hamon, 29.

[2]Ibid., 13.

[3]John and Elizabeth Sherrill, *The Happiest People on Earth* (Grand Rapids: Chosen, 1975), 19–20.

[4]Hamon, 66.

[5]Bruce Yocum, *Prophecy* (Ann Arbor: Servant, 1976), 115.

[6]Pat Robertson, *Bring It On* (Nashville: W Publishing, 2003), 224–5.

[7]David Blomgren, *Prophetic Gatherings in the Church* (Portland, OR: Bible Temple Publishing, 1979), 59–60.

Week Eight

[1]Pat Robertson, *The Secret Kingdom* (Nashville: Thomas Nelson: 1984).

Week Nine

[1]Oswald Chambers, *My Utmost for His Highest* (Uhrichsville, OH: Barbour, 2003).

[2]Blaine Smith.

[3]Squire D. Rushnell, *When God Winks: How the Power of Coincidence Guides Your Life* (Atria Books, 2002).

[4]Blaine Smith.

[5]Bob Sorge, *The Fire of Delayed Answers* (Canandaigua, NY: Oasis House, 1996).

Week Ten

[1]Robert Jeffress, *Hearing the Master's Voice* (Colorado Springs, CO: Waterbrook, 2001).

[2]Ken Gire, *Intimate Moments with the Savior* (Grand Rapids: Zondervan, 1989), 47–50.

[3]Blaine Smith, 144–5.

[4]Ibid., 145.

Real Problems... Real People... Real Life... Real Answers...
THE INDISPUTABLE POWER OF BIBLE STUDIES

Through the Bible in One Year
Alan B. Stringfellow • ISBN 1-56322-014-8

God's Great & Precious Promises
Connie Witter • ISBN 1-56322-063-6

Preparing for Marriage God's Way
Wayne Mack • ISBN 1-56322-019-9

Becoming the Noble Woman
Anita Young • ISBN 1-56322-020-2

Women in the Bible — Examples To Live By
Sylvia Charles • ISBN 1-56322-021-0

Pathways to Spiritual Understanding
Richard Powers • ISBN 1-56322-023-7

Christian Discipleship
Steven Collins • ISBN 1-56322-022-9

Couples in the Bible — Examples To Live By
Sylvia Charles • ISBN 1-56322-062-8

Men in the Bible — Examples To Live By
Don Charles • ISBN 1-56322-067-9

7 Steps to Bible Skills
Dorothy Hellstern • ISBN 1-56322-029-6

Great Characters of the Bible
Alan B. Stringfellow • ISBN 1-56322-046-6

Great Truths of the Bible
Alan B. Stringfellow • ISBN 1-56322-047-4

The Trust
Steve Roll • ISBN 1-56322-075-X

Because of Jesus
Connie Witter • ISBN 1-56322-077-6

The Quest
Dorothy Hellstern • ISBN 1-56322-078-4

God's Solutions to Life's Problems
Wayne Mack & Joshua Mack • ISBN 1-56322-079-2

A Hard Choice
Dr. Jesús Cruz Correa • Dr. Doris Colón Santiago
ISBN 1-56322-080-6

11 Reasons Families Succeed
Richard & Rita Tate • ISBN 1-56322-081-4

The Fear Factor
Wayne Mack & Joshua Mack • ISBN 1-56322-082-2

Embracing Grace
Judy Baker • ISBN 1-56322-083-0

Courageous Faith
Keith Bower • ISBN 1-56322-085-7

5 Steps to Financial Freedom
James D. Wise • ISBN 1-56322-084-9

Forged in the Fire — Shaped by the Master
Tim Burns • ISBN 1-56322-086-5

7 Keys to Hearing God's Voice
Craig Von Buseck • ISBN 1-56322-087-3

Problemas Reales... Gente Real... Vida Real... Respuestas Reales...
EL INDISCUTIBLE IMPACTO DE LOS ESTUDIOS BÍBLICOS

A través de la biblia en un año
Alan B. Stringfellow • ISBN 1-56322-061-X

Preparando el matrimonio en el camino de Dios
Wayne Mack • ISBN 1-56322-066-0

Mujeres en la Biblia
Sylvia Charles • ISBN 1-56322-072-5

Parejas en la Biblia
Sylvia Charles • ISBN 1-56322-073-3

Decisión Difícil
Dr. Jesús Cruz Correa & Dra. Doris Colón Santiago •
ISBN 1-56322-074-1